POSTCARD HISTORY SERIES

The Grand Haven Area 1905–1975

IN VINTAGE POSTCARDS

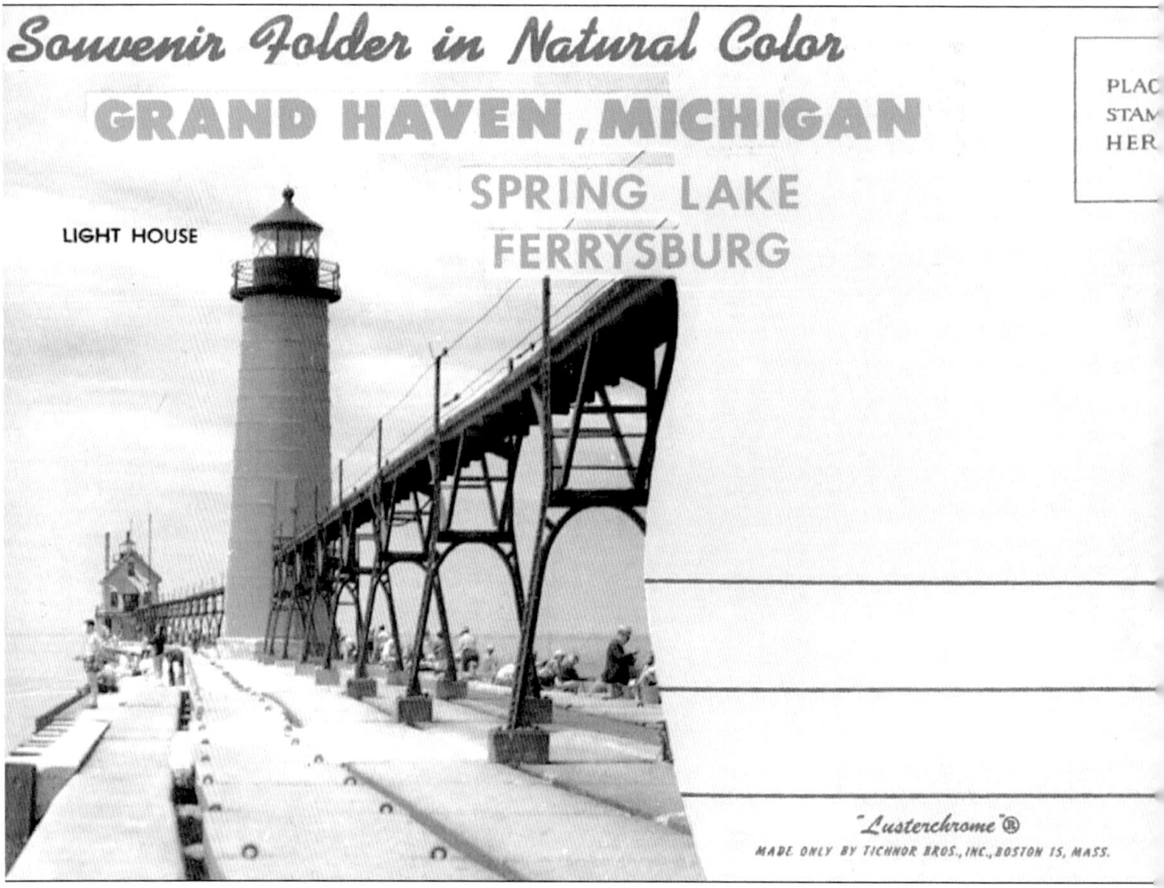

Postcard folders were another way of preserving memories. This one contains 12 views of popular sights in and around the Tri-Cities of Grand Haven, Spring Lake, and Ferrysburg. The unmailed folder dates to about 1960.

Cover Picture: Packets like the *Fanny M. Rose* carried people, freight, and mail between Grand Rapids, Spring Lake, and Grand Haven. In this 1907 postcard view, the *Fanny Rose* is ready to drop off its passengers at the Washington Street dock. The packet was built in Grand Haven in 1893.

POSTCARD HISTORY SERIES

The Grand Haven Area 1905–1975

IN VINTAGE POSTCARDS

Wallace K. Ewing, Ph.D. and
David H. Seibold, D.D.S.
for the Tri-Cities Historical Museum

ARCADIA
PUBLISHING

ISBN 978-0-7385-2337-8

Published by Arcadia Publishing,
Charleston, South Carolina

Printed in the United States of America

Library of Congress Catalog Card Number: 2003103778

For all general information contact Arcadia Publishing at:
Telephone 843-853-2070
Fax 843-853-0044
E-Mail sales@arcadiapublishing.com
For customer service and orders:
Toll-Free 1-888-313-2665

Visit us on the Internet at www.arcadiapublishing.com

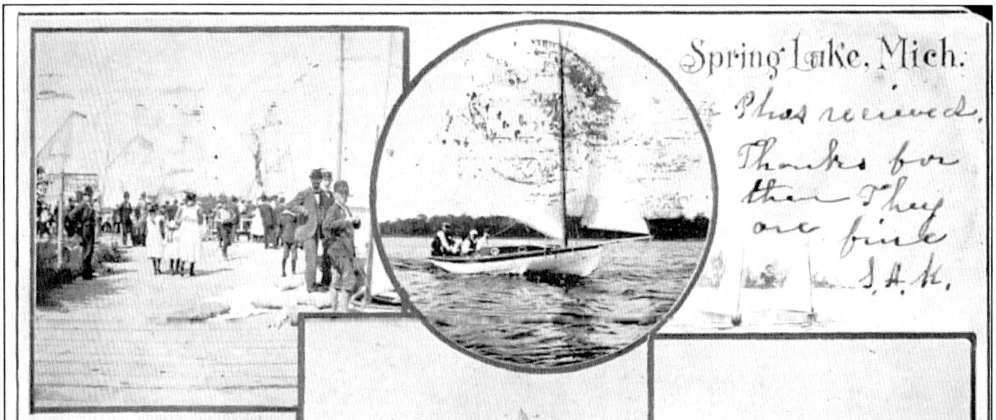

Sailing for sport and pleasure was a well-established activity on Spring Lake by 1904, the date of this postcard. It looks as if the boat in the lower right corner had capsized, but the four men seem to be enjoying themselves nevertheless!

Contents

ACKNOWLEDGMENTS

This collection of picture postcards represents a collaborative effort between the Tri-Cities Historical Museum and the communities it serves. Many of the cards shown here were donated to the museum by local residents who recognized their importance in preserving history as it was seen through the camera's eye during most of the 20th century. We thank those donors for their generosity, their foresight, and their trust in the museum to keep those precious items in a safe but accessible place. The remainder of the images came from the private collection of Wally Ewing and local residents Robert Pushaw, Fred Peterson, and Tom Fisher. Our thanks to each of them for sharing their rare and valuable cards. It is a special treat not only to include them in this book, but to see them at all and to savor the history they reveal.

Jeanette Weiden, Assistant Curator at the museum, was especially helpful in selecting the postcards for inclusion, and for attending to the many critical details incurred in such an undertaking. We thank her for sharing her perspective and for keeping us on schedule.

We also extend sincere thanks to the museum's Board of Directors and to Denny Swartout, the museum's Executive Director, for their enthusiastic support. Their confidence in the project provided the inspiration to keep at it. Finally, we want to express our gratitude to Hoch Schultz, Margaret Babcock, Bruce Baker, and Tad Poel for the historical information they provided for some of the captions.

Wallace K. Ewing, Ph.D.
David H. Seibold, D.D.S.

INTRODUCTION

Picture postcards were to the early 1900s what email is to the early 21st century: an easy, efficient, and economical way to correspond with friends and family. "Having a wonderful time, wish you were here," came about in the heyday of the picture postcard. Many cards were never mailed, but were saved as personal reminders of a trip or vacation to someplace new and exotic, such as the Grand Haven area. Either way, the surviving cards provide a tantalizing glimpse into our past.

Postcards as we know them today were a long time developing. It took over a century just for the spelling to evolve from "postal card" to "post card" to "postcard," the term and spelling that is in general use today. One of the early, formidable barriers to its development was the Post Office regulation that required an envelope for all correspondence. And then there were early detractors who thought it improper to mail a message on cards that anyone, especially the servants, could read!

The direct ancestors of the postcard were envelopes printed with comic figures, valentines, music, and patriotic images issued during the Civil War. The first postal-type card similar to that used today was copyrighted in 1861. Post Office officials eventually recognized its potential popularity and, on May 13, 1873, issued America's first penny postal card. The simple penny postal was sold at Post Offices throughout the country for the next 70 years.

Early entrepreneurs also saw the worth of post cards and began mailing what became known as exposition cards, which were used for advertising and not intended to be souvenirs. The earliest known exposition card appeared in 1873 and showed the InterState Industrial Exposition in Chicago.

The first cards published as souvenirs were placed on sale in 1893 at the Columbia Exposition in Chicago. However, the postage was two cents, whereas the government-printed post cards remained at one cent. Public pressure eventually ended this Post Office "monopoly." By an Act of Congress on May 19, 1898, publishers of printed mailing cards, or postcards, were granted permission to sell cards to the general public that could be mailed for one cent, the same as the Post Office card. But, as with the government postals, writing was still on the front, or picture side, of the card with the address on the opposite side.

A major breakthrough came in 1907 when the divided back card was introduced, which allowed one side to be used exclusively for the picture while the other side provided spaces for both message and address. This revolutionary innovation ushered in the "Golden Age" of postcards.

Deltiology, the collecting of postcards, is the third largest collectable hobby in the world,

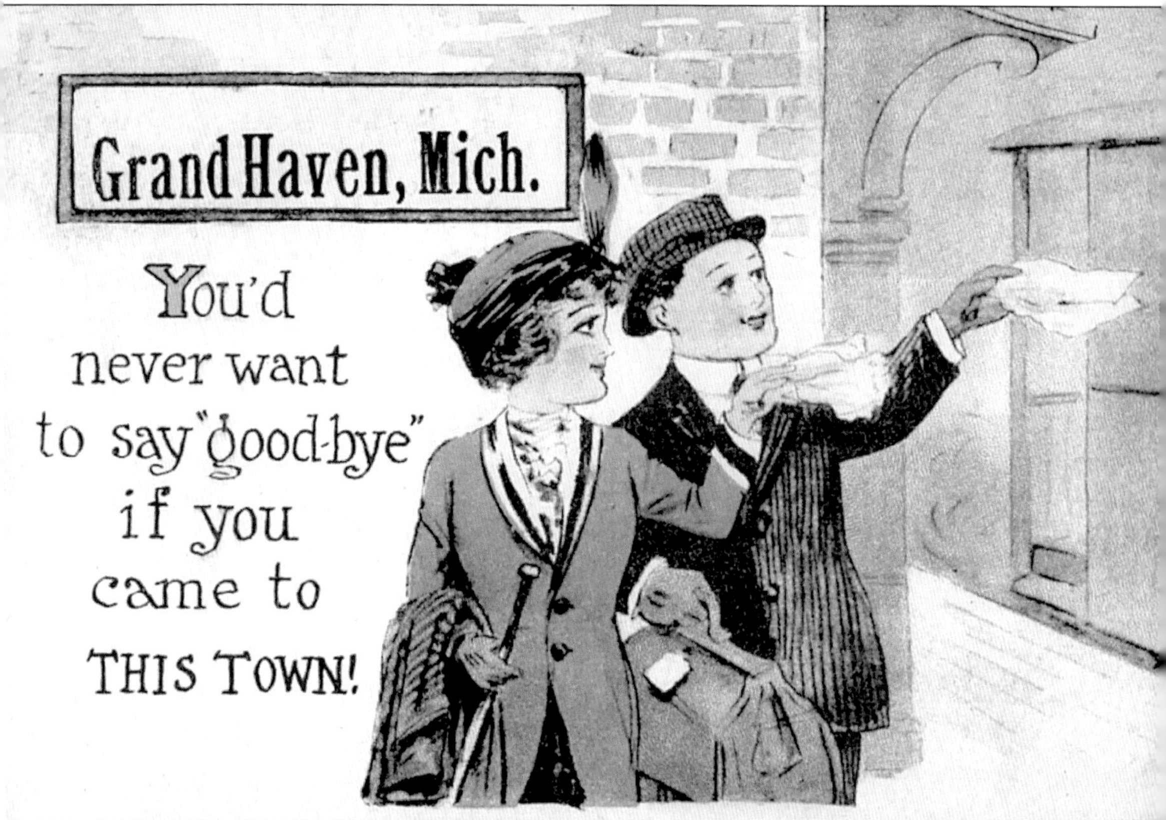

Some postcards, like this one, consisted of whimsical cartoon-like characters in humorous situations. Although the card features Grand Haven, the name of any city could have been printed in the box. The card is undated.

surpassed only by coin and stamp collecting. The evolution of the postcard can be divided into seven overlapping eras: Pioneer,1870–1898; Private Mailing Card, 1898–1901; Undivided Back, 1901–1907; Divided Back, 1907–1915; Early Modern or White Border, 1916–1930; Linen, 1930–1945; and Photochrome, 1939–present. By referring to these eras, collectors can approximately date a card even without a postmark. Part of the postcards' appeal was that publishers took the liberty of improving scenes to make them "perfect." Although all the cards in this book are black and white, most of them originally were "colorized" for distribution. Throughout most of the 20th century, the astonishing detail and clarity of "real photo" postcards made them consistently popular and always favored by collectors. As the name suggests, real photo cards were reproduced by photographic means rather than a rapid printing process. Other variations were the "double panel" fold-out postcard, which offered a panoramic "wide angle" view, and the split view, which offered more than one scene on a standard-sized card.

Occasionally publishers printed postcards in packets, using an accordion-like hinge that allowed as many as a dozen views to be mailed as a unit. The earliest known packet from the Grand Haven area was postmarked 1907 and contained 12 miniature views of local landmarks, each measuring two by three inches.

In this collection the reader will see samples of all types of cards, and we hope each will convey at least a taste of what life was like in the Grand Haven area in those bygone days.

One

Safe Harbor

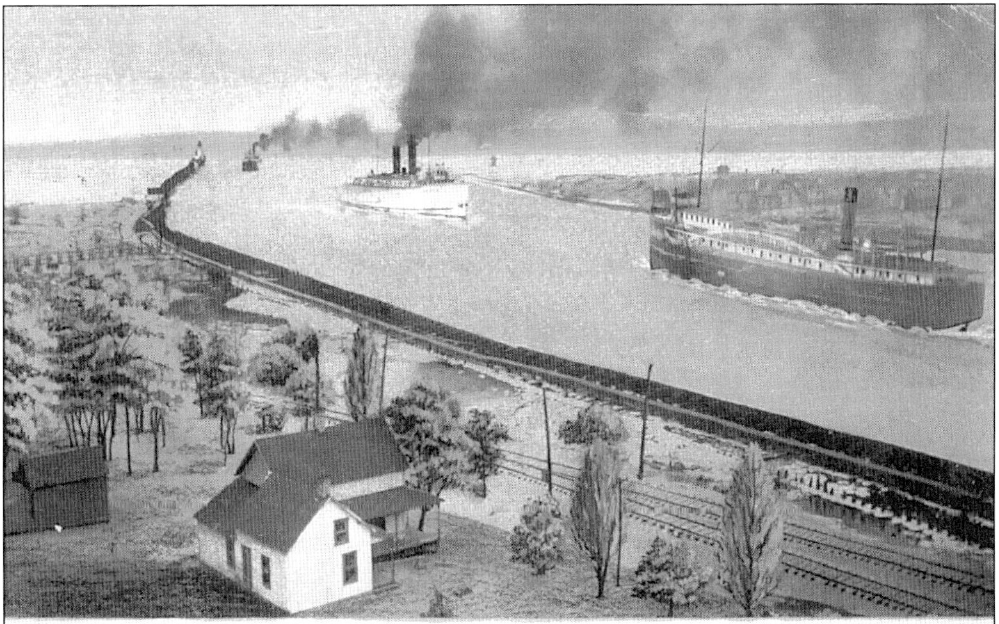

Nat Brown, a Grand Haven photographer, copyrighted this postcard in 1908. As with many picture postcards, the scene was enhanced to make it more appealing. Even an extra track for the Interurban was added! The outward bound ship is the steamer *Nyack* and the incoming vessel appears to be one of the Grand Trunk ferry boats. There is a third, unidentified ship at the far end of the south pier.

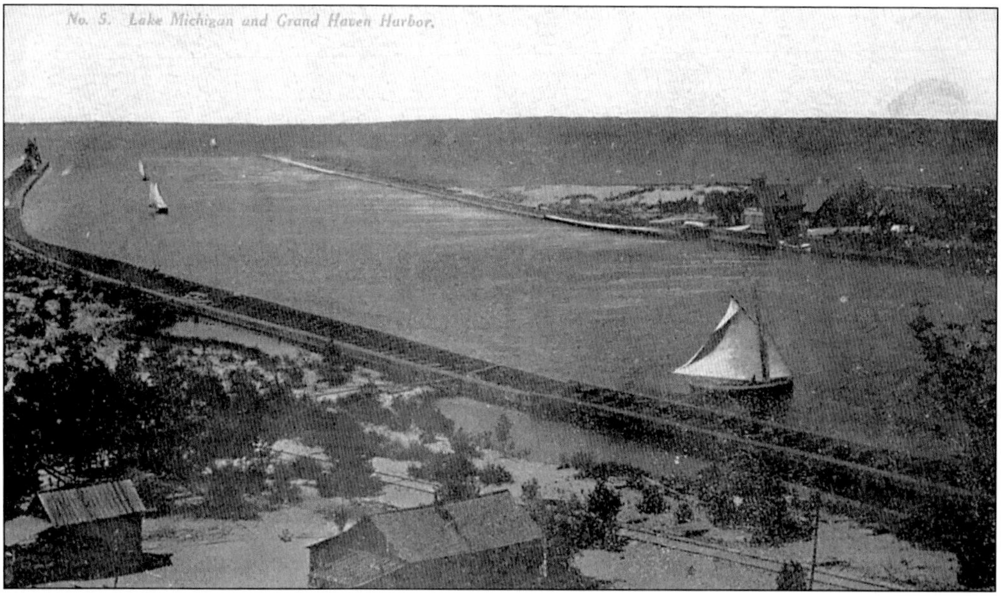

The view in this unmailed postcard presents a more realistic scene than the previous one, including the rustic farm house. The single Interurban track can be seen between the sheds in the foreground and the revetment. The Life Saving Service Station across the channel is somewhat hidden by the shadows. It is rare to see small recreational boats in the channel in these early years.

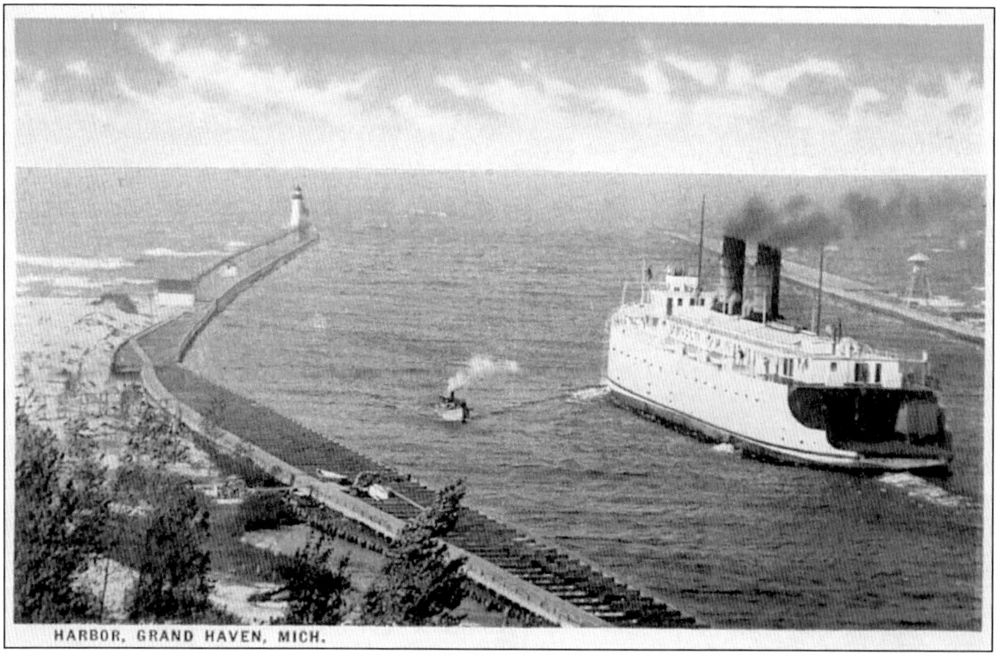

The Grand Trunk Railroad ferried entire freight trains between Grand Haven and Milwaukee. After reaching the other side of Lake Michigan, the cars could continue their journey east or west. The sun is just catching one end of a boxcar in the ship's large hold, as shown in this card postmarked 1910. The south pier was extended to its present length in 1893, but the beacon on the bluff remained the primary guiding light until 1905.

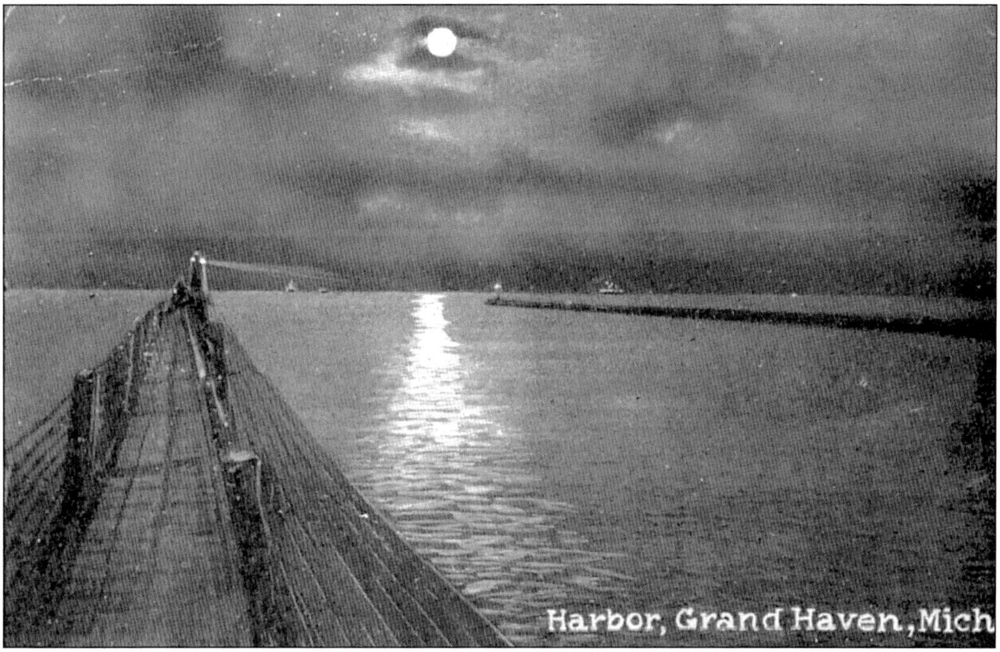

Although touched up by an artist to make it more romantic, this 1915 card displays a rare night scene with the moon setting over the entrance to Grand Haven Harbor. There appear to be about a half dozen well-lighted ships dotting the horizon. The picture was taken from the catwalk that allowed a lighthouse keeper to traverse the pier even in a fierce storm.

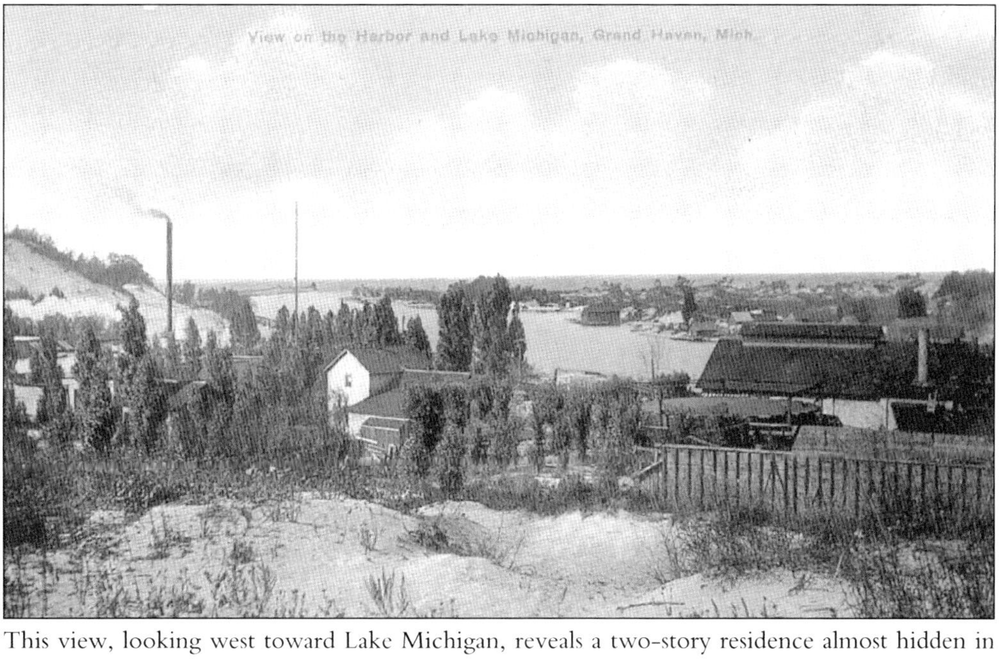

This view, looking west toward Lake Michigan, reveals a two-story residence almost hidden in the wooded dunes. The large factory at right of center appears to be the American Mirror & Glass Beveling Company, now the site of Sandpiper Condominiums. The tall chimney on the left was part of the early Grand Haven Water and Light plant. The card is dated 1908.

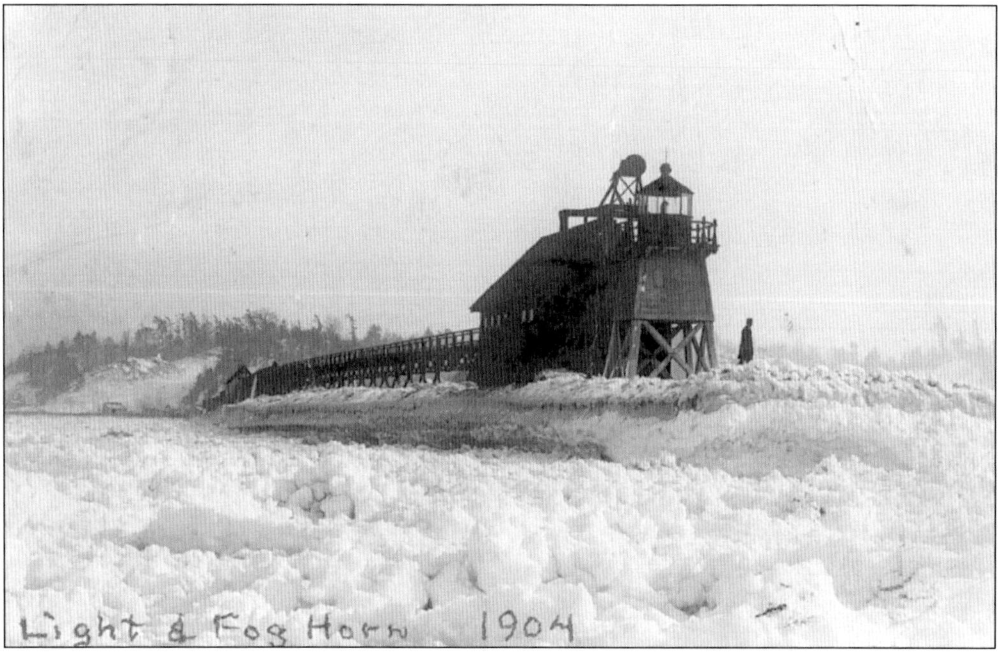

This unusual view shows the lighthouse and fog horn shed as they appeared in 1904 to its present length. The uniformed man standing at the end of the pier looks like Captain Frank Fraga, the lighthouse keeper from 1900 to 1911. The card is dated 1904.

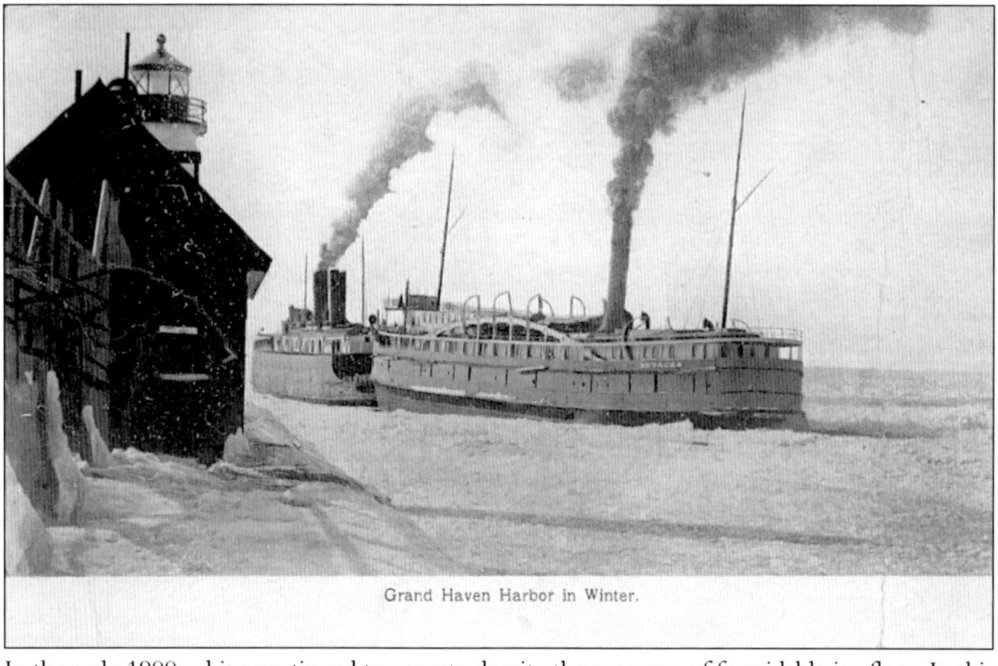

In the early 1900s, ships continued to operate despite the presence of formidable ice floes. In this undated photo, the carferry *Grand Haven* breaks a path through the ice for the steamer *Nyack* as it heads out of harbor. The 52-foot lighthouse behind the foghorn on the south pier was placed at the end of the pier in 1905 and was moved back 600 feet to its present position two years later.

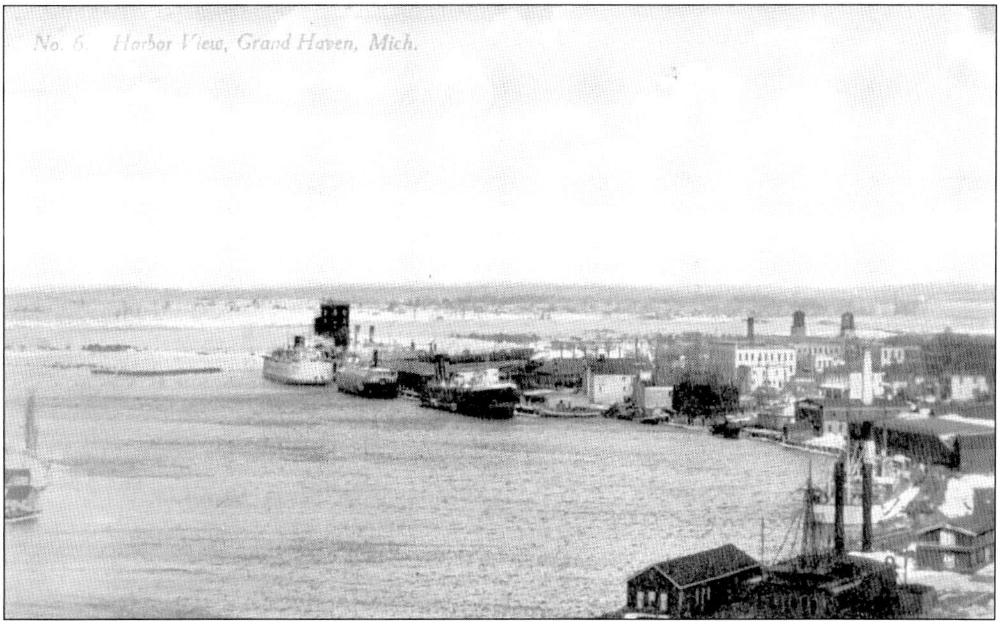

The seven-story grain elevator, built around 1890, is the dominant structure near the center of this undated and unmailed postcard. There are at least five large ships moored, four of them near the elevator. To the right of center is the three-story Gildner Hotel, currently known as the Kirby Grill, with the two-story Andre House, now the Tip-A-Few and Wessel's Garage, to the right of the Gildner. The grain elevator was destroyed by fire in 1914.

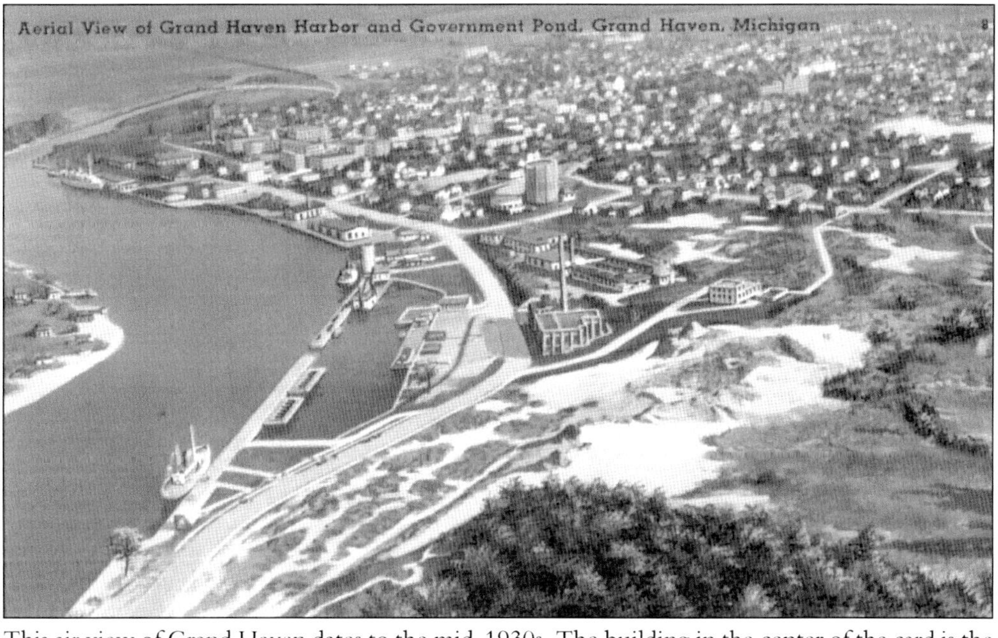

This air view of Grand Haven dates to the mid-1930s. The building in the center of the card is the Grand Haven Board of Light and Power. Slightly to its right is the city's Water Filtration Plant, while behind it is Michigan Brass Company. Sherman was not yet a through street. The *Escanaba* was in port, as was the steamer *Alabama*, farther upstream.

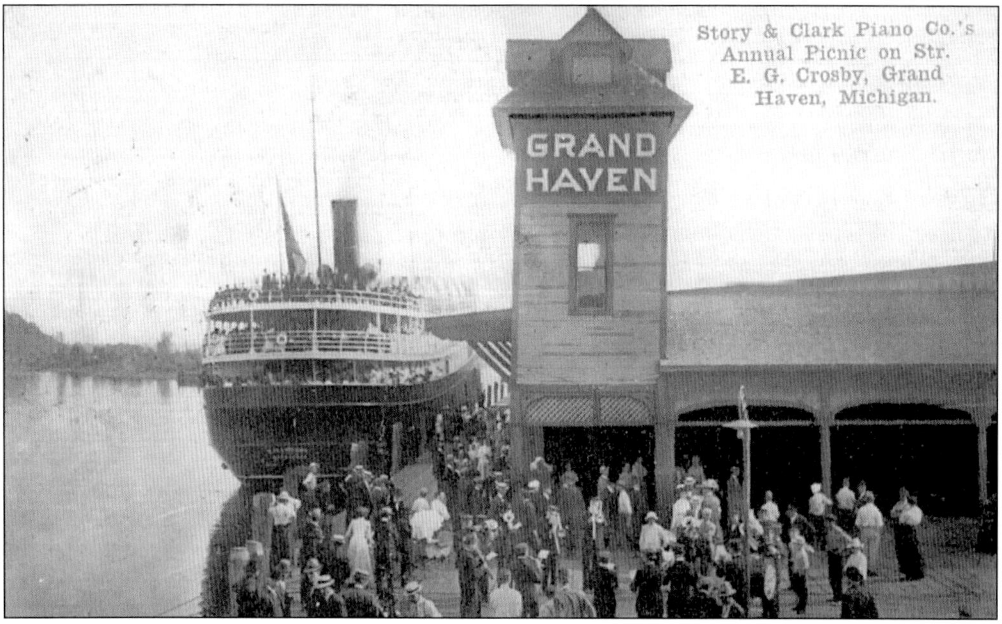

The caption on this 1914 postcard lets the viewer know that the crowd of people waiting to board ship for their annual picnic were employees of the Story & Clark Piano Company. A band in the center foreground helps get the crowd in proper spirit. The steamer *E.G. Crosby* appears to be well loaded with people before the final boarding. The dock was at the foot of Washington Street.

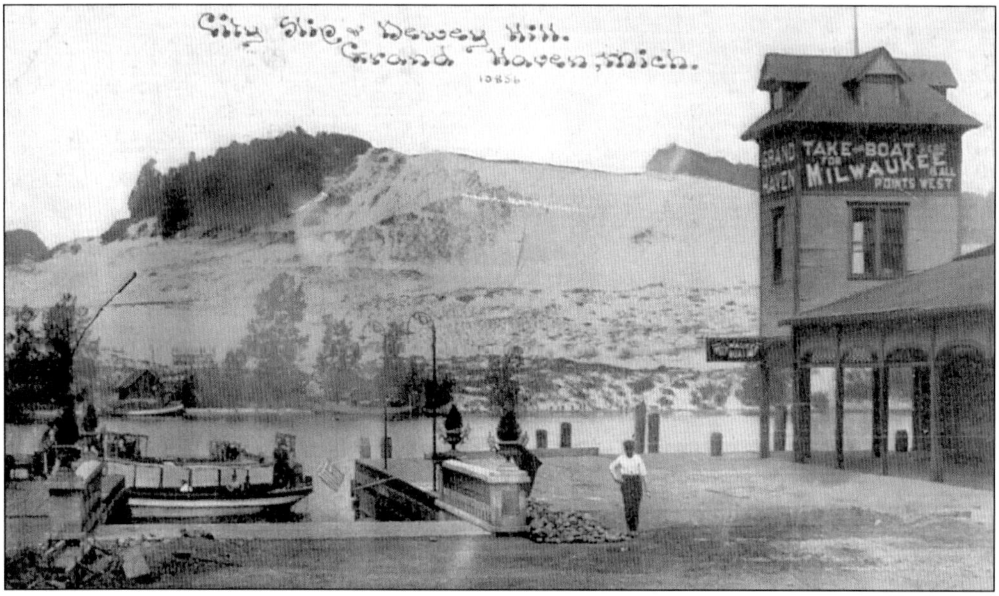

The E.G. Crosby Transportation Company operated steamships out of Grand Haven. Its office was at the foot of Washington Street, in a building attached to the Grand Trunk Railway Depot. Riders could come into Grand Haven on the train and continue their journey to Milwaukee and "points west" by walking a few steps to the dock and boarding ship. A slip for smaller boats can be seen at the left in this 1910 postcard. A large sign across the river advertises the Goodrich Line, which offered passenger service to Chicago.

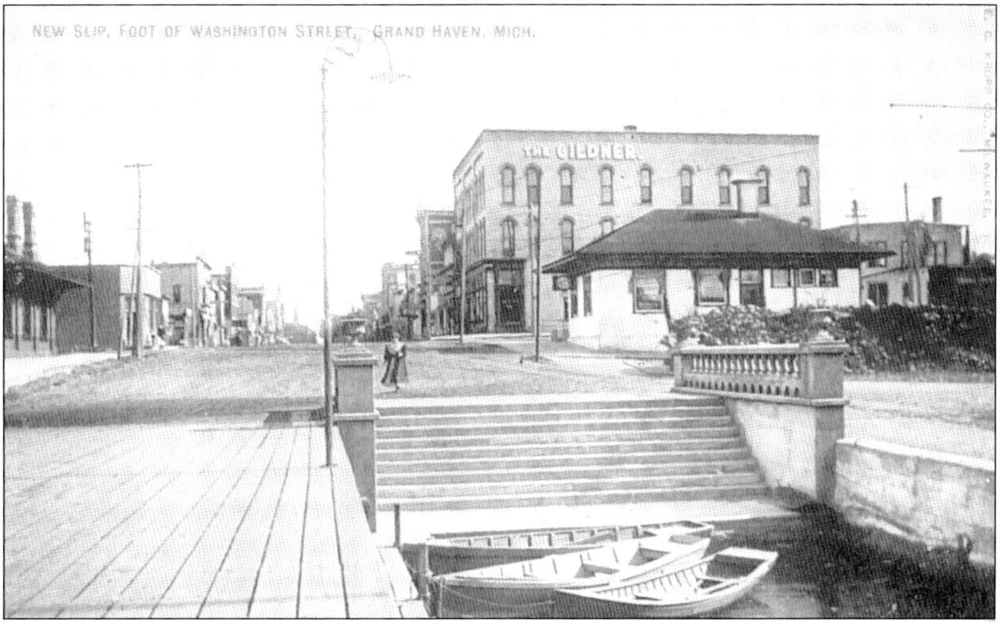

The steps at the foot of Washington Street led to a landing for small boats. The building at the right was Nat Robbins's office, now headquarters for the Chamber of Commerce, and across Harbor Drive was the three-story Gildner Hotel. The end of the Grand Trunk Railway Depot can be seen to the left, and the concrete-block building on the northeast corner of Harbor and Washington is Bruce Hewitt's Saloon. Not far beyond that is William Hanrahan's Saloon, and the next structure is the Story & Clark office building.

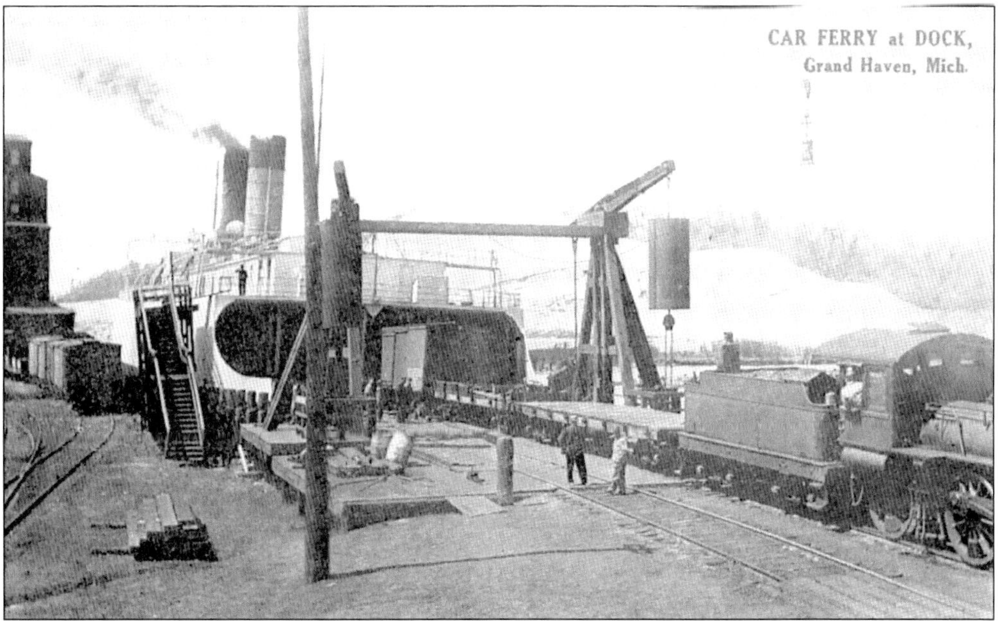

This scene shows in detail how freight cars were loaded onto a carferry to continue their trip across Lake Michigan. The dock area is now part of Chinook Pier. The seven-story grain elevator is visible at the left edge of the postcard and Dewey Hill can be seen across the Grand River.

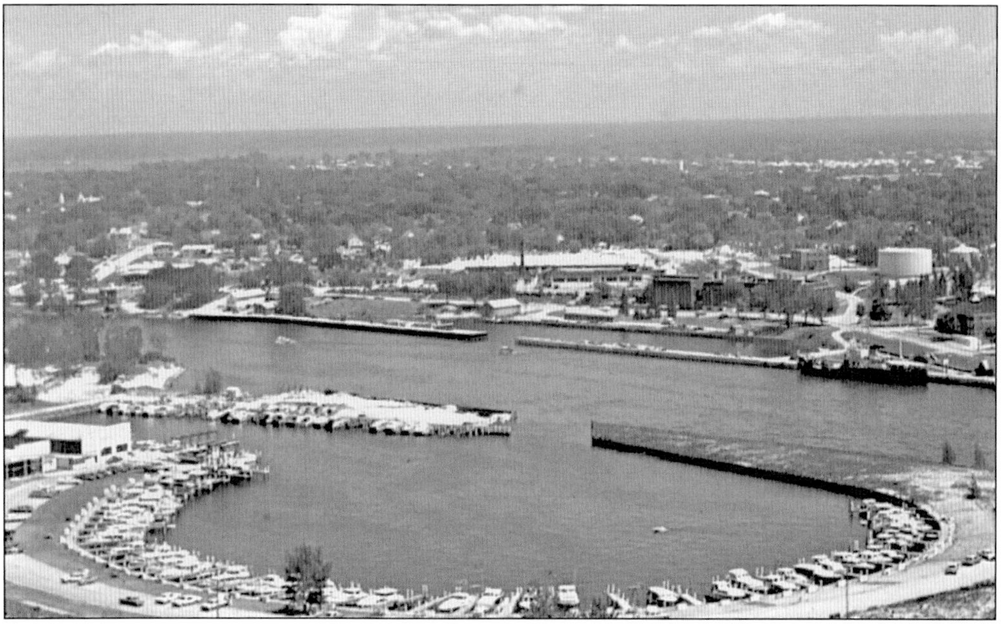

In 1952, Clare Jarecki of Grand Rapids purchased 85 acres on the north side of the channel and developed North Shore Marina. This aerial view dates to the mid-1960s, before Sandpiper Condominiums replaced Michigan Brass Company on Harbor Drive. The caption on the reverse of the postcard noted that this was "one of West Michigan's largest and most complete marinas."

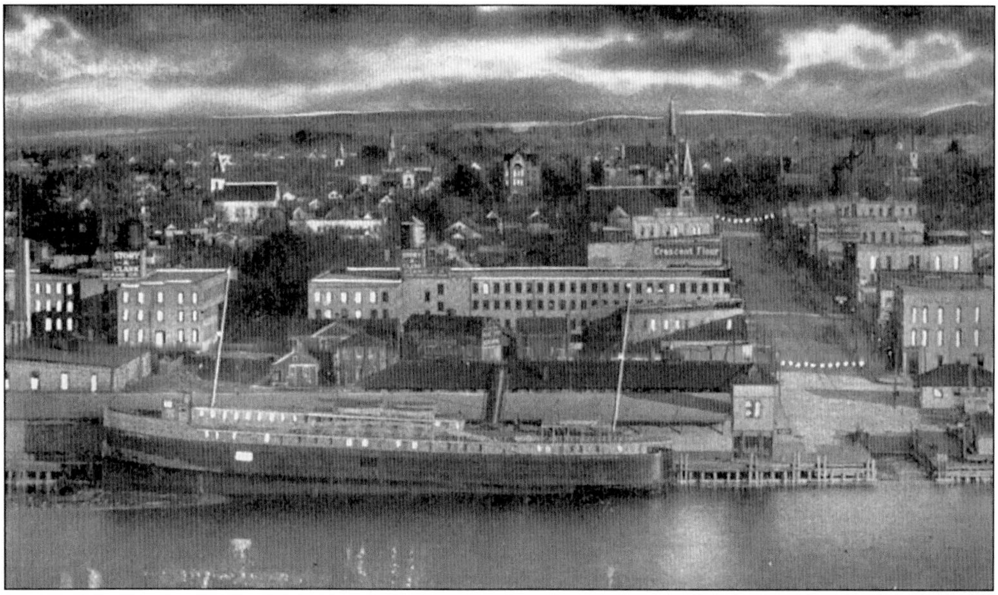

This rare nighttime view, taken by Nat Brown from Dewey Hill, shows remarkable detail, including lights in many of the windows. The two Story & Clark Piano buildings are near the center of the card. Nat Robbins's office is near the right edge, and across from that is the Gildner Hotel. At the time of this photograph, a warehouse was still attached to the Grand Trunk Depot, now the home of the Tri-Cities Historical Museum. The lights strung across Washington Street must have marked a special celebration—or may have been added by the photographer.

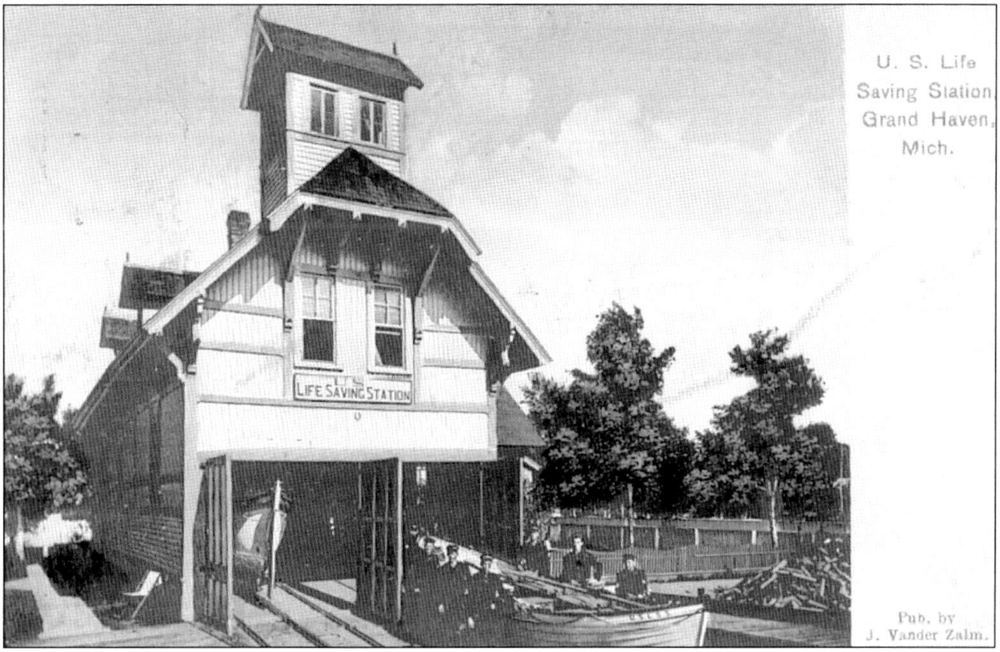

A volunteer life-saving group was organized in Grand Haven in 1871 under the leadership of Captain William R. Loutit, and six years later it became part of the United States Life Saving Service. In 1878 a life-saving station was constructed on the North Shore. That station, pictured in this 1908 card, served until a larger building was put into use in 1922.

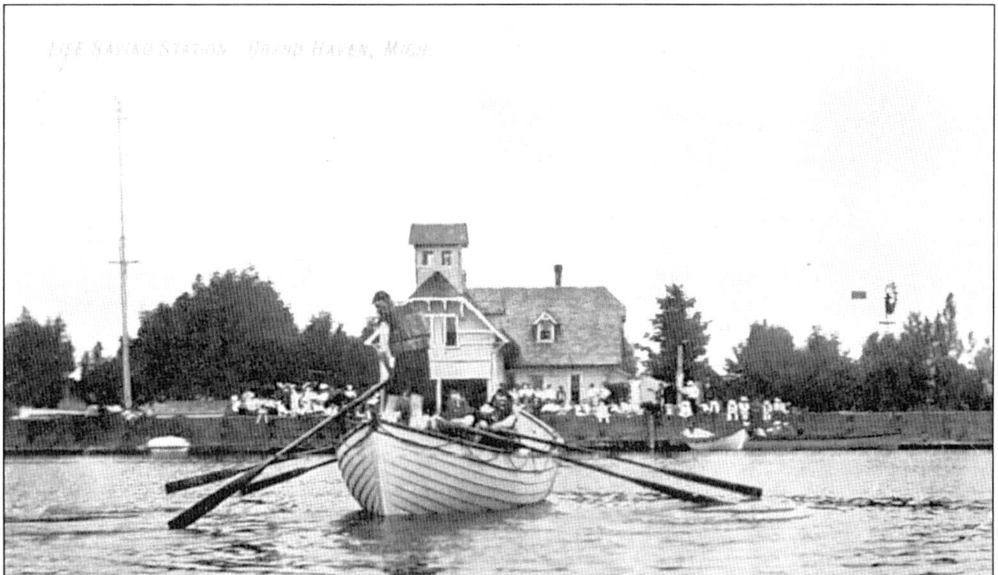

By act of Congress, the United States Life Saving Service merged with the Revenue Cutter Service in 1915 to form the Coast Guard. In this scene, which dates to about 1910, the crew of the USLSS are putting on a life saving demonstration for several dozen people observing from the riverbank. The building was located not far from the beach on the North Shore.

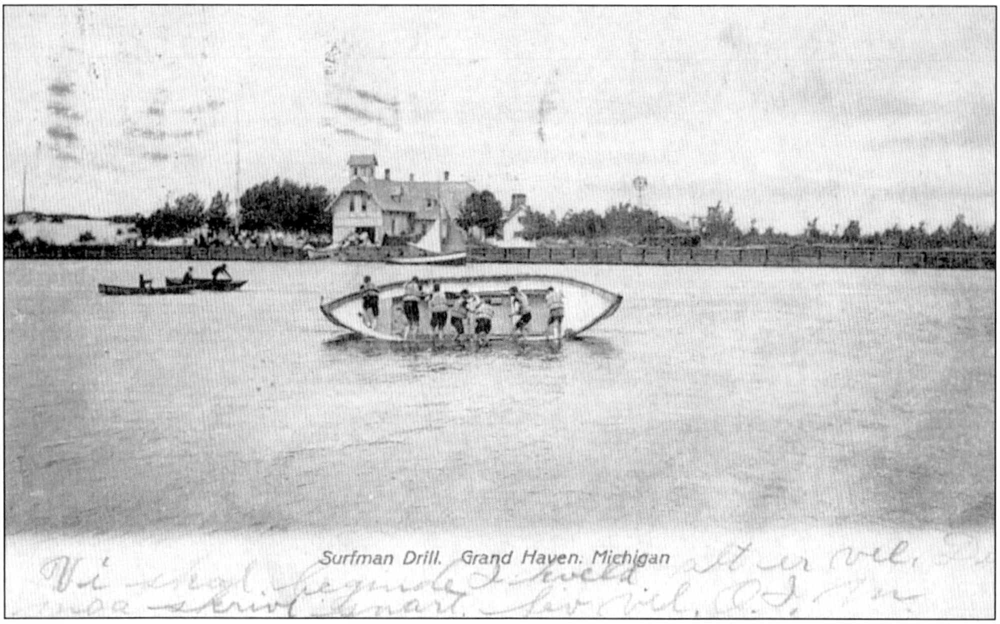

This card, dating to 1906, provides a clear view of the enlisted men demonstrating a capsize drill. The Station on the opposite shore was built in 1878 and served until 1922. The only way to reach the North Shore at the time of this picture was by boat. Still, a crowd of spectators made the short boat trip and stood on the north revetment to view the exercises. The crew members in the boat were referred to as "surfmen."

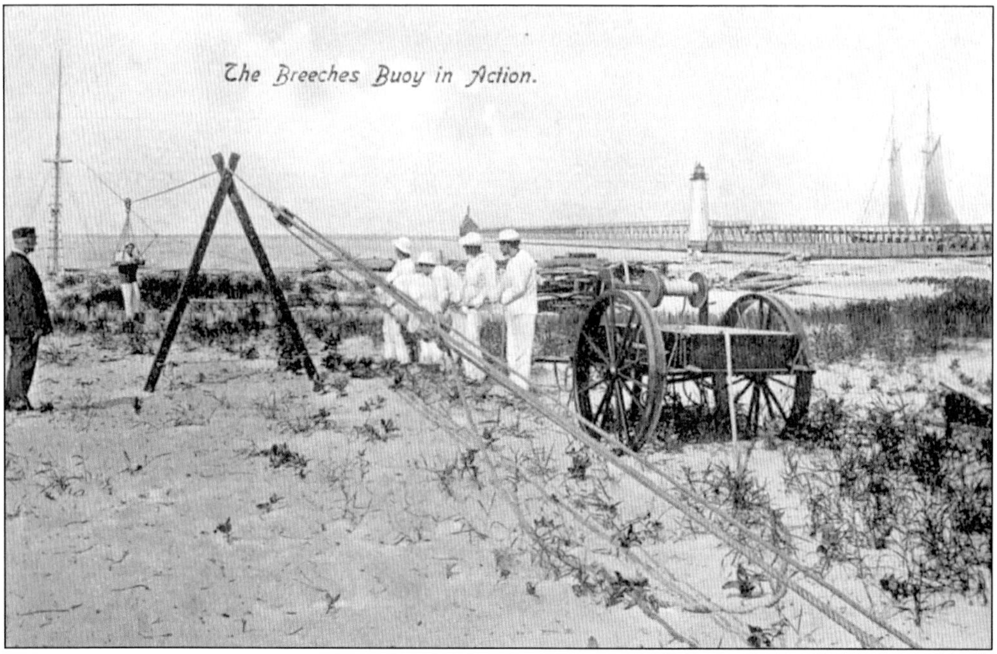

With the familiar south pier in view, the Life Saving crew practices using the breeches buoy, sometimes the only method by which the men on a ship marooned offshore could be brought to safety. Note the gaff-rigged schooner passing between the pierheads. The card dates to about 1906.

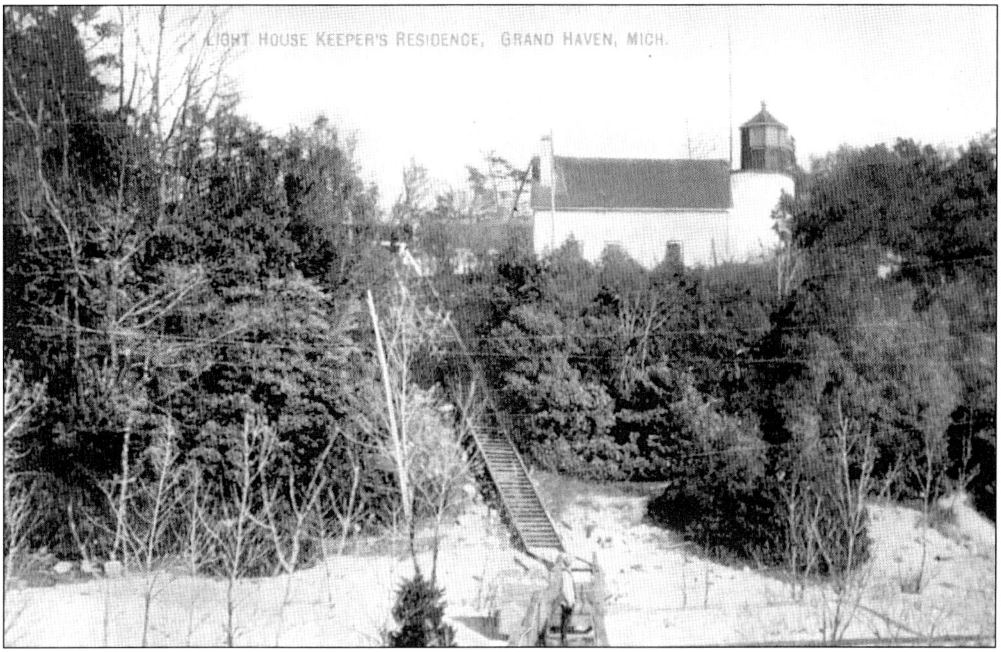

Although the tower has long since disappeared, the basic structure of the lighthouse that once stood upon the wooded, sandy bluff near the entrance to Grand Haven Harbor can still be seen. The original lighthouse operated from 1855 to 1905. The tracks at the bottom of the card carried the Interurban that ran slightly south of Highland Park. The card is postmarked 1911.

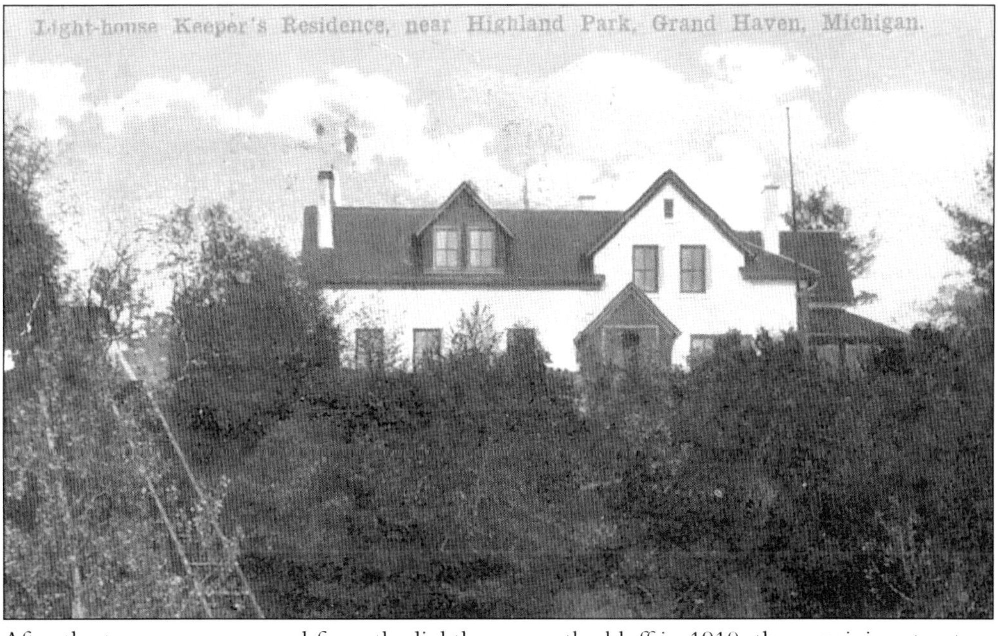

After the tower was removed from the lighthouse on the bluff in 1910, the remaining structure was improved and expanded to include 13 rooms. It was used as a residence for the lighthouse keeper and his family until 1939. Since 1956, it has served as an apartment complex with an address of 900 Harbor Drive. The card is postmarked 1912.

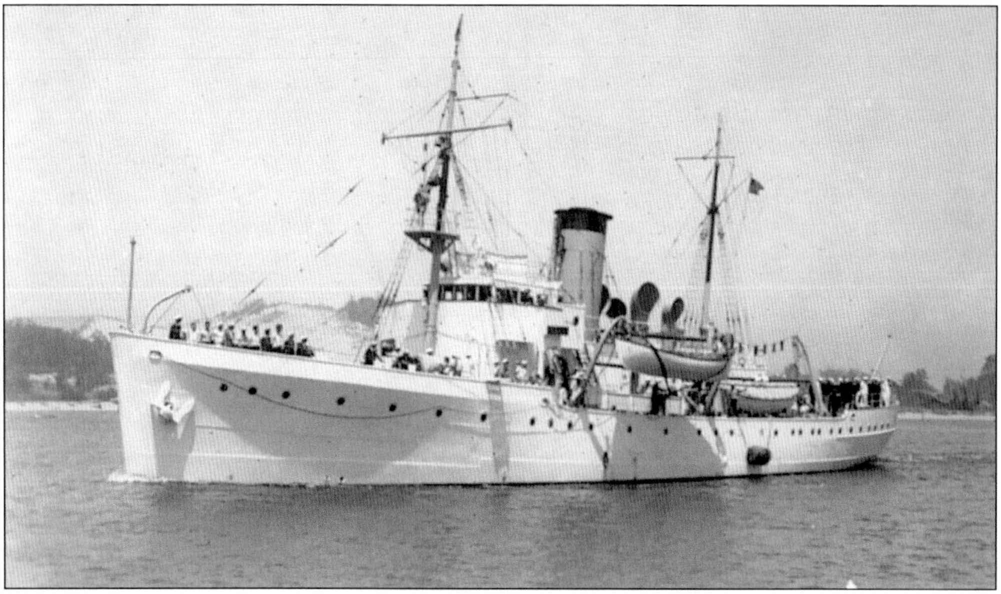

The Coast Guard Cutter *Escanaba* steamed into port on a cold, blustery day in December, 1932. The sleek, white cutter was a fixture in Grand Haven Harbor for nearly a decade. Called to convoy duty in the North Atlantic during World War II, she was sunk on June 13, 1943 with the loss of all but two of her 103-man crew.

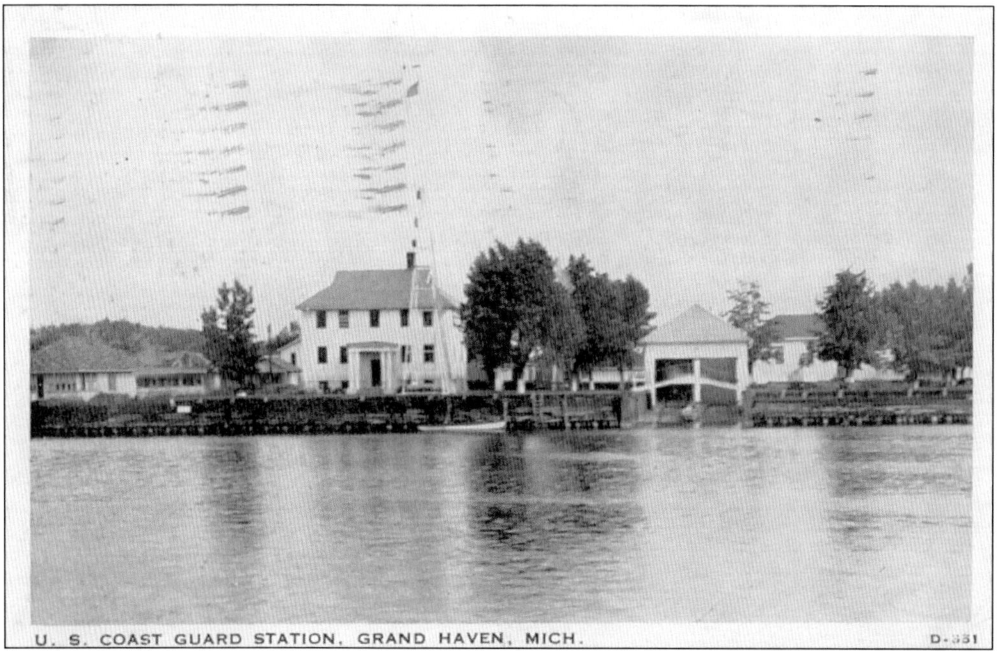

In 1922, the Coast Guard constructed new headquarters and a two-stall boathouse slightly down river from the original Life Saving Service building. These structures served Coast Guard needs until 1989, when the administration building was sold to a private party and remodeled into a residence. The original photograph was taken before 1938, the year the Coast Guard replaced the two-stall boathouse with a four-track launchway.

Two

Ships, Boats, and Packets

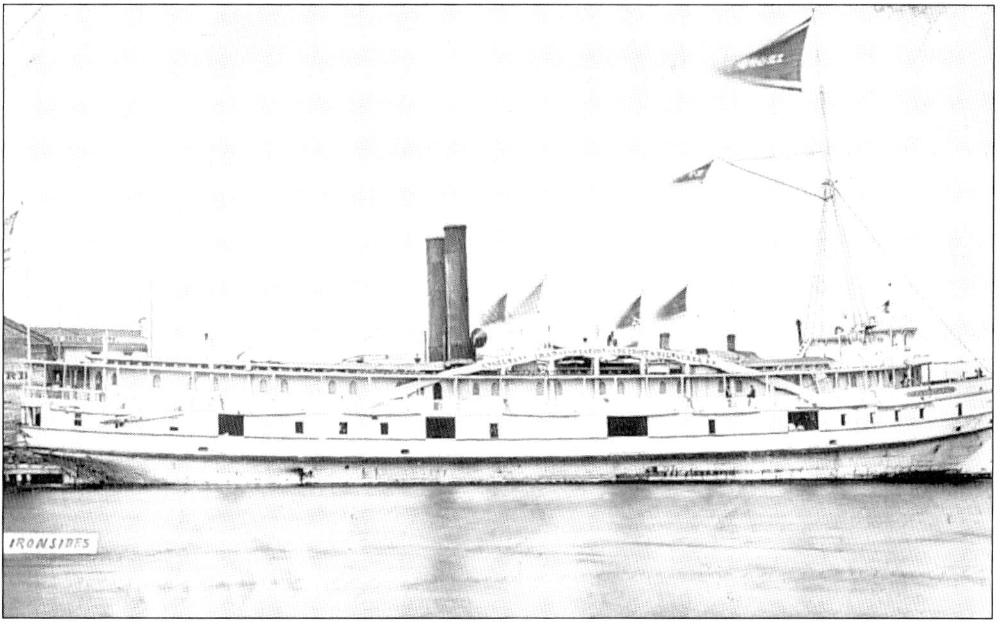

The wooden hull steamer *Ironsides* was destroyed in a late summer storm as she approached Grand Haven Harbor in the early morning of September 15, 1873. Constructed in 1864 to carry iron ore over the Great Lakes, the ship had been overhauled for passenger service earlier that year. Of the 52 crewmen and passengers aboard her that fateful morning, 23 lost their lives. The valiant efforts of the newly-formed volunteer lifesaving crew out of Grand Haven kept the number from being larger. The lettering on the arch reads, "Engelmann Transportation Co. Detroit & Milwaukee R.R." The picture was not taken in Grand Haven and the card is not dated, but clearly it was printed long after the ship went down.

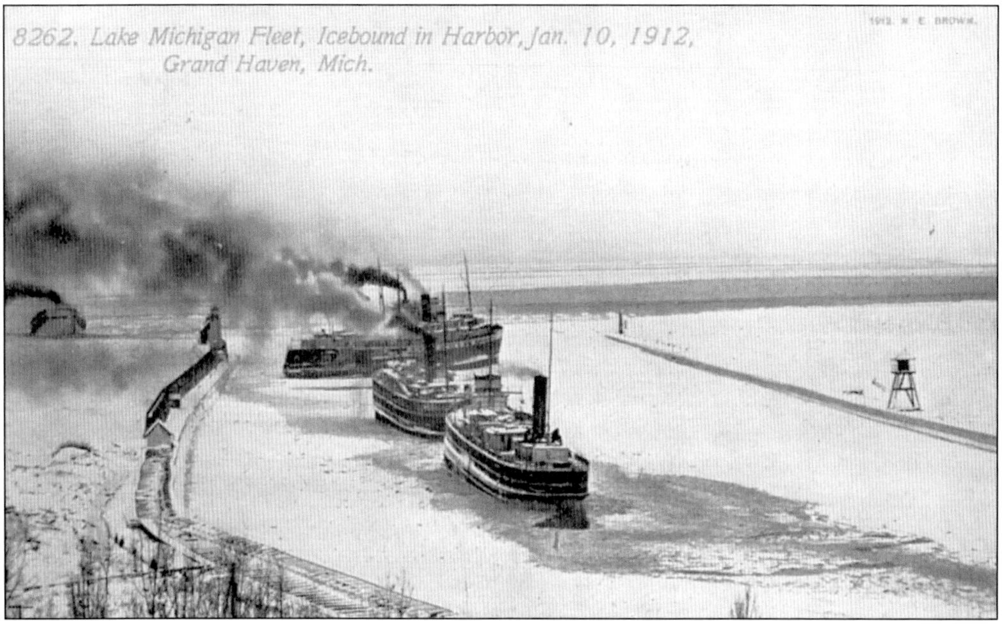

Commercial shipping continued to come into Grand Haven Harbor even in the depths of winter, sometimes under difficult circumstances. This card, dated January 10, 1912, shows four of the big ships between the pier heads trying to make it through the ice to open water. A fifth, off to the left, is waiting to enter port. Nat Brown was the photographer.

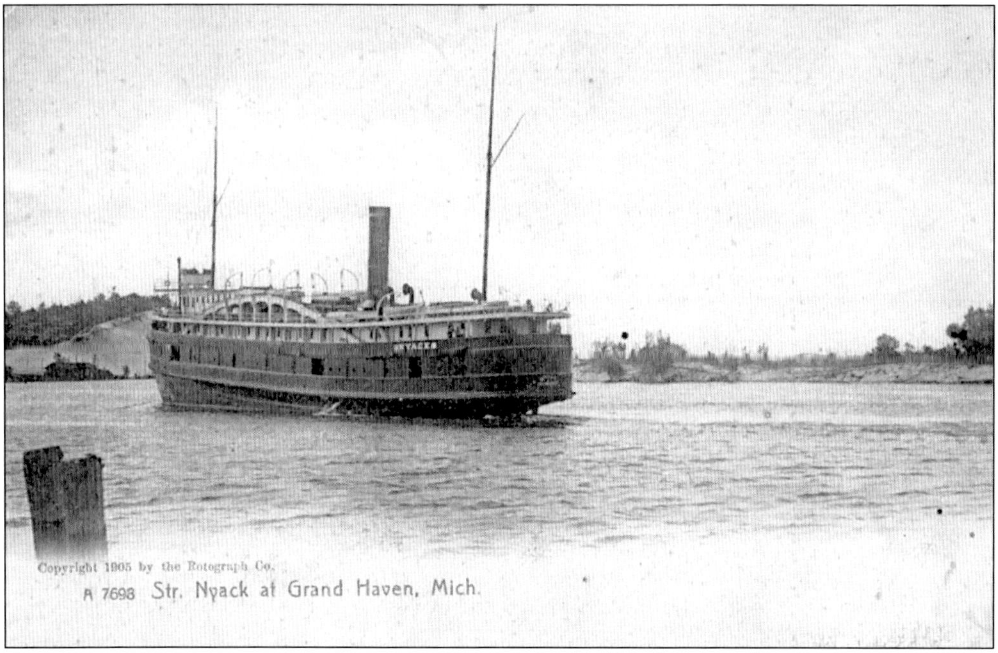

This 1905 postcard shows the steamer *Nyack* heading out of Grand Haven Harbor, carrying passengers and freight to Milwaukee. Built in 1878, the wooden-hull ship was destroyed by fire in Muskegon Harbor on December 30, 1915. Present day Kitchel Dunes Preserve is across the river to the right.

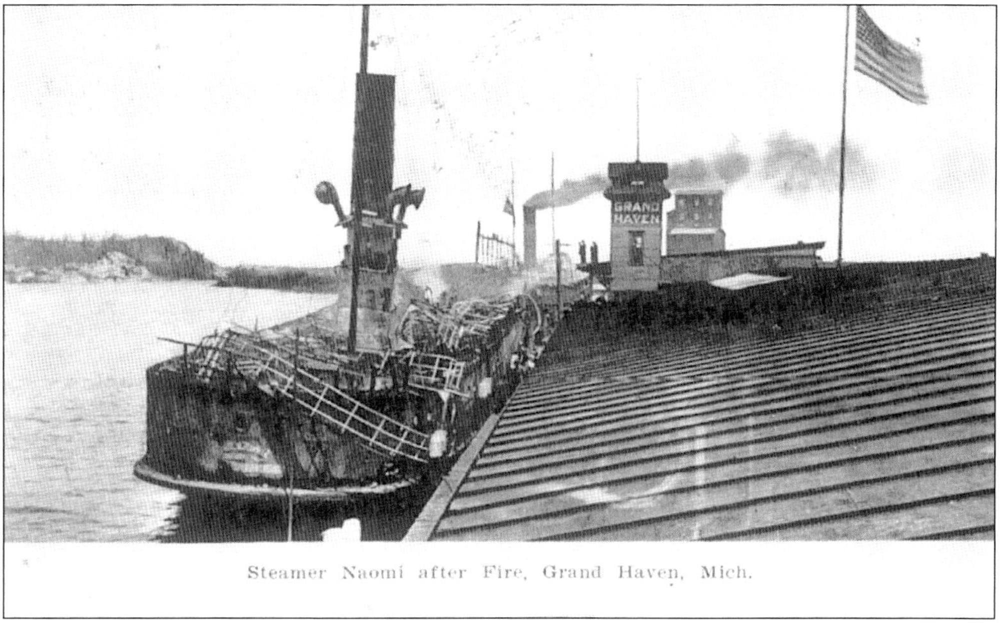

Fire destroyed the steamer *Naomi* on May 22, 1907 in the middle of Lake Michigan, while the vessel was on its way from Milwaukee to Grand Haven. All 51 passengers made it safely to lifeboats, but five of the 31 crewmen lost their lives. The hulk was towed back to Grand Haven and moored along side Nat Robbins's warehouse. *Naomi* was rebuilt the next year and continued operating for more than 20 years under four different names, until she sank in a fall storm in 1929.

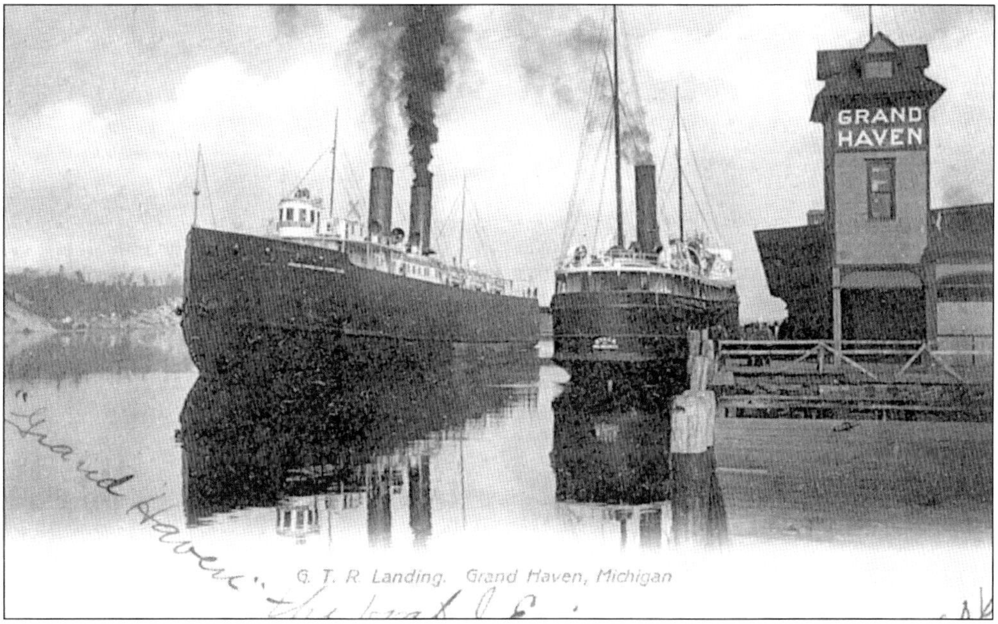

The Crosby and Goodrich passenger lines had adjacent docks at the foot of Washington Street. In this early 1900s view, the *City of Grand Haven*, part of the Grand Trunk Car Ferry system, is headed out of port, while the Crosby's *Nyack* takes on passengers. The "Grand Haven" tower was behind the Grand Trunk Depot and served as the Crosby Line office.

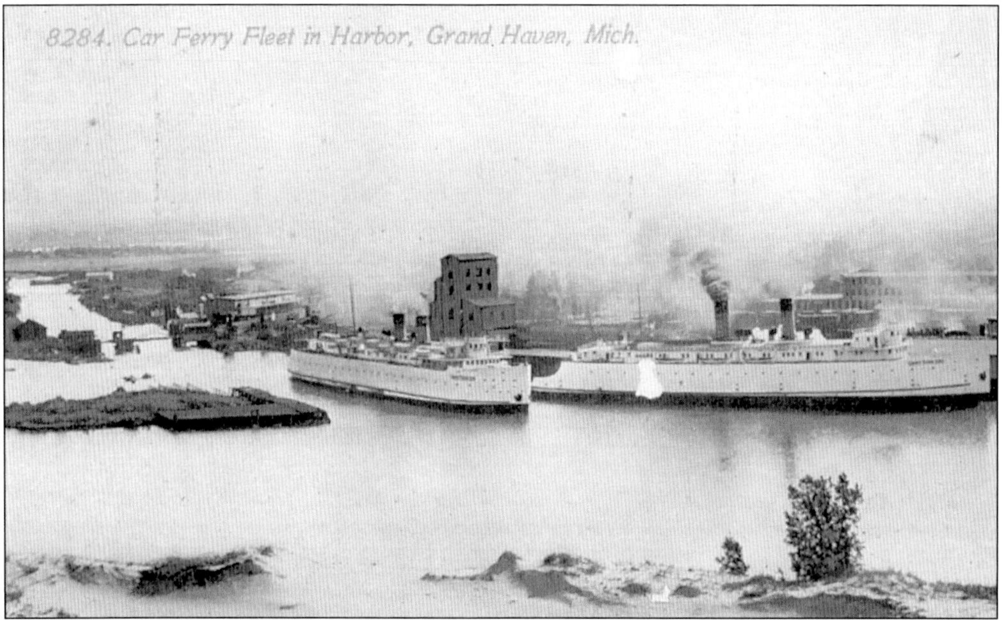

Grand Haven photographer Nat Brown copyrighted most of his postcards, such as this one with a date of 1911. Taken from Dewey Hill—one of his favorite vantage points—the scene shows two of the large Grand Trunk ferry boats getting ready to load or unload freight cars. The tall structure in the center was the grain elevator. The First Street Bridge is also visible to the left.

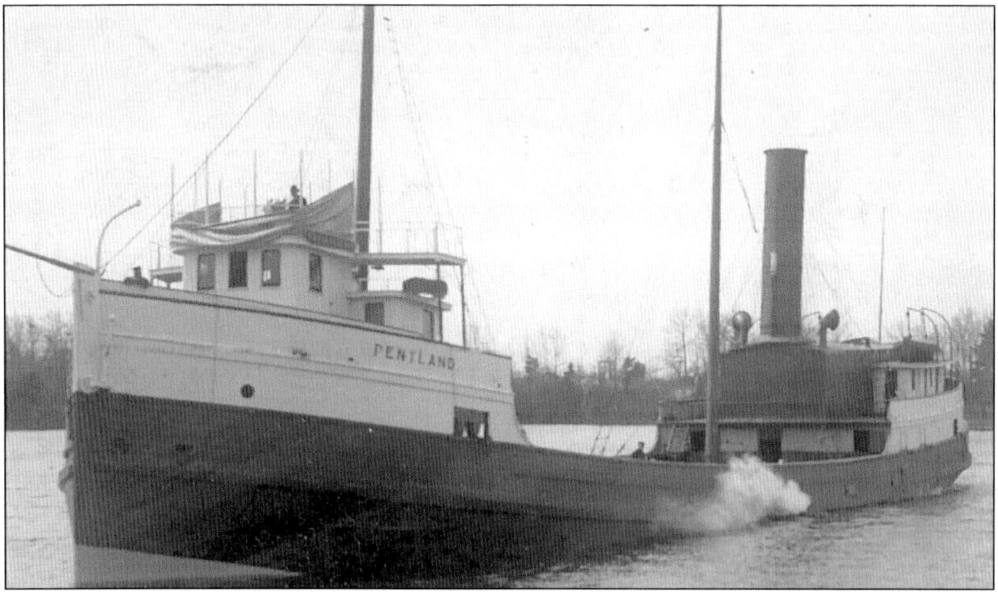

Among the many ships built at Duncan Robertson's shipyards in Grand Haven was the wooden hull *Pentland*, launched in 1894. Captain William R. Loutit was the owner. The 160-foot craft was steam-powered and screw-driven. She was a frequent visitor to Spring Lake in the early 1900s, hauling ore from the Upper Peninsula to the iron foundry at Fruitport. In 1928 the *Pentland* ran into a breakwall in Ontario, Canada, and was destroyed beyond repair. The card's postmark is blurred, but dates to around 1908.

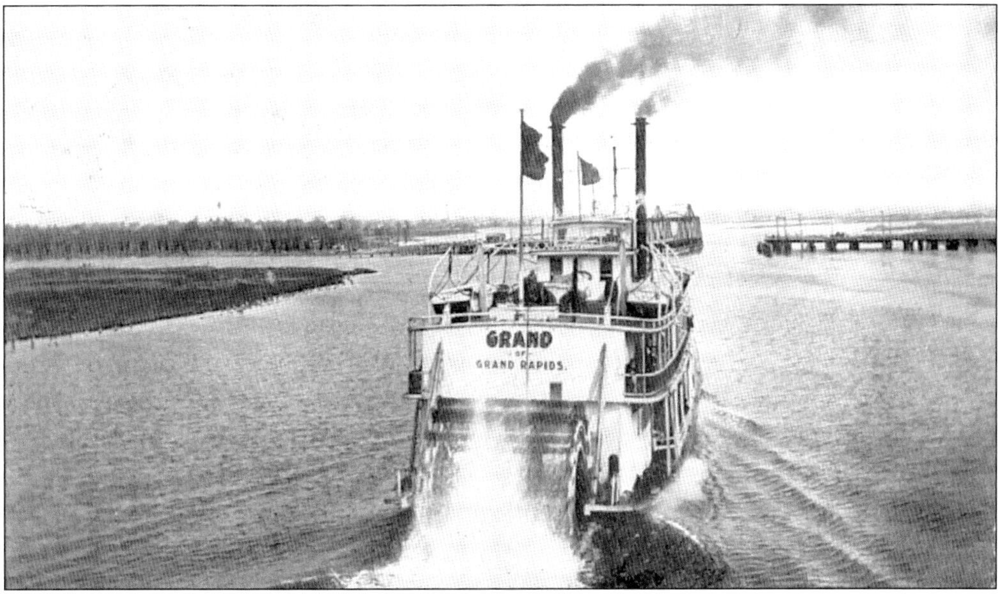

The sternwheeler *Grand* was launched in Grand Rapids in 1905. The steamer is seen here on its way to Grand Haven around 1908. The 1870 railroad bridge in the distance is open to allow passage. The 134-foot classic riverboat with dual smokestacks plied the river between "The Rapids" and "The Haven" for just two years and then began to perform similar duty on the Ohio and Mississippi Rivers. The boom at the bow was used to load and unload freight.

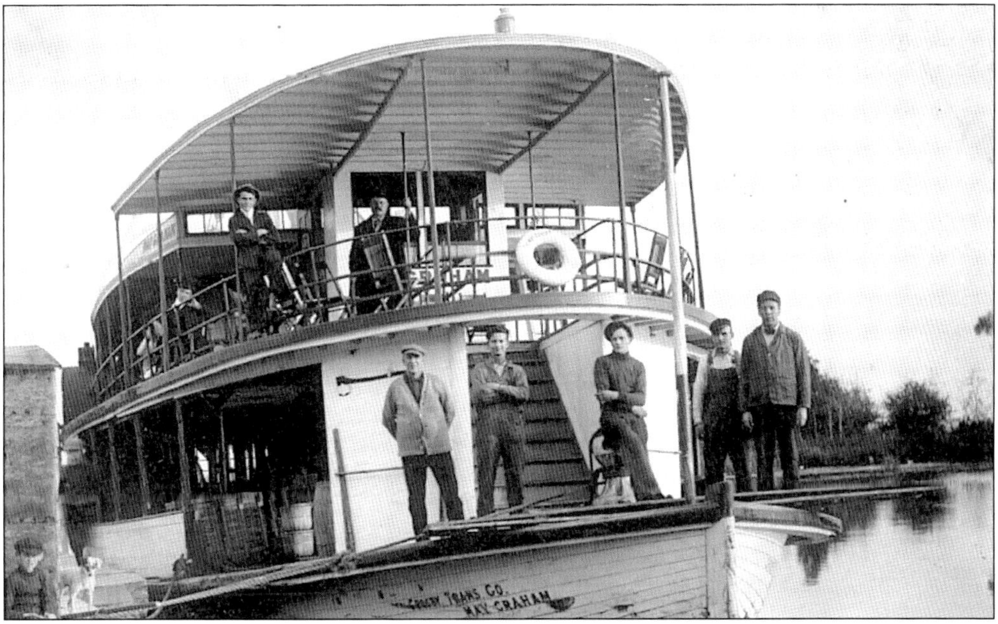

The packet *May Graham* appears ready to retire from its job of moving passengers, freight, and mail up and down the Grand River. The vessel was taken out of service in 1918 and its pilot house, seen in this postcard view, was converted to a cottage on North Shore Cove. When North Shore Marina was constructed in 1952, the cabin was razed. The lettering on the prow confirmed that the *May Graham* was owned by Crosby Transportation Company.

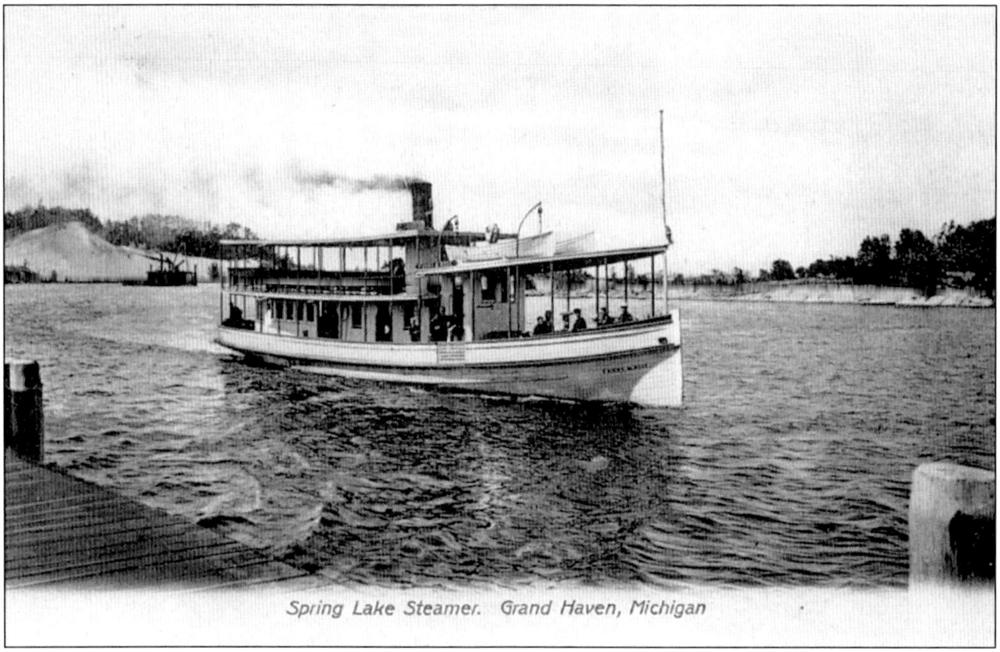

The waterways provided a convenient and efficient route to transport people, freight, and mail. Small steamboats called packets were especially popular, such as the *Fanny M. Rose*, shown in this unmailed postcard. This packet was launched in 1893 and steamed between the shores of Spring Lake and Grand Haven Harbor.

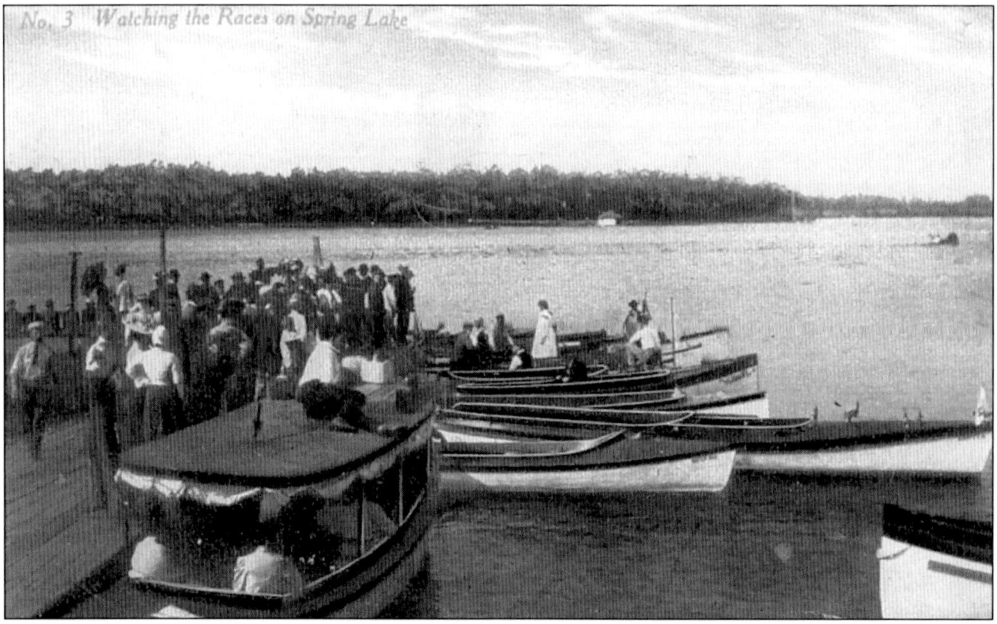

The spectators in this picture are gathered on a dock to watch Nat Brown go for a cruise in his propeller-driven boat. He is the small figure in the lake, near the right edge. The yacht *Ensing* in the foreground is packed with people as well. This picture was taken from Hammond's Boat Livery, located at the foot of Buchanan Street in Spring Lake. The card is postmarked 1913.

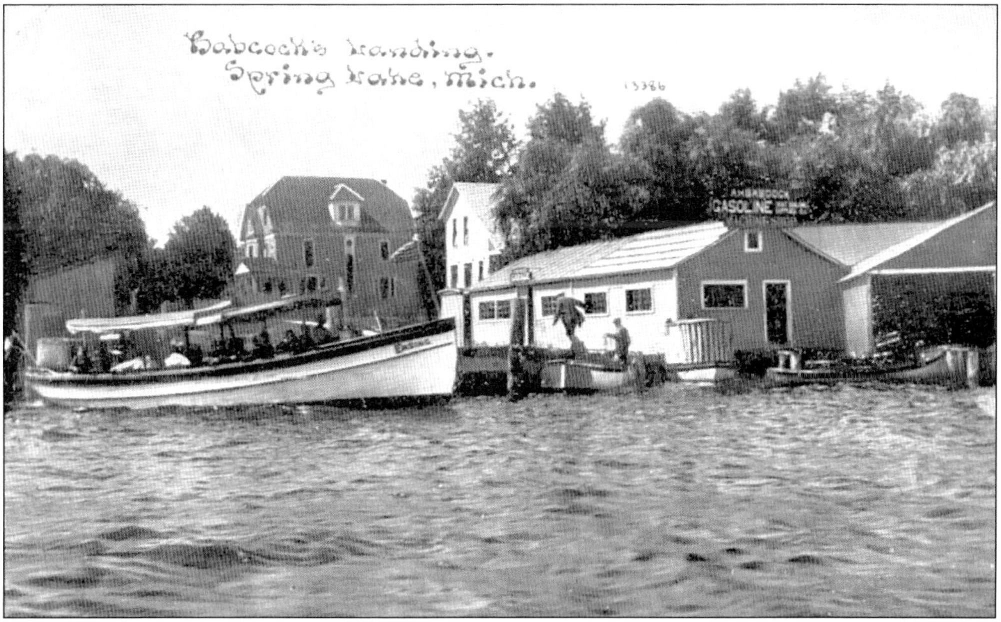

Albert Babcock owned a boat repair shop and offered marine fuel at Babcock's Landing, near the foot of Jackson Street in Spring Lake Village. The packet approaching the landing is the *Ensing*. The card is postmarked 1911.

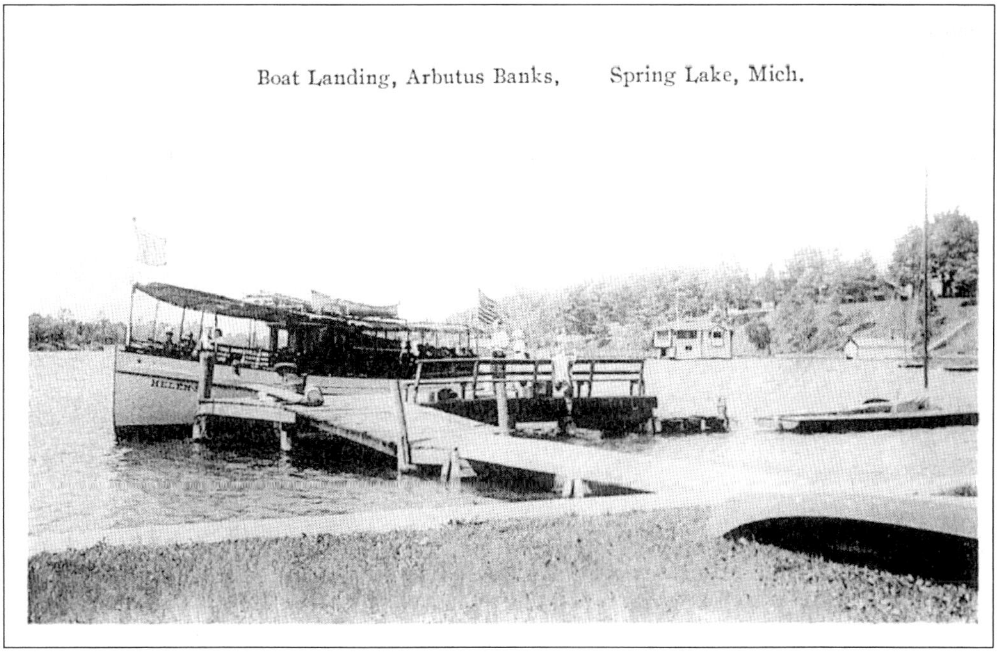

The boat at the dock of Arbutus Banks resort was named *Helen B.* In 1910 it was brought to Spring Lake from St. Joseph, Michigan by Captain Guy L. Boswell to carry passengers between Grand Haven, Spring Lake, and Fruitport. Four years later Boswell added another boat, the *Hazel B.* The card was not mailed.

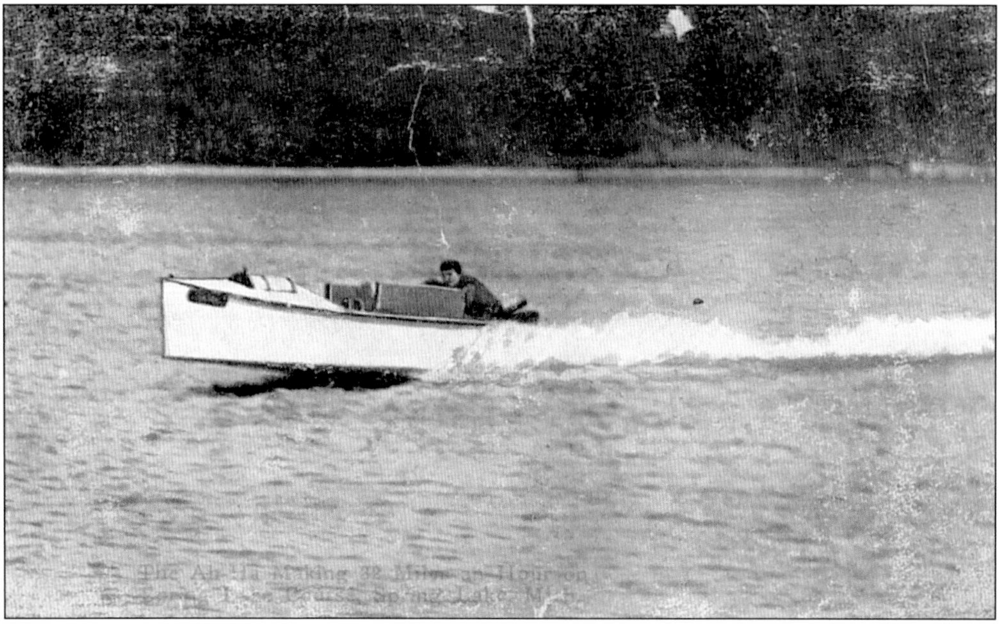

Private sailboats were popular on the lakes by the latter part of the 19th century, but motorboats soon took their place as an important water sport. The caption on this card reads, "The Ah-Ha Making 38 Miles an Hour on Spring Lake Course." In 1908, the Spring Lake Yacht Club accepted motorboating as a legitimate water sport and listed the officers and members of its new Motor Boat Club.

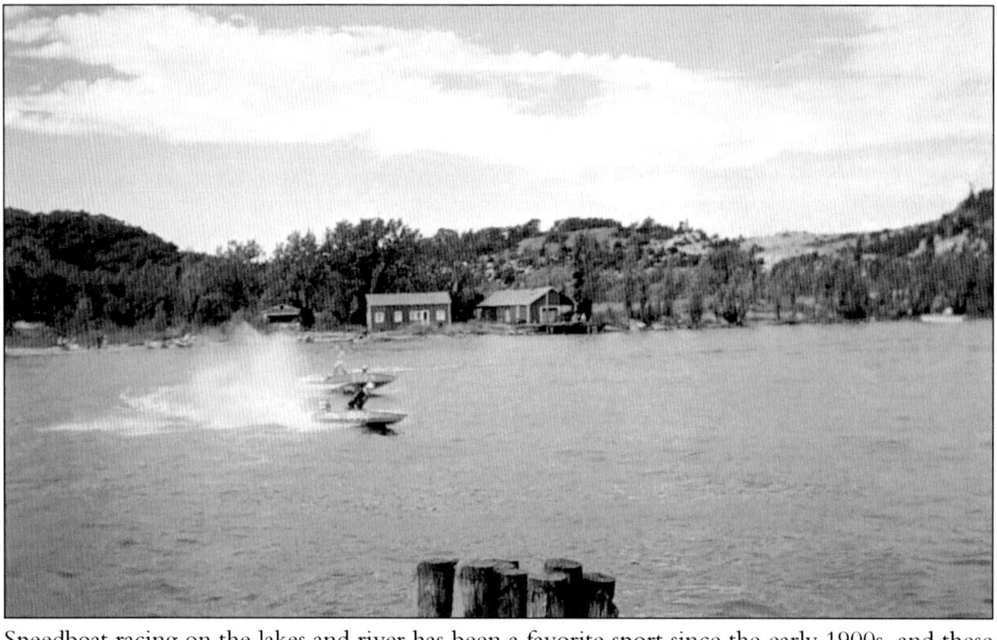

Speedboat racing on the lakes and river has been a favorite sport since the early 1900s, and these two small boats have just made a turn at full throttle. 88V appears to be just slightly ahead of 859M. The buildings across the river are a cottage and two storage barns, all now gone. The card is undated, but the picture probably dates to about 1960.

Motorboats were used for pleasure as well as racing. According to the caption, the name of the boat was "Easy Life." The railroad bridge in the background was constructed in 1870 and still spans the Grand River. Although the caption states the boat is entering Spring Lake, it actually appears to be in the river headed west toward Grand Haven. The card is dated 1918.

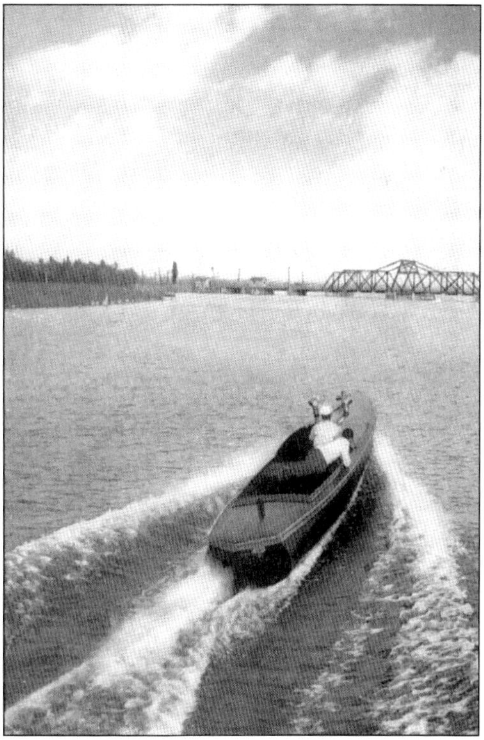

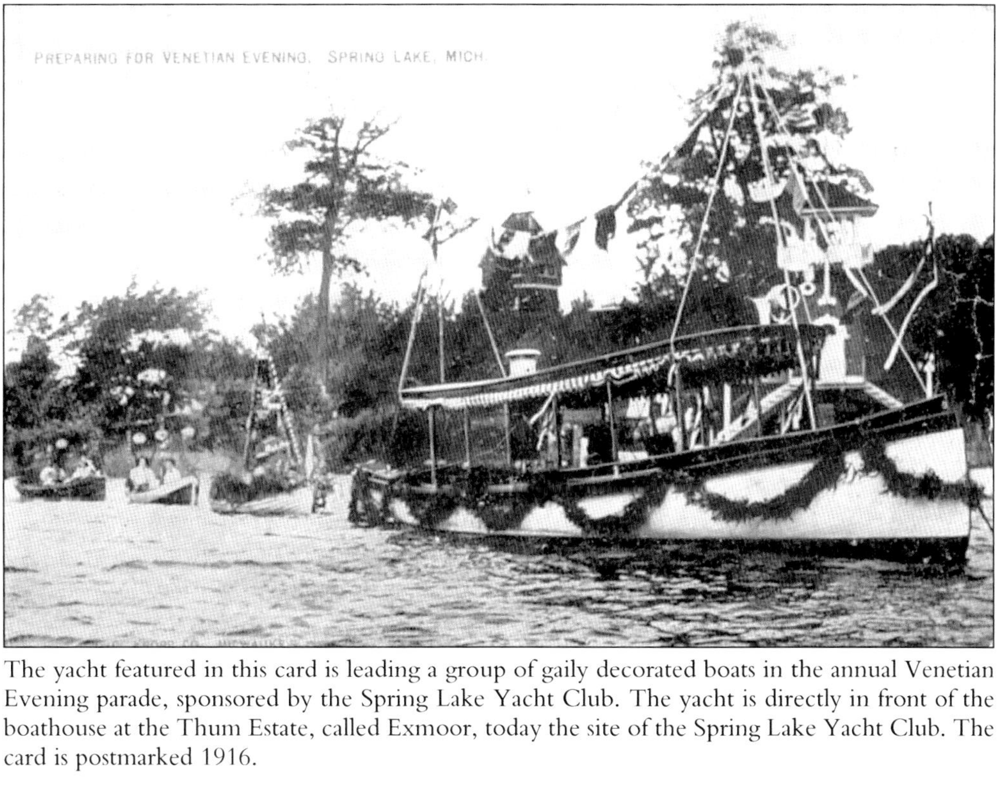

The yacht featured in this card is leading a group of gaily decorated boats in the annual Venetian Evening parade, sponsored by the Spring Lake Yacht Club. The yacht is directly in front of the boathouse at the Thum Estate, called Exmoor, today the site of the Spring Lake Yacht Club. The card is postmarked 1916.

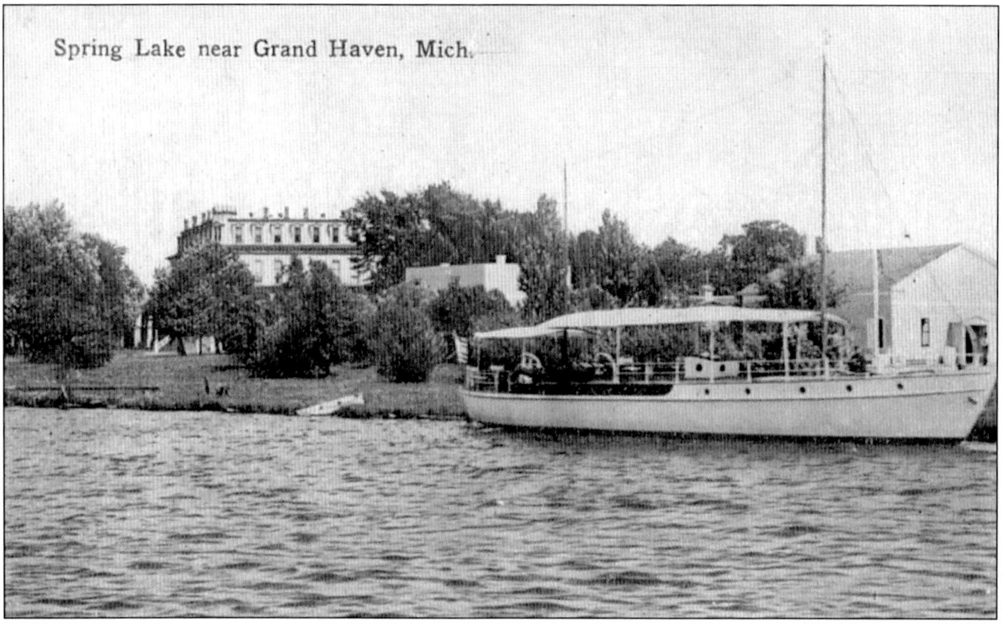

When the Spring Lake Yacht Club was organized in 1897, it used the former Barber School as a clubhouse. In this scene a yacht is moored alongside the shoreline, not far from the Yacht Club and the majestic Spring Lake House. Although undated, the card predates 1916, the year the hotel burned down.

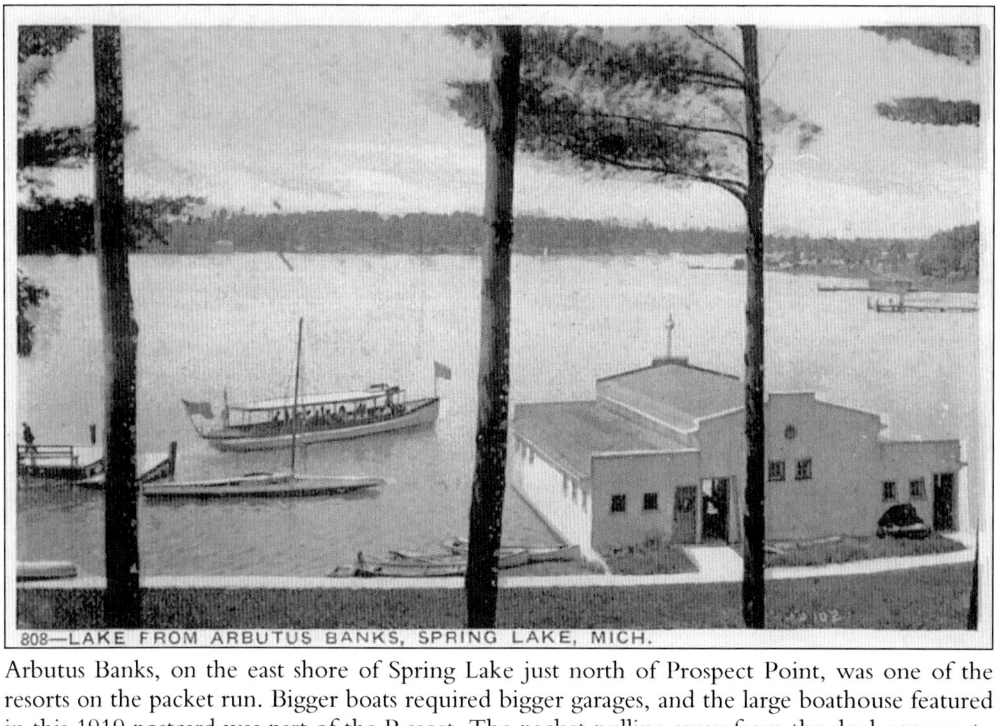

Arbutus Banks, on the east shore of Spring Lake just north of Prospect Point, was one of the resorts on the packet run. Bigger boats required bigger garages, and the large boathouse featured in this 1919 postcard was part of the Resort. The packet pulling away from the dock appears to be the *Helen B.*

Three

Summer Hideaways

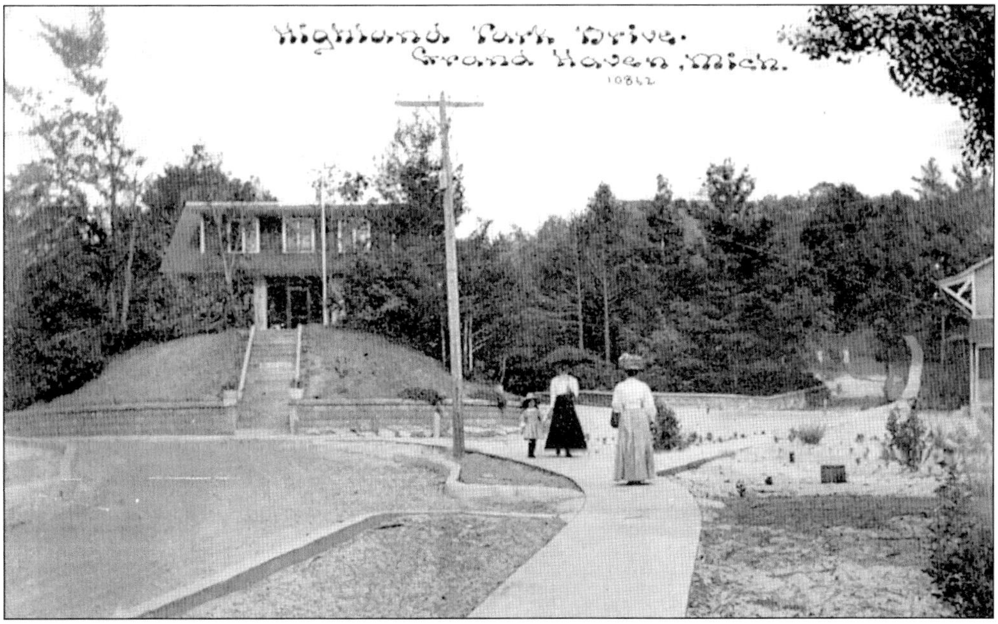

Although postmarked 1925, this photograph appears to have been taken some years earlier, judging from the women's dresses and the unpaved street. By the early 1900s Highland Park had grown to 107 cottages nestled in the wooded dunes. The cottage atop the slight rise near the west end of Lake Avenue was named "Beech Holme."

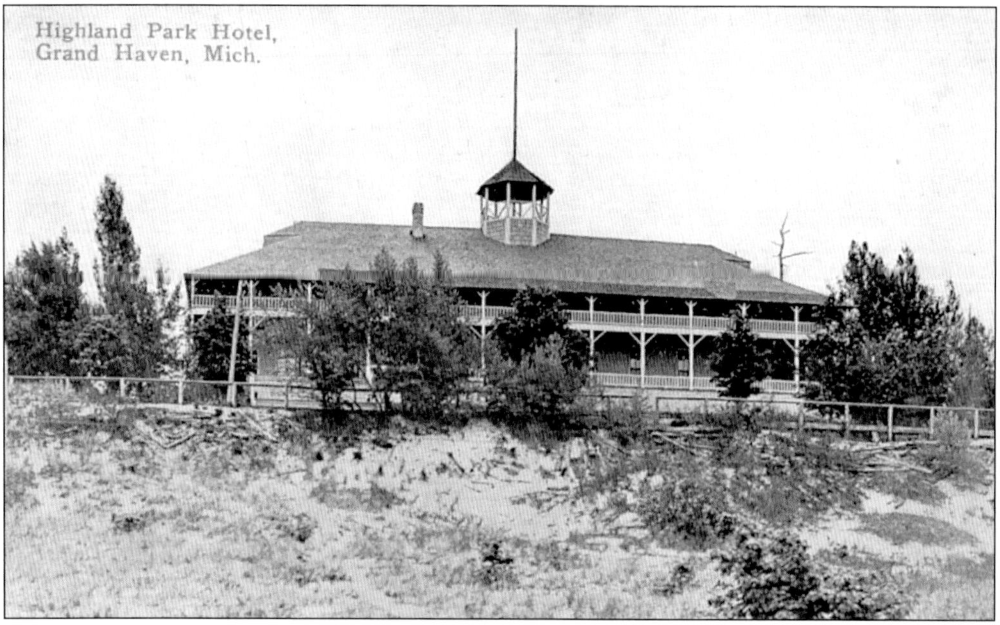

For nearly 80 years the impressive Highland Park Hotel sat high on a wooded bluff overlooking Lake Michigan. Guests from throughout the Midwest came to the hotel by train, boat, and automobile. The three-story frame building was said to rival Mackinac Island's Grand Hotel. This card was mailed in 1915.

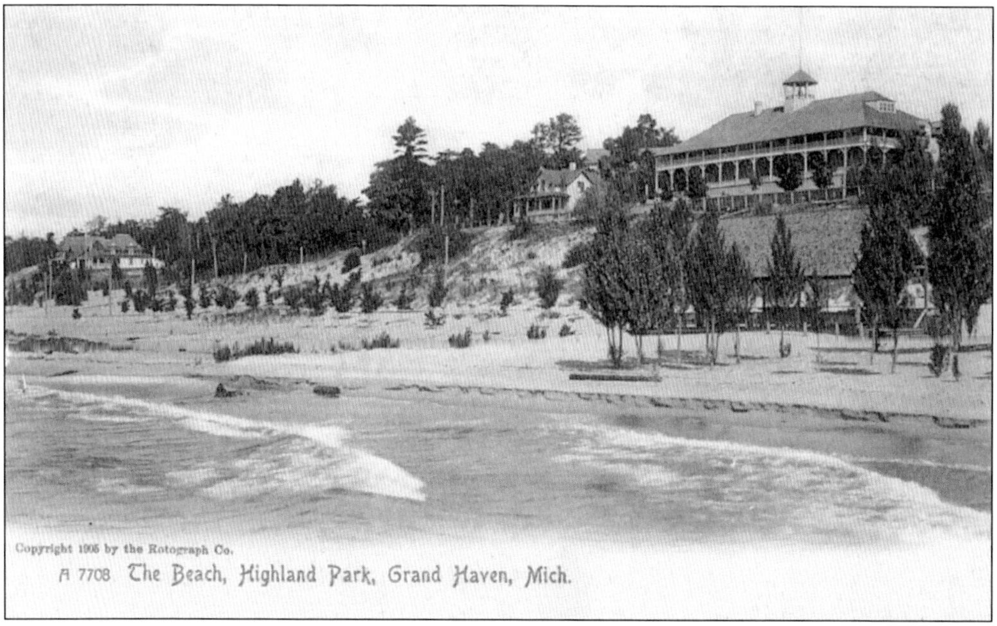

This view of Highland Park Hotel shows it atop a sandy dune near the Lake Michigan beach. The large frame structure with its imposing open porches and cooling lake breezes attracted tourists who wanted to escape the heat of the big cities. The Interurban station is on the beach, partially concealed by the grove of trees. This card has a 1905 copyright date. The hotel was destroyed by fire the night of December 21, 1967.

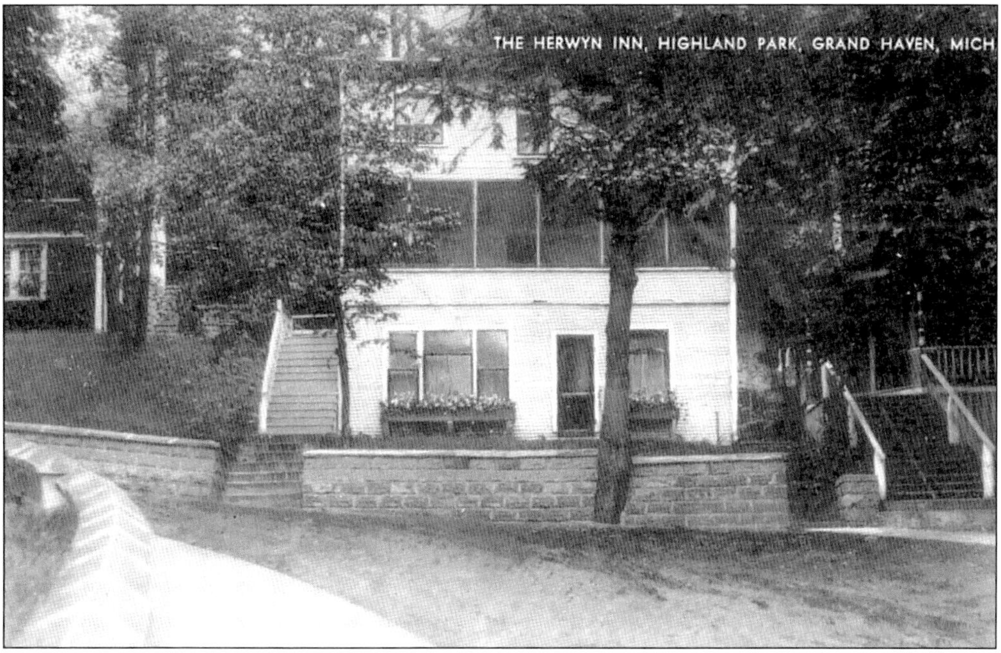

The Herwyn Inn, owned and managed by Jane Van Herwyn and her sister, provided comfortable rooms and served home-cooked meals to its guests. The Inn sat opposite today's Bil-Mar Restaurant and offered easy access to the beach and pavilion. Jane's husband, Ed Peters, owned the business that preceded the Bil-Mar Restaurant. Today, the former inn is a private residence.

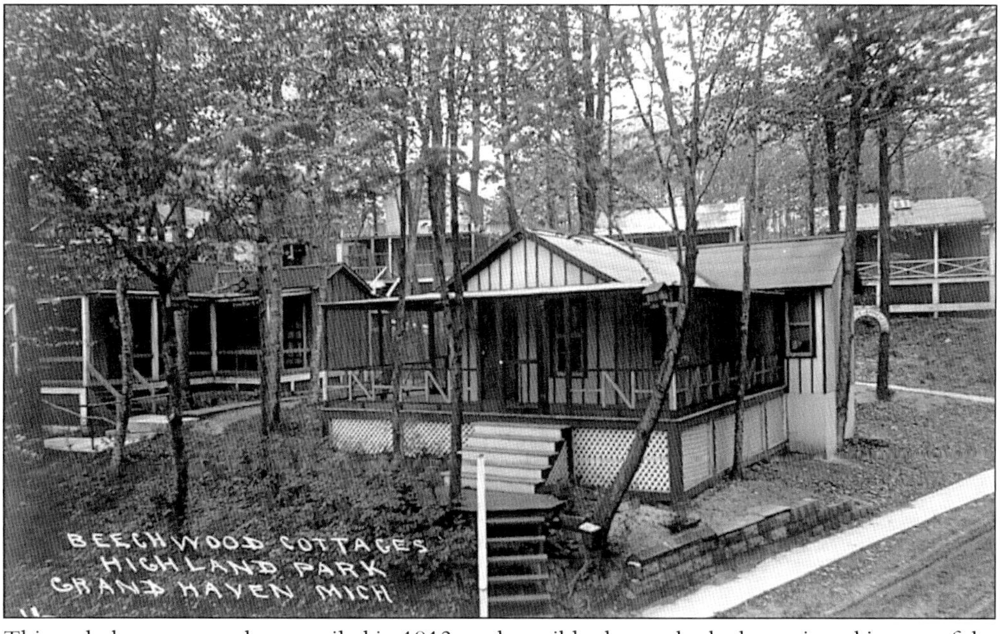

This real photo postcard was mailed in 1913, and possibly the sender had vacationed in one of the Beechwood Cottages in Highland Park. Although most of the cottages in Highland Park were privately owned, some were used as investments and rented during the summer months. A small, arched sign identifying "Beechwood" can be seen near the right edge of the card.

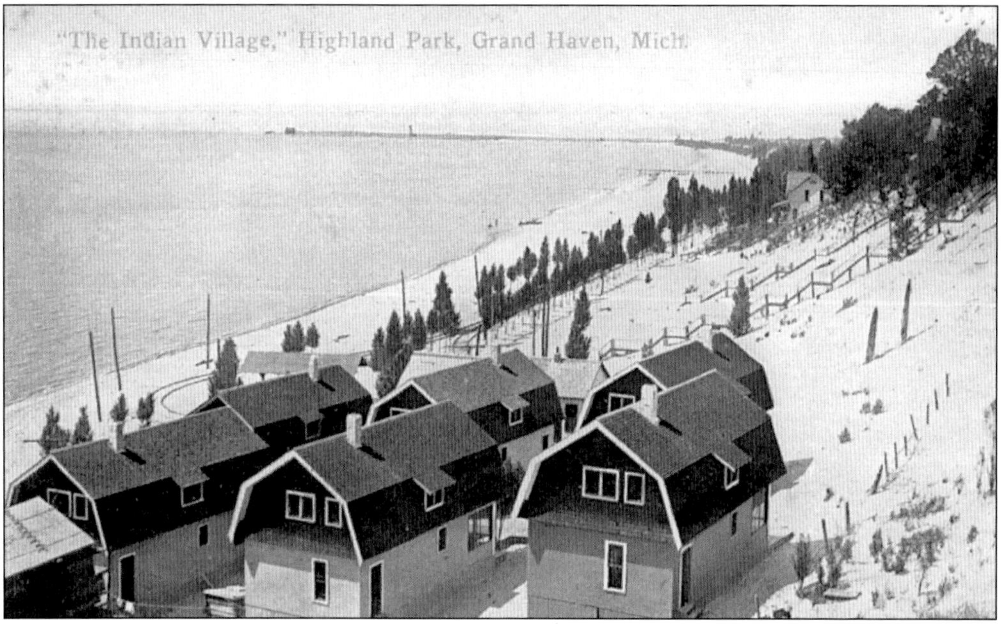

Built by Gerrit Bottema immediately south of Highland Park, this cluster of six modest cottages of similar barn design was known as Indian Village. The loop marking the end of the Interurban line is visible on the beach. An 1893 map showed that developers at that time planned to lay a railroad from Grand Haven, along the beach, and over the dunes eastward toward Grand Rapids. The Interurban tracks followed that early route as far as Indian Village. The card is postmarked 1912.

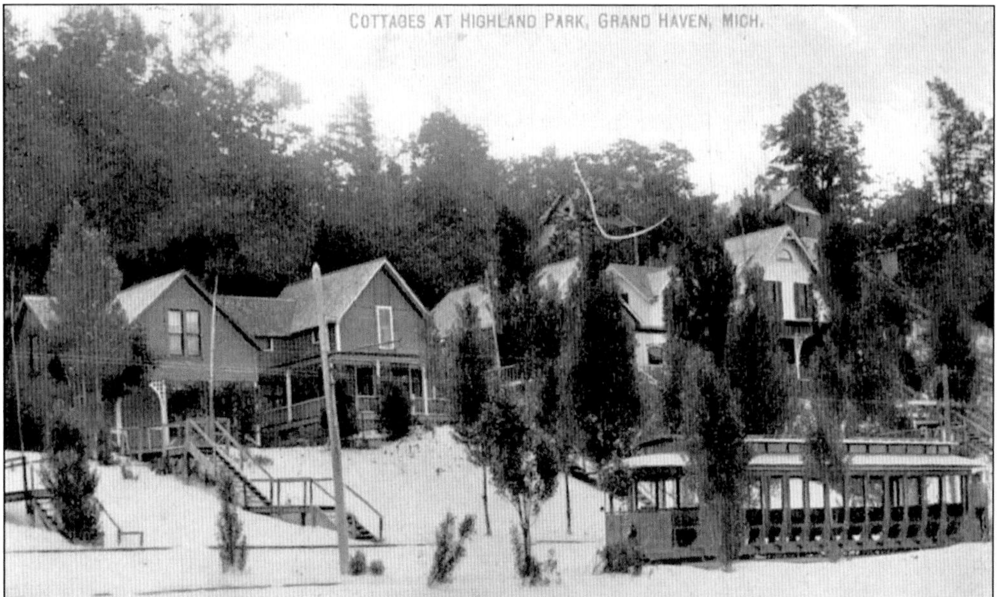

Before Harbor Drive was extended to the lake front in 1922, the Interurban provided transportation for visitors to Highland Park and three other stops along the route. One of the Interurban cars conveniently stopped for the photographer in this 1909 postcard. The conductor is standing at the far end of the car. This group of cottages below Edward Street was considered part of Highland Park.

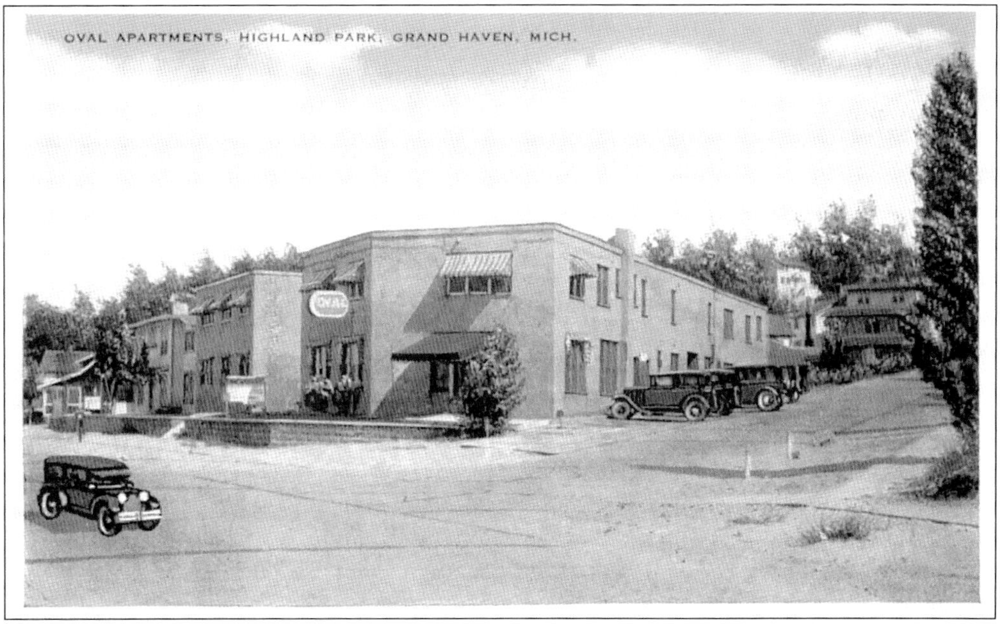

In 1926 Frank and Florence Reghel purchased the newly-constructed Oval Inn, located on Harbor Drive across from Grand Haven State Park. By adding the "Grand Haven Apartments" and the "Miami Apartments," the new owners could offer a total of 40 rooms to summertime visitors. Food service was provided from 9:00 a.m. to midnight. This picture must have been taken not long after the Reghels finished their additions.

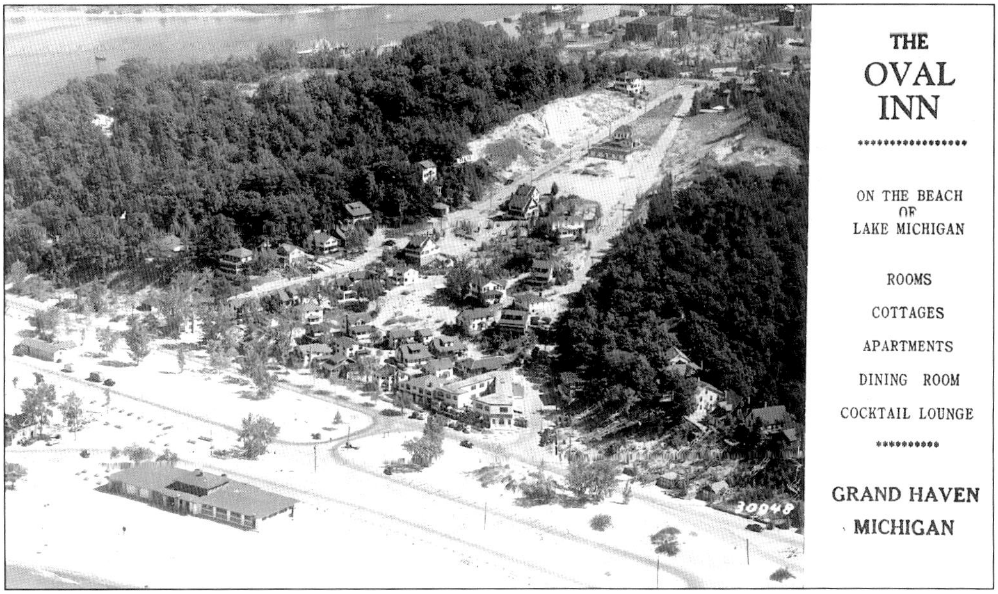

Picture postcards also were used for advertising. This real photo card was distributed by the Oval Inn, but also provides a detailed view of Five Mile Hill, the Oval, and Grand River. At the very top, near the right edge, the building that housed Michigan Brass Company is visible. It was replaced by Sandpiper Condominiums. The Coast Guard ship *Woodbine* is docked at Escanaba Park. The card is postmarked 1952.

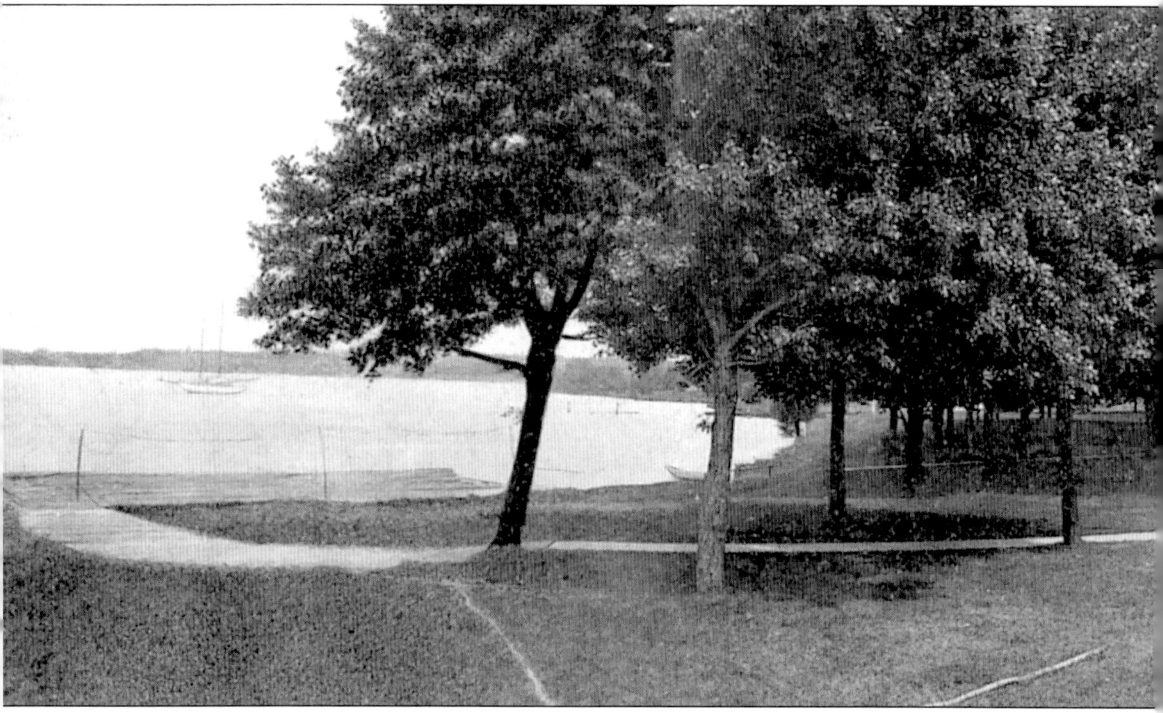

The Spring Lake House was one of the first resort hotels to attract summer visitors to the area. As this panoramic, two-panel postcard shows, the hotel was situated close to the wooded shoreline of Spring Lake. The resort's cottages are visible behind the hotel. A chauffeur sits at the right-

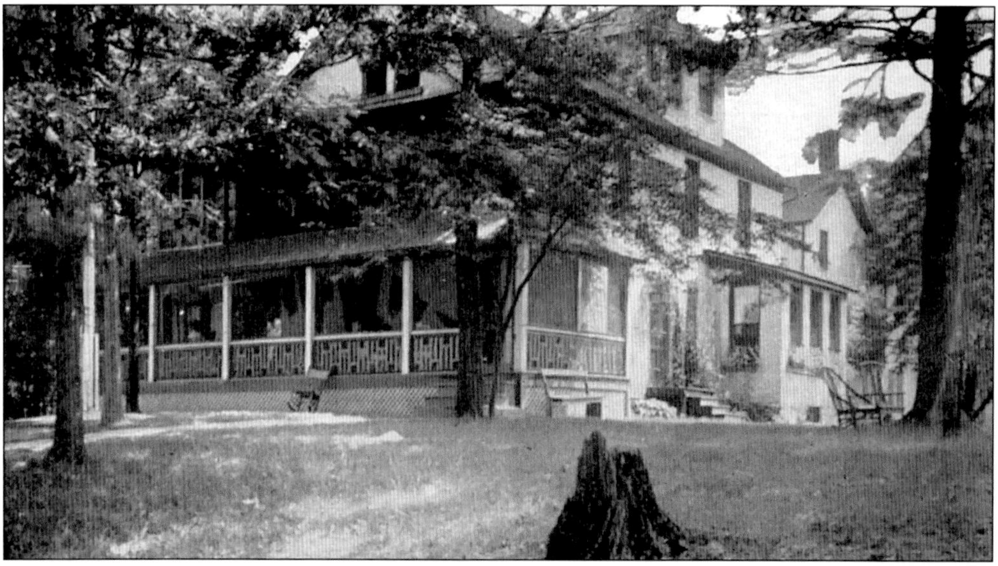

In 1893 Chauncey and Mary Blakeslee built a residence on their 40-acre property on the east shore of Spring Lake. Two years later, they erected a larger structure and called it Arbutus Banks Hotel. The Blakeslees ran the resort 19 years. It then was owned and managed by different individuals until 1946, when it closed as a resort and was used as a private home. The hotel is shown in this undated card.

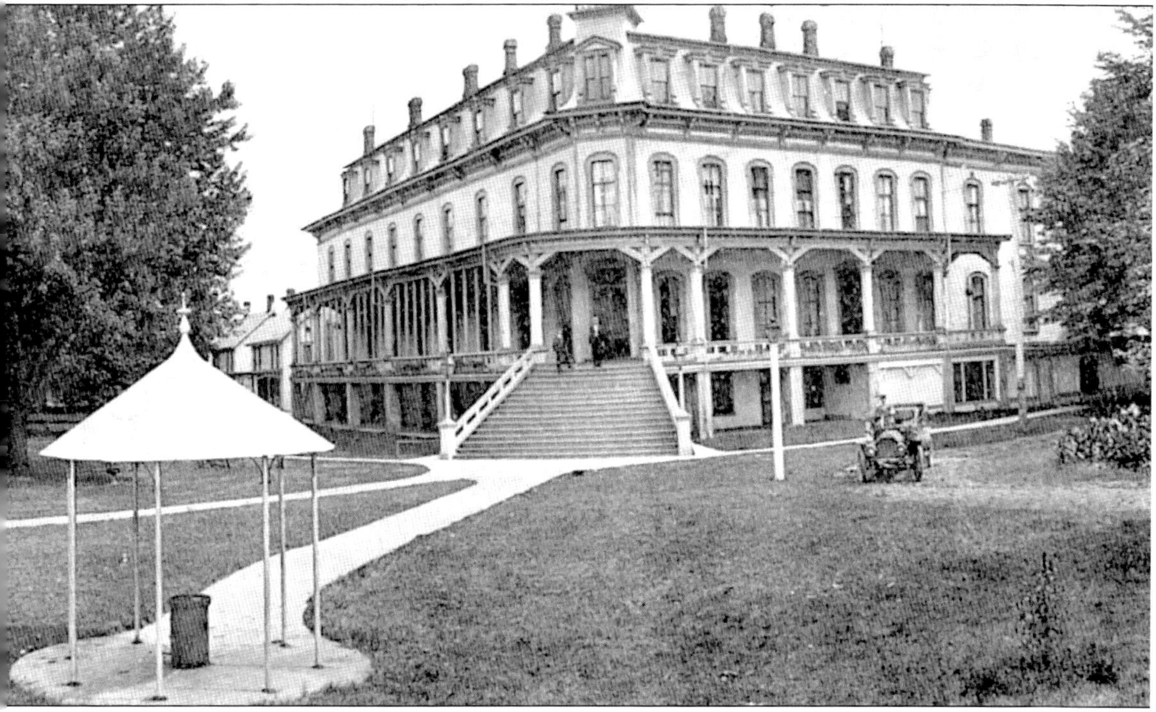

handed steering wheel of the old touring car. The small canopy shields the well that provided the mineral waters. The resort's cottages are visible behind the hotel. The hotel, which opened in 1871, burned down on June 16, 1916.

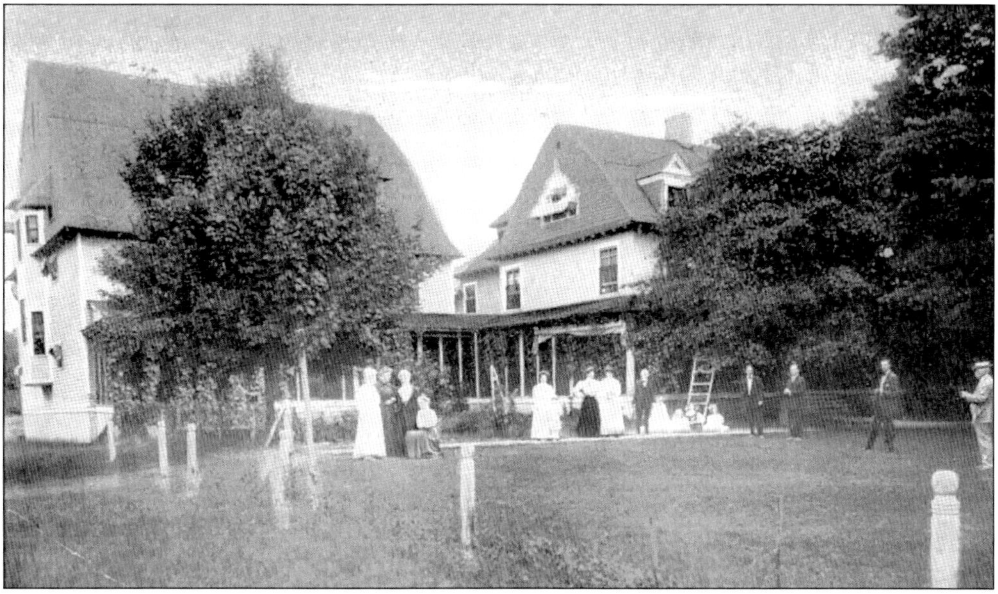

One of the many summer resorts dotting the shores of Spring Lake was the Pines, located on the west side. The 90-room resort was built by Frank Baker in 1895. Its dock was large enough to accommodate the large boats that provided convenient transportation to the Village and Grand Haven. The Pines was destroyed by fire in 1928.

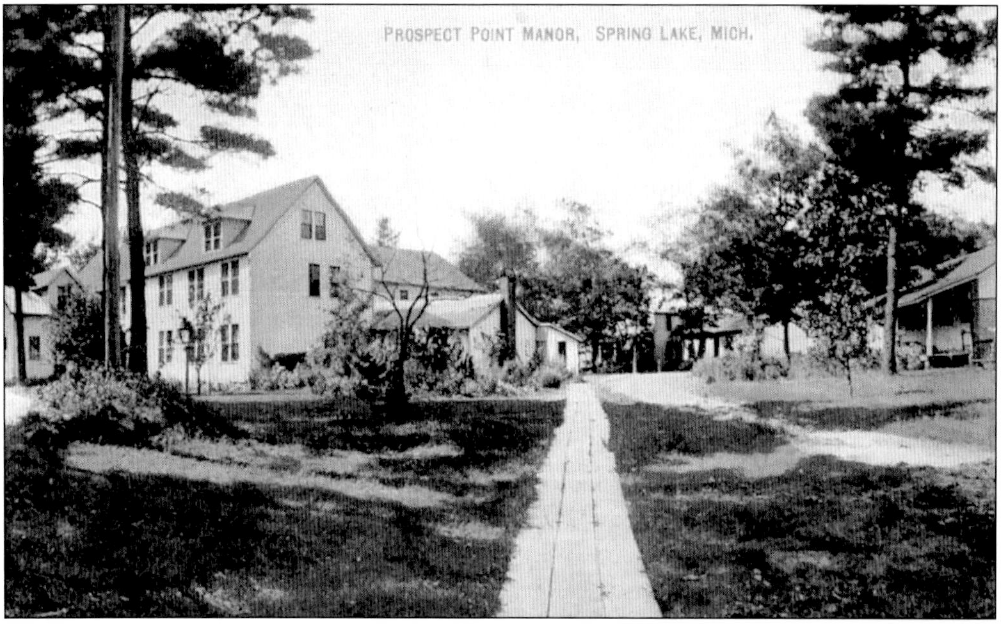

Prospect Point Resort, near Petty's Bayou in Spring Lake, consisted of several large buildings and cottages with a total of 60 rooms for seasonal rental. The resort advertised "Modern Lodge and private Hotel Cottages. Accommodations for 150 guests. Unusual meals... private beach... golf and tennis nearby... shuffleboard... motion pictures... water sports... organized entertainment. Midnight snacks. Select clientele."

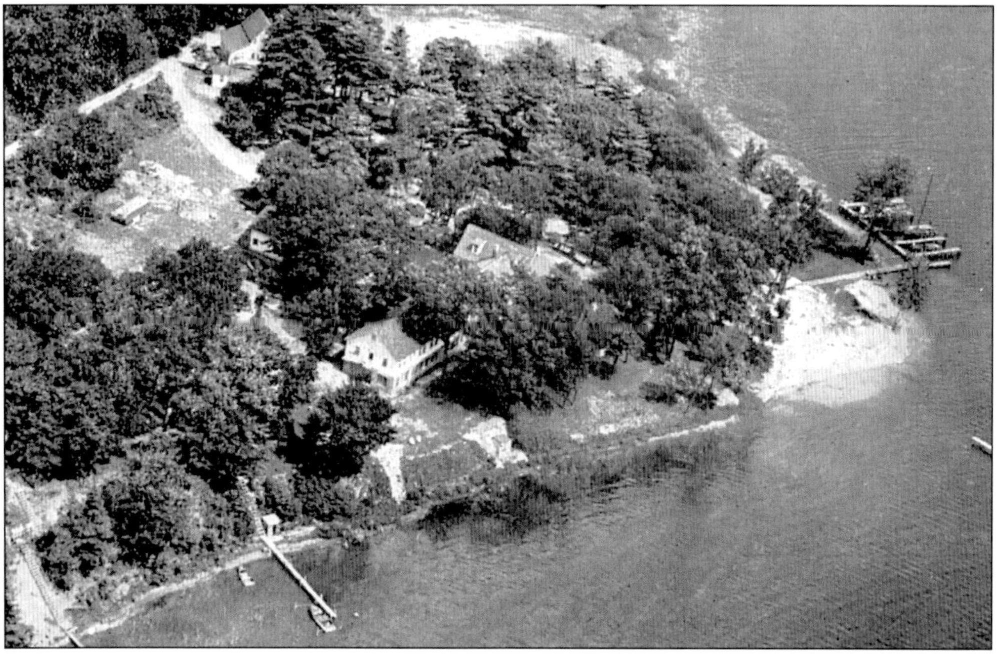

This 1949 aerial view shows the entire grounds of Prospect Point Resort. Built in the late 1800s, it served as a popular summer gathering place into the 1960s, but was destroyed by fire in 1968. Prospect Point Condominiums now occupy the site.

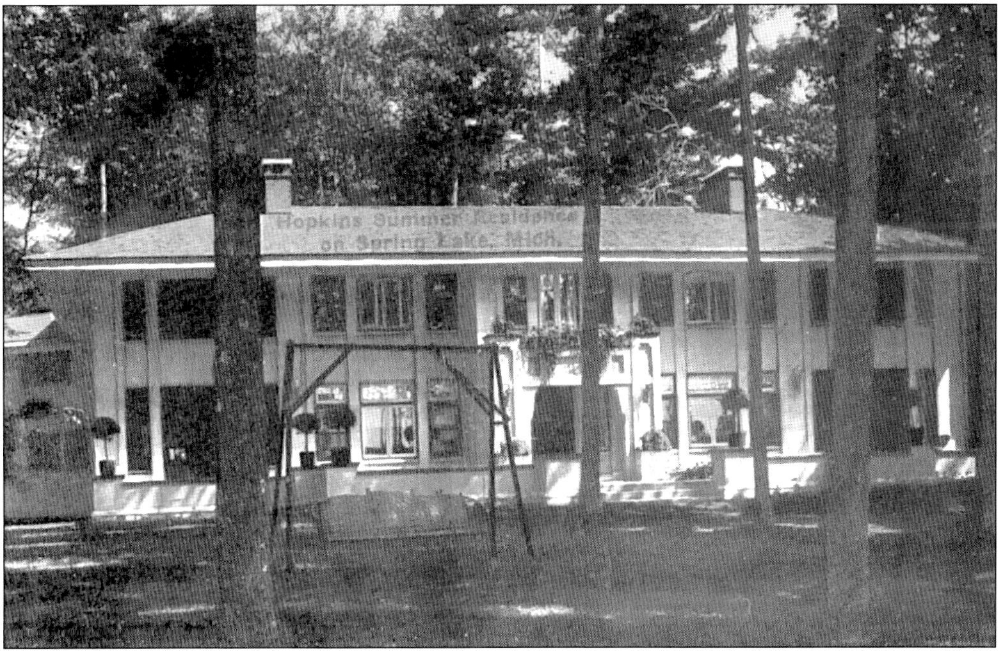

Claude Hopkins became a success in the advertising field by coining such phrases as "It Floats" and "Keep that Schoolgirl Complexion." His summer home on Spring Lake, named Pineycrest, was located on the north end of the lake. The card is postmarked 1914.

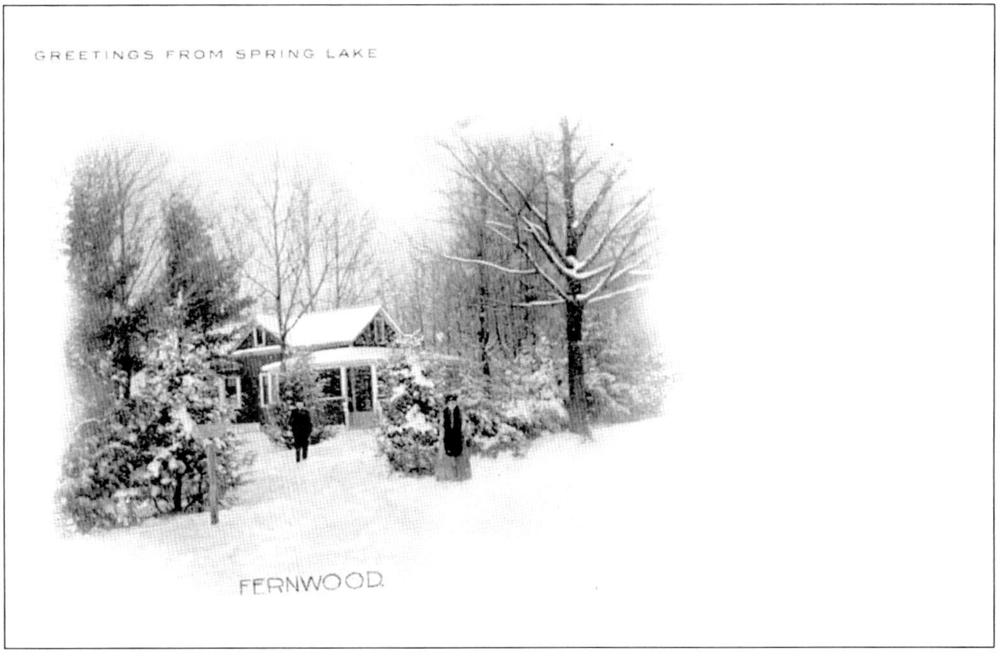

The home that looks so snug and cozy in this wintry scene was part of the Fernwood Resort. Located on Cornelius Bayou, in the northeast corner of Spring Lake, the property originally was a summer resort with a large hotel and dock that were in operation around 1900. Cottages, such as this one, were added later. The people are not identified. The card predates 1907.

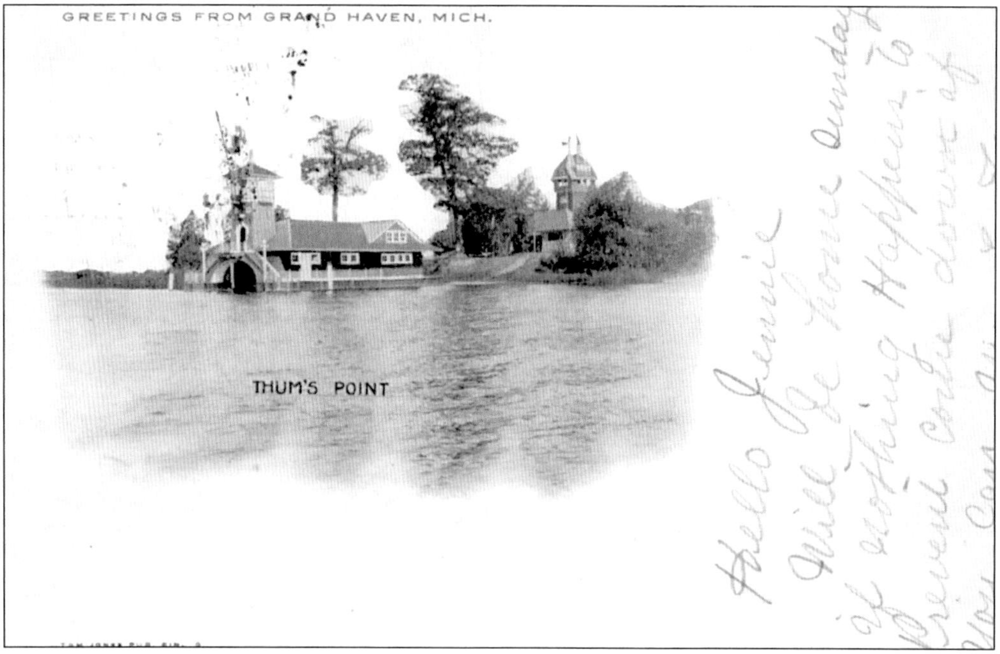

Postcards distributed before 1907 contained a small space under or around the picture for a message, while the other side was devoted exclusively to the address. This card, postmarked 1905, shows the Thum family estate known as "Exmoor," now the site of the Spring Lake Yacht Club.

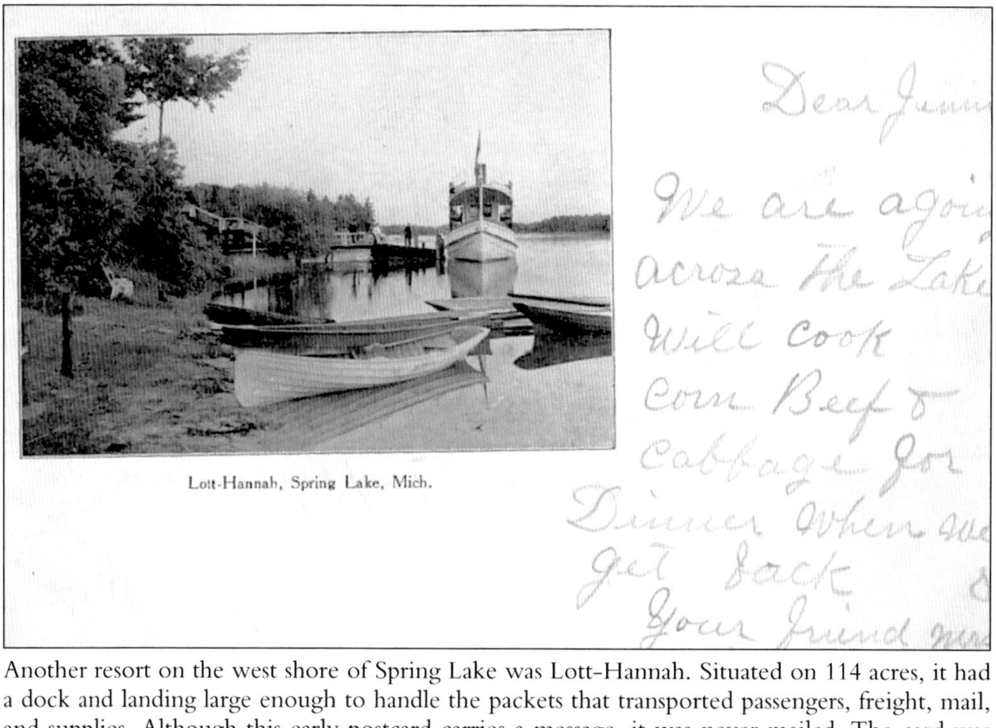

Another resort on the west shore of Spring Lake was Lott-Hannah. Situated on 114 acres, it had a dock and landing large enough to handle the packets that transported passengers, freight, mail, and supplies. Although this early postcard carries a message, it was never mailed. The card was printed before 1907.

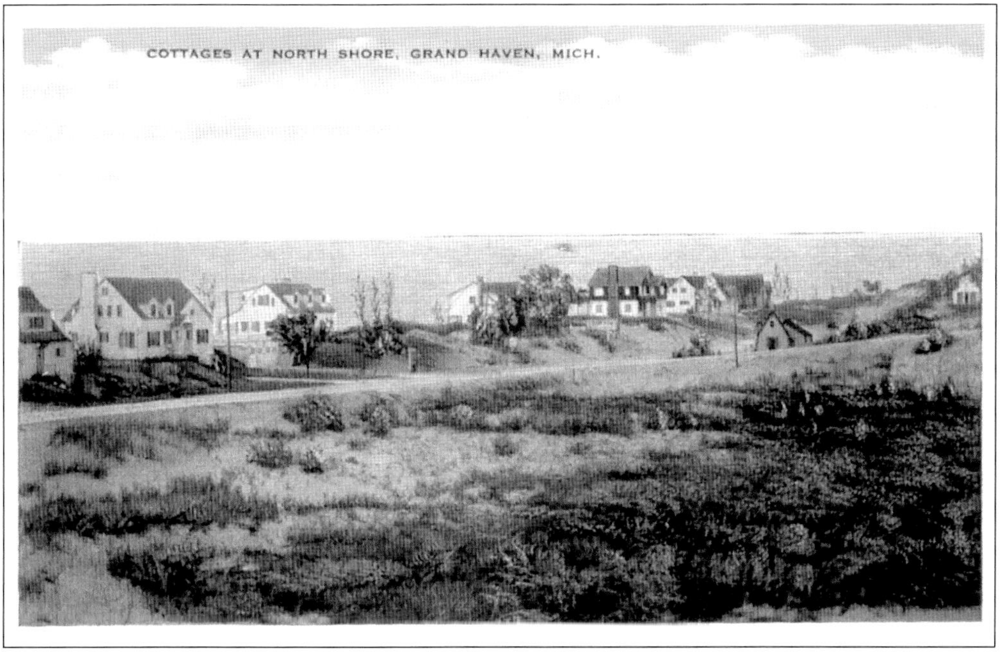

Not long after a road was put through from Ferrysburg to the North Shore in 1928, Harold Worm's development attracted widespread attention. The back of this undated postcard promoted the area: "The North Shore group is a colony of very fine summer homes built on the sandy beach, with delightful wooded hills as a background, all modern conveniences." The card was published by Reichardt's of Grand Haven.

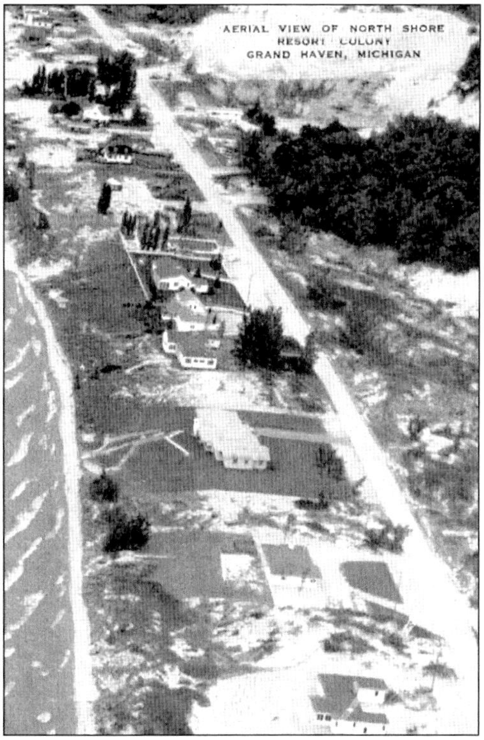

By the early 1950s, North Shore boasted a number of residences and summer cottages. This aerial view, dated 1954, is looking in a northerly direction along the Lake Michigan beach and North Shore Road. The printed caption on the message side reads, "These beautiful cottages overlook Lake Michigan and are close to Spring Lake and Grand River. This district has the advantages of natural gas, electric lights and beautiful roads."

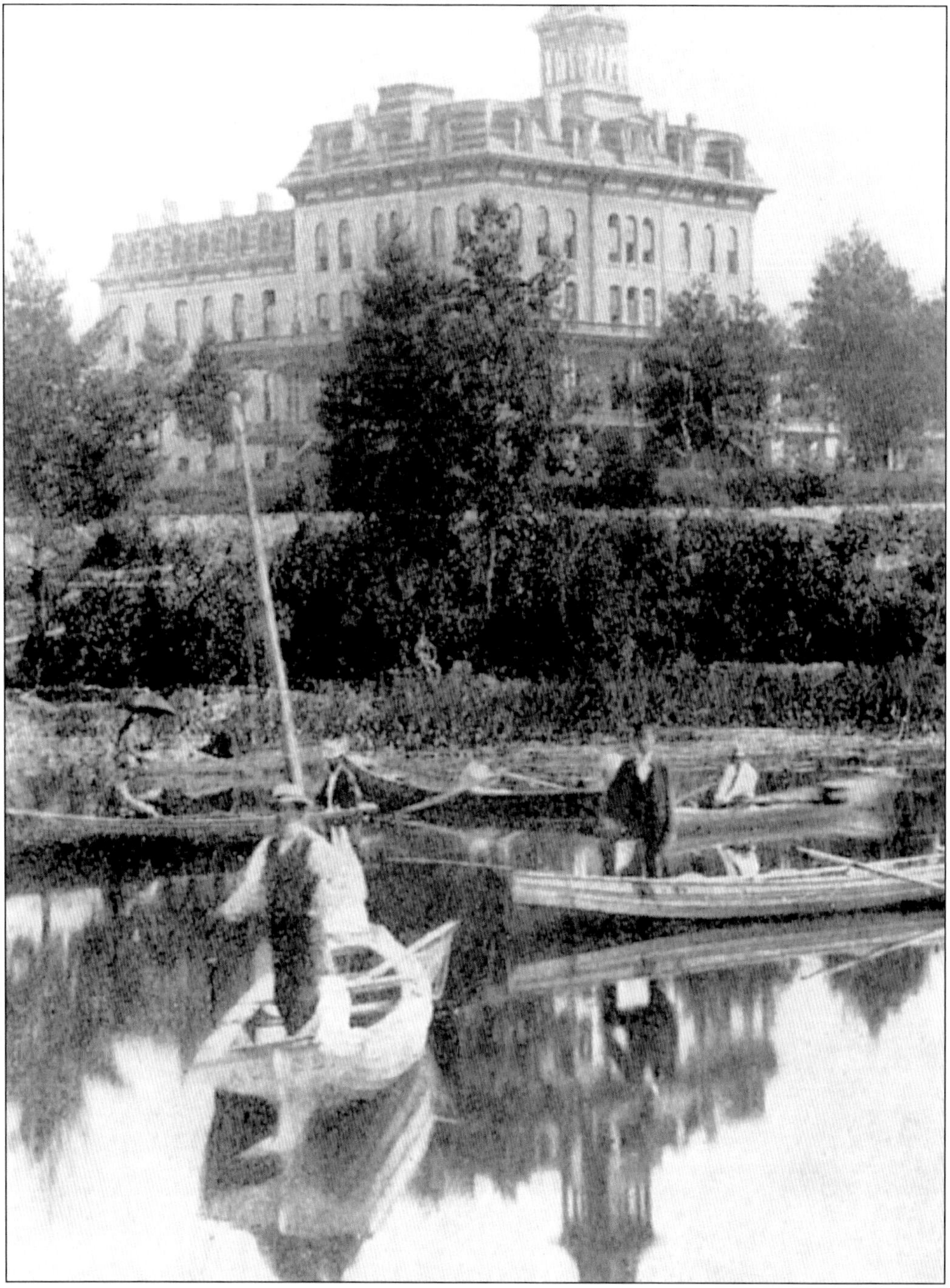

The discovery of mineral waters at the north end of Spring Lake opened the way for a syndicate out of Chicago to construct the imposing four-story Pomona House in 1870. It was the first resort hotel in the area, although similar structures were soon to follow in Spring Lake and Grand Haven. Located in Fruitport, the Pomona House was built with white brick and trimmed in brownstone. The resort burned down in the mid-1870s, was immediately rebuilt, and was again destroyed by fire in 1881. It never reopened. The card was not dated.

Four

SURF, SAND, AND SUN

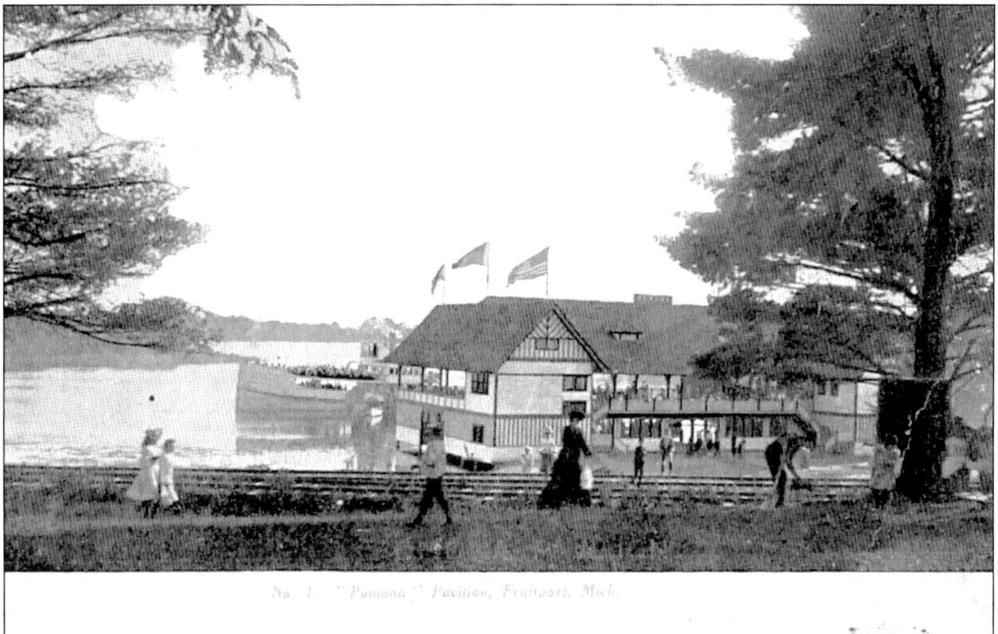

Fruitport Pavilion, built near the site of the once-famous Pomona House at the north end of Spring Lake, was a popular dancing spot. From the early 1900s through the 1950s, a variety of "big bands" entertained people of all ages on this waterfront spot. The Pavilion was destroyed by fire in 1963.

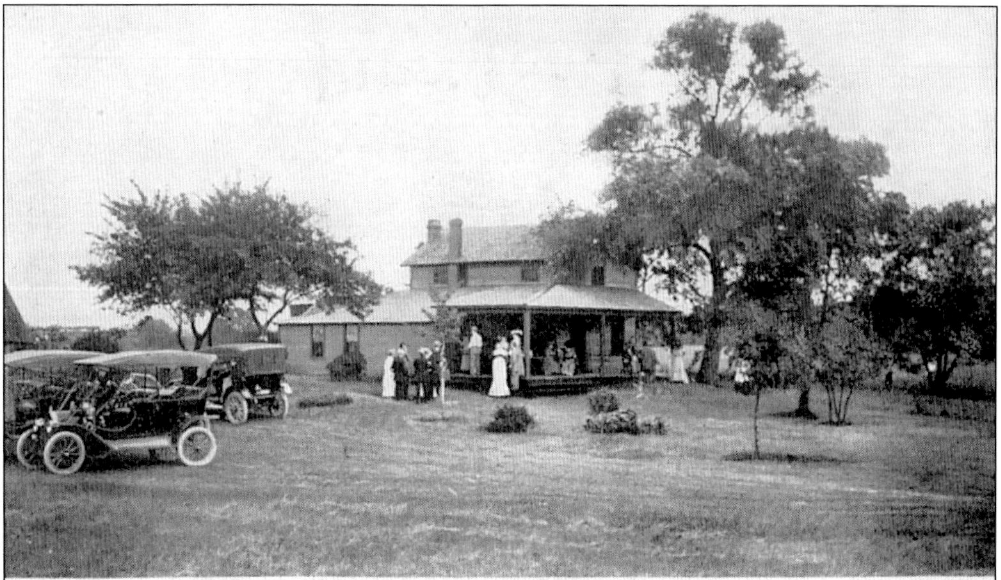

Spring Lake Country Club. (Near Grand Haven, Mich.)

The Spring Lake Country Club started in 1911 when a group of local residents purchased the 140-acre Benjamin Soule farm, not far from the lake. The farmhouse, pictured here, was converted to a clubhouse, while a nearby barn was used as the men's locker room. The nine-hole course soon was expanded to eighteen holes.

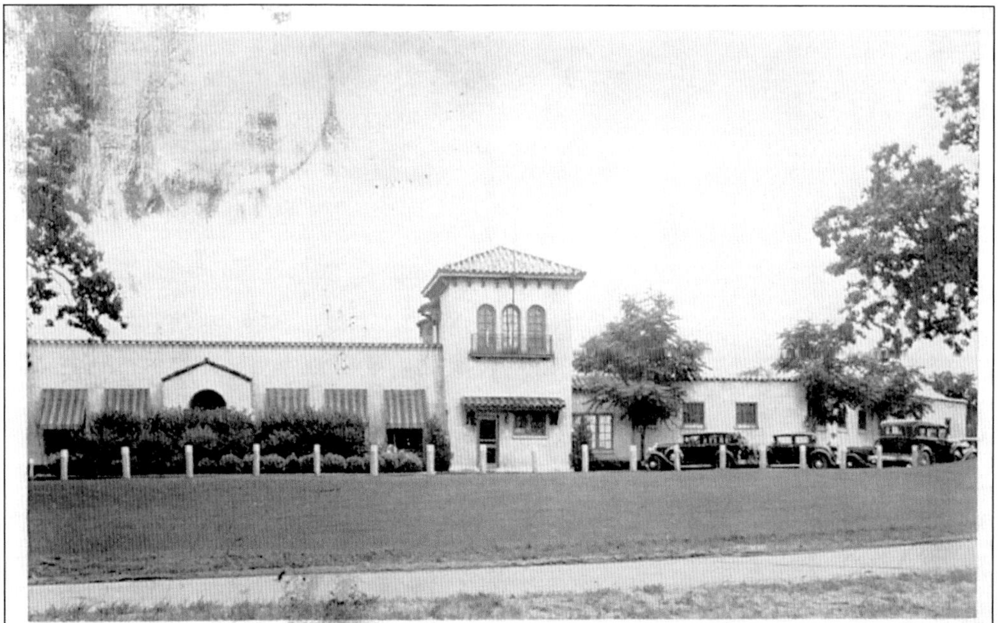

COUNTRY CLUB, SPRING LAKE, MICH. D-364

In 1925 the Spring Lake Country Club raised funds for the construction of a Spanish-style clubhouse, which was built not far from the original farmhouse. Additions and improvements have been made to the clubhouse since then, but the building now looks much as it did in the mid-1920s. This card is postmarked 1936.

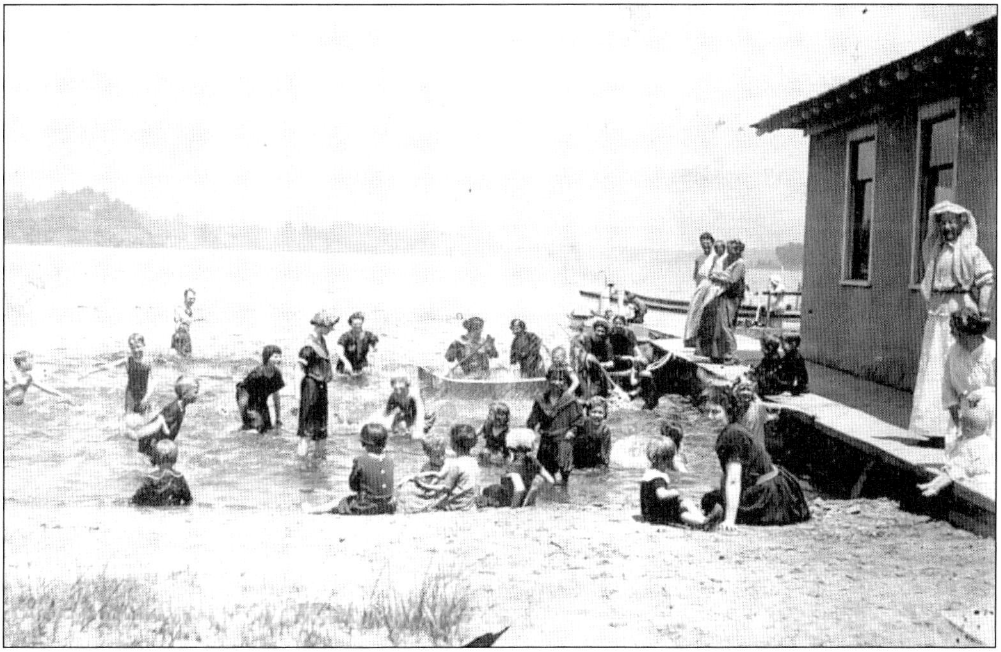

Lake Avenue in the Village comes to an end at the Spring Lake shoreline. There, the road right-of-way provided ample room for a public beach that remains in use today. The building to the right was called Lakeside Pavilion. The four young women in the canoe look thoroughly soaked—but happy! The pavilion offered food, ice cream, and tobacco products.

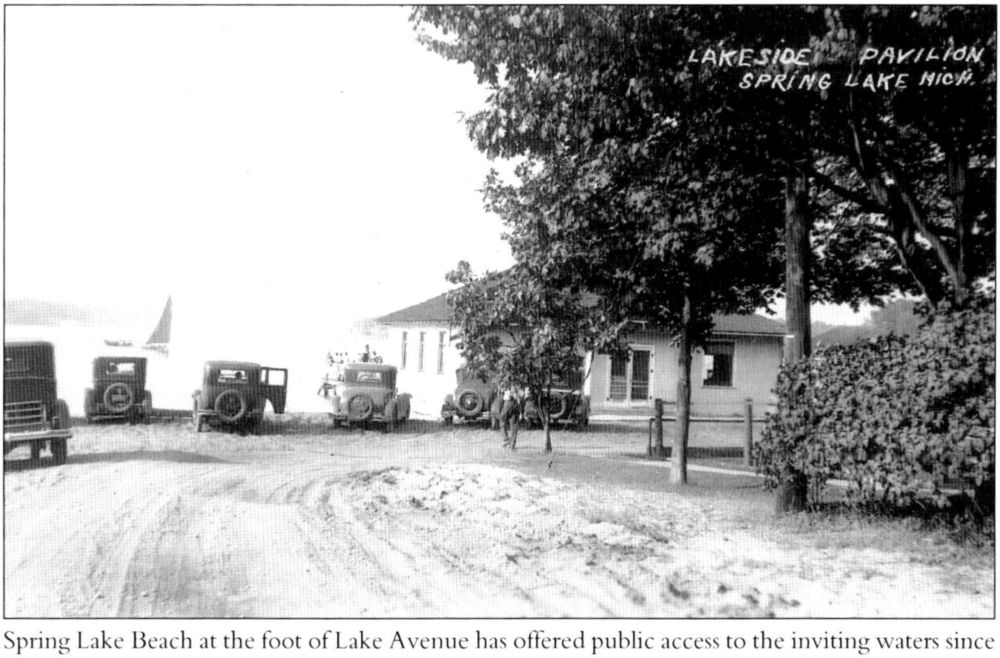

Spring Lake Beach at the foot of Lake Avenue has offered public access to the inviting waters since the mid-1890s. In this view a number of youngsters are gathered at the end of the pier, ready to test the temperature. Judging from the cars, the photo was taken in the mid-1930s. The pavilion was razed in the summer of 2002.

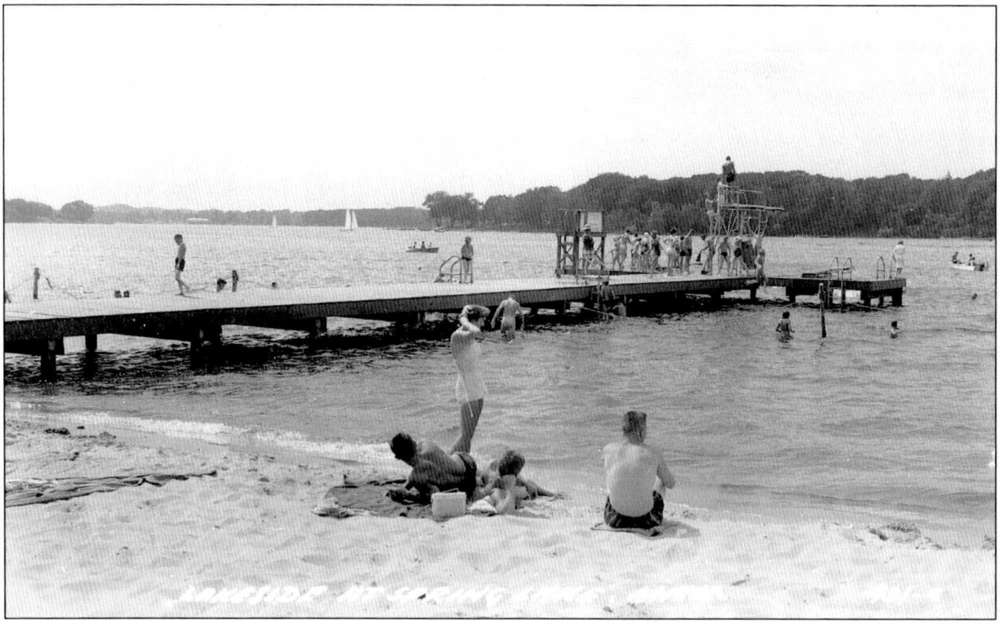

The swimming beach maintained by Spring Lake Village at the north end of Lake Avenue included a substantial pier, as well as a pavilion. A pier similar to the one shown here served as a stop on the steamboat run. It must have been a pleasant summer day to entice so many people into the water for swimming, diving, and sailing. This real photo postcard was unused.

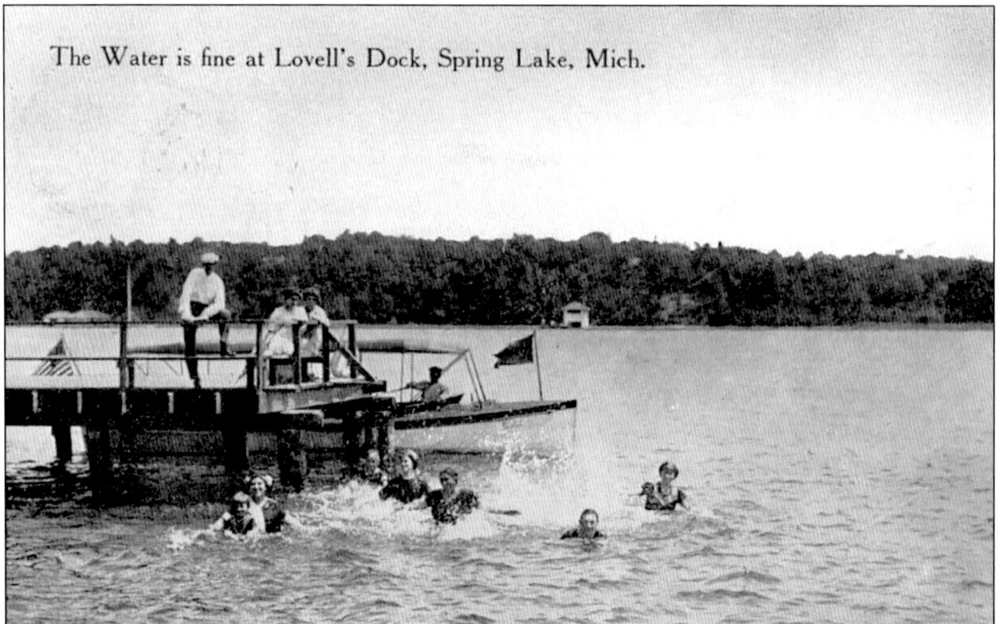

George Lovell, an early settler in Spring Lake, was well known for his fruit trees. He planted some of his trees on a large parcel of land on the west side of the lake. After his death in 1901, the site became known as Summerland Park and was a popular gathering place in the summer. This 1914 card shows a group of people enjoying the water off Lovell's Dock.

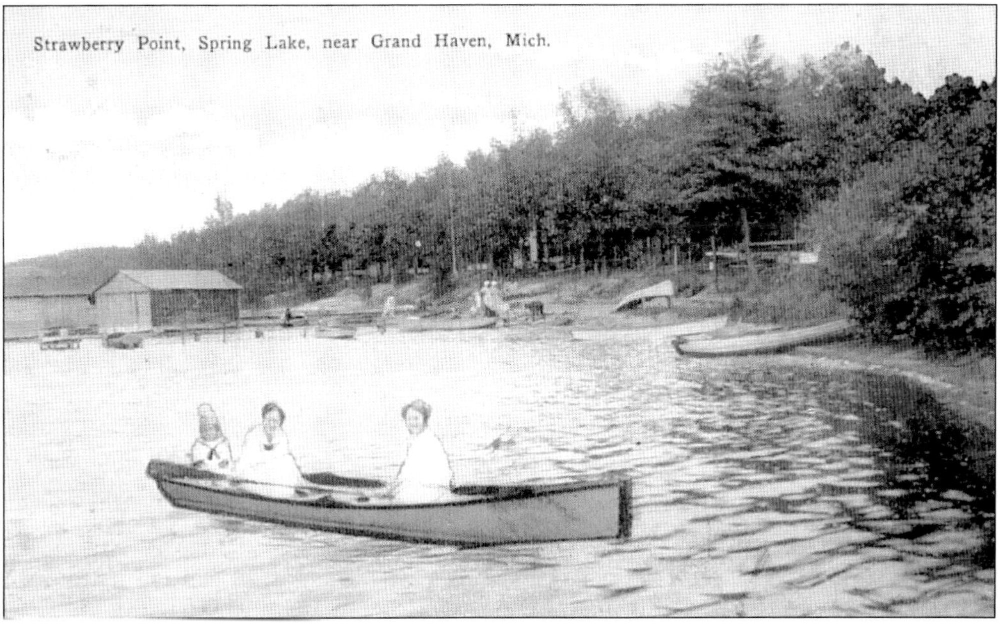

Strawberry Point, on the southeast end of Spring Lake, was a favorite spot for summer cabins throughout the 1900s. Today many of the cabins have been remodeled for year-round living. In this view, two women and a girl enjoy some exercise and fresh air in a rowboat. The card is postmarked 1926. The area was named for the "luscious wild strawberries" that once were found there in the shade of the oak trees.

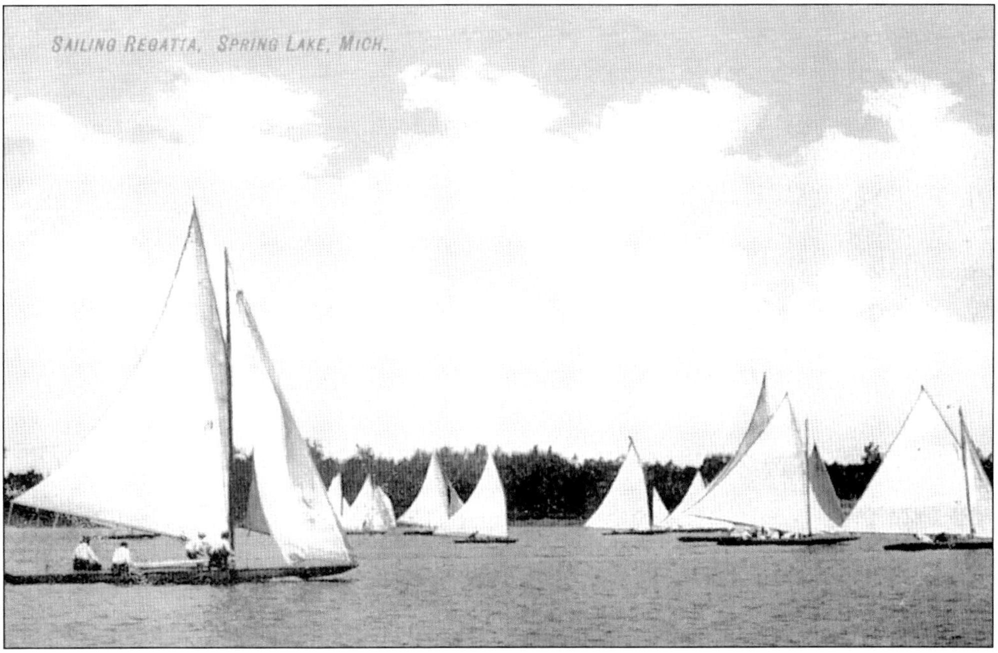

By the third quarter of the 19th century, sailing for recreation and sport had become a common sight on Spring Lake. The postcard capturing this regatta is dated 1907. The featured boats were designed specifically for racing.

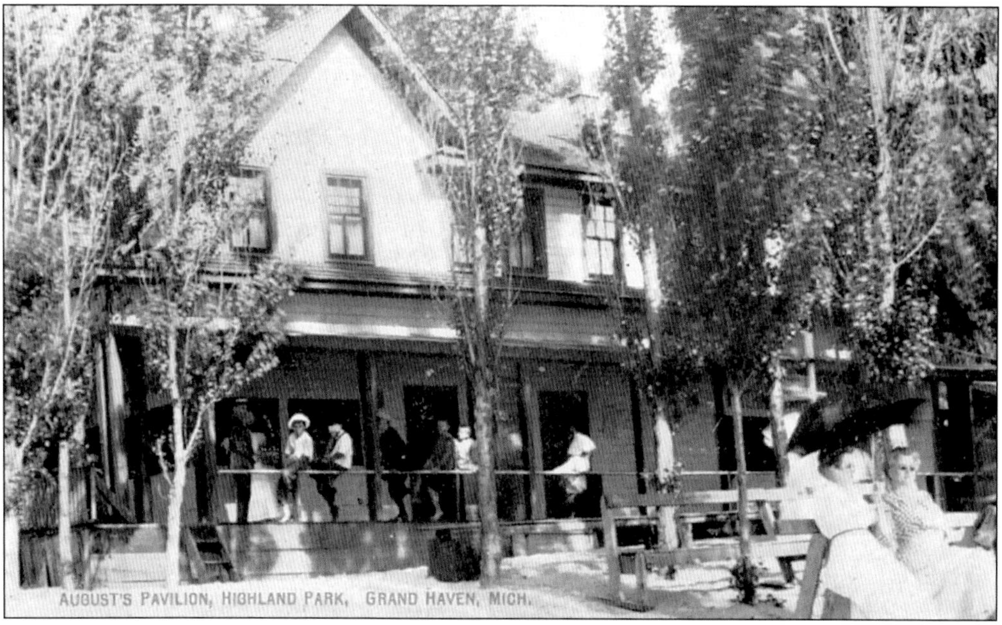

Prior to 1900, Highland Park Pavilion was operated by Captain Walker with August Boseker as his assistant. In 1901 Boseker bought the pavilion from Walker for $100 and renamed it August's Pavilion. Boseker added bathhouses, rented rowboats and swimsuits, and each year built a pier out into Lake Michigan. Boseker, his wife, Henrietta, and their two daughters lived on the second floor. The card, dated 1909, was published by Reichardt's of Grand Haven.

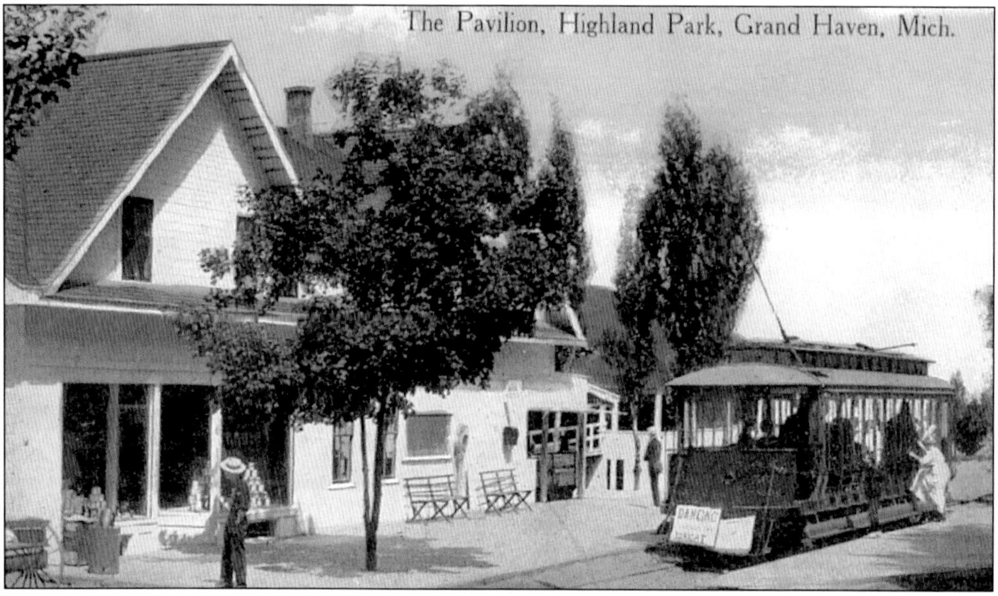

August Boseker's Pavilion also served as one of the stops along the Interurban route. Today the Bil-Mar Restaurant is located in these buildings, but in the early 1900s they housed a grocery store, ice cream parlor, bathhouses, boat rental, and other attractions. The sign on the front of the Interurban car advertises "Dancing Tonight." The roof of the dance hall can barely be seen through the trees in the center of the card.

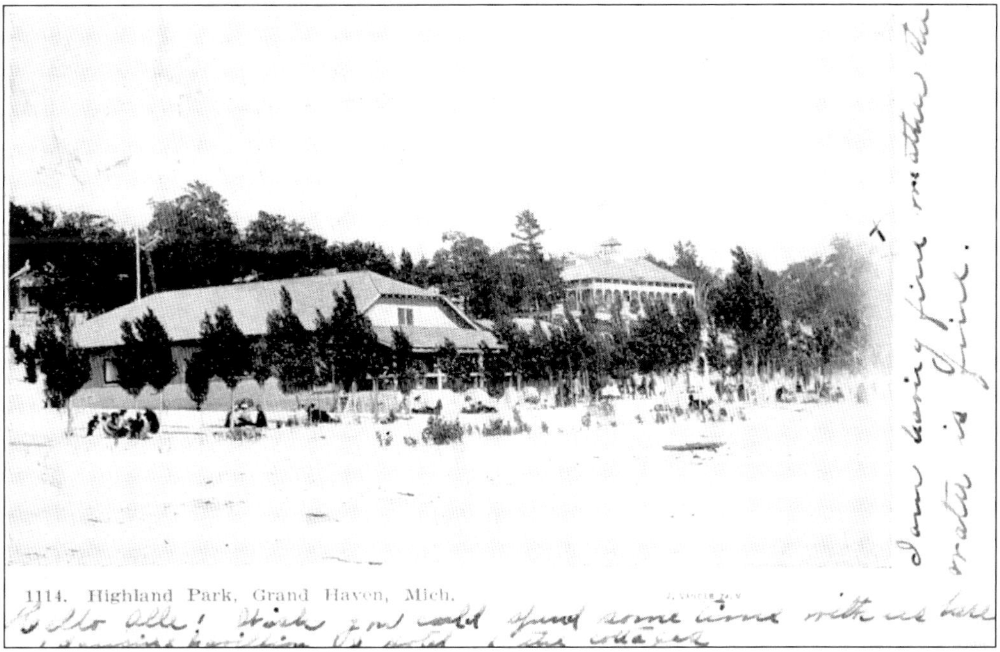

In 1907 August Boseker bought the frame building that had served as a dance hall and station on the Interurban route. He moved it to the beach just below Highland Park Hotel, adjacent to his Pavilion. He first situated it perpendicular to the shoreline, as shown in this early card, postmarked 1908. Not long afterward, he turned it parallel to the beach, perhaps to keep it safe from Lake Michigan waves and erosion. It was called Highland Park Dance Hall, and later Hyland Gardens.

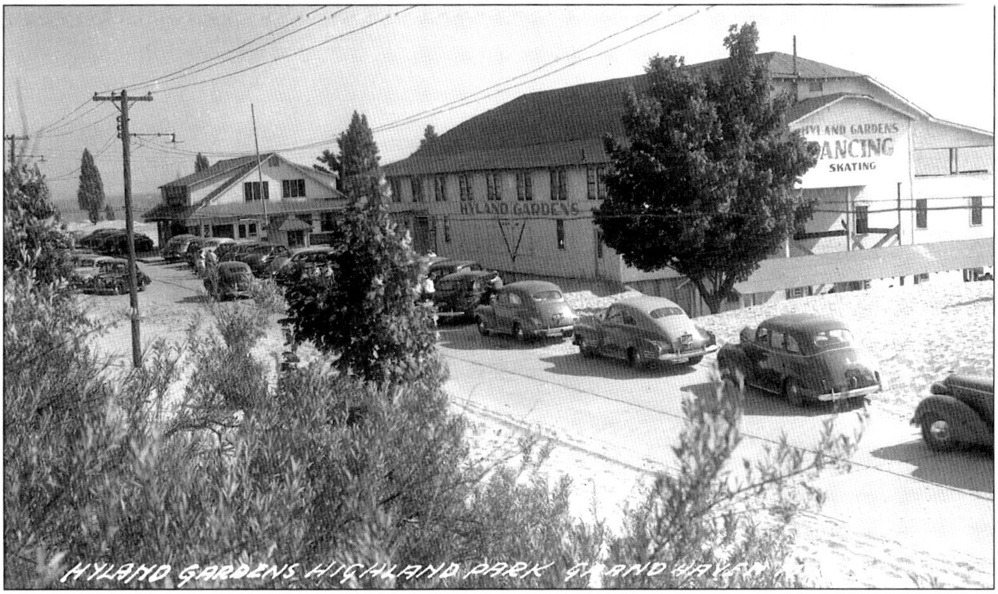

Boseker's large frame building eventually became known as Hyland Gardens and was a popular spot for dancing and skating. The dance hall went through several modifications in its 50-year history. A condominium now occupies the site. The structure next door houses Bil-Mar Restaurant today. This real photo postcard was never mailed.

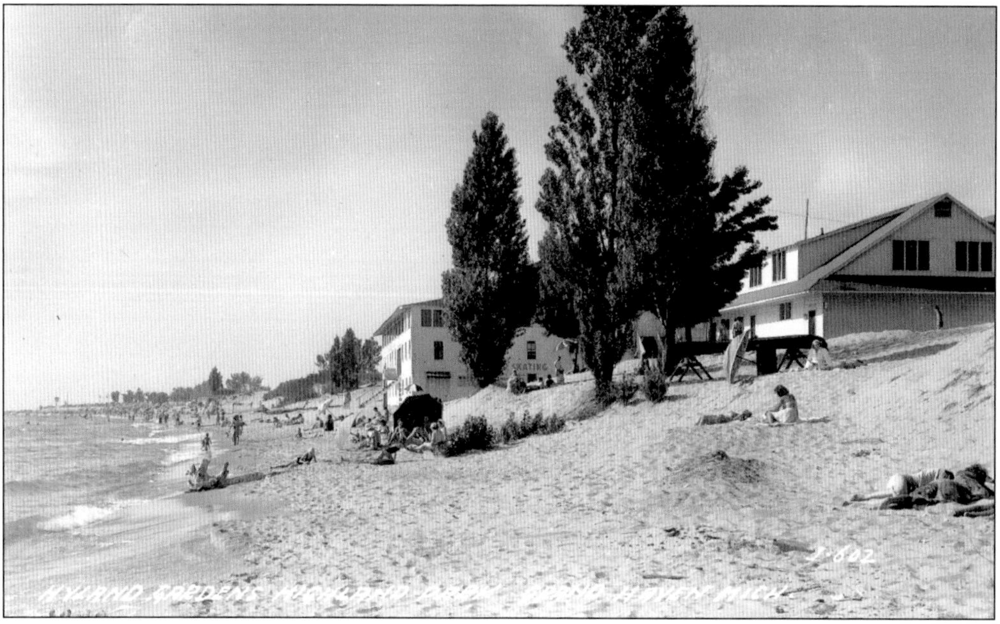

Low water level in 1940 made the Lake Michigan beach at Highland Park especially wide and inviting. Peeking behind one of the tall poplar trees is part of Hyland Gardens' frame structure, where skating and dancing were popular forms of recreation. The frame building on the right now houses Bil-Mar Restaurant.

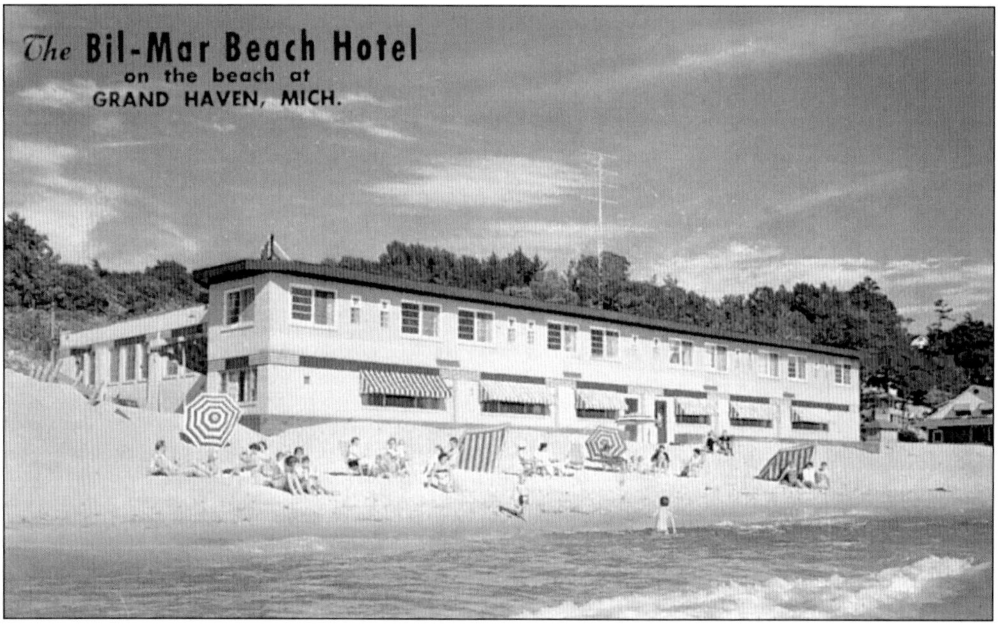

In 1953 the original large frame structure known as Hyland Gardens was replaced by a 21-room, concrete block summer lodge called the Bil-Mar Beach Hotel. This pink structure was badly damaged by a winter storm in 1974, torn down, and replaced by the Lighthouse condominium complex that now stand on the site. The Bil-Mar restaurant can be seen at the far right edge of the card. The postcard is undated.

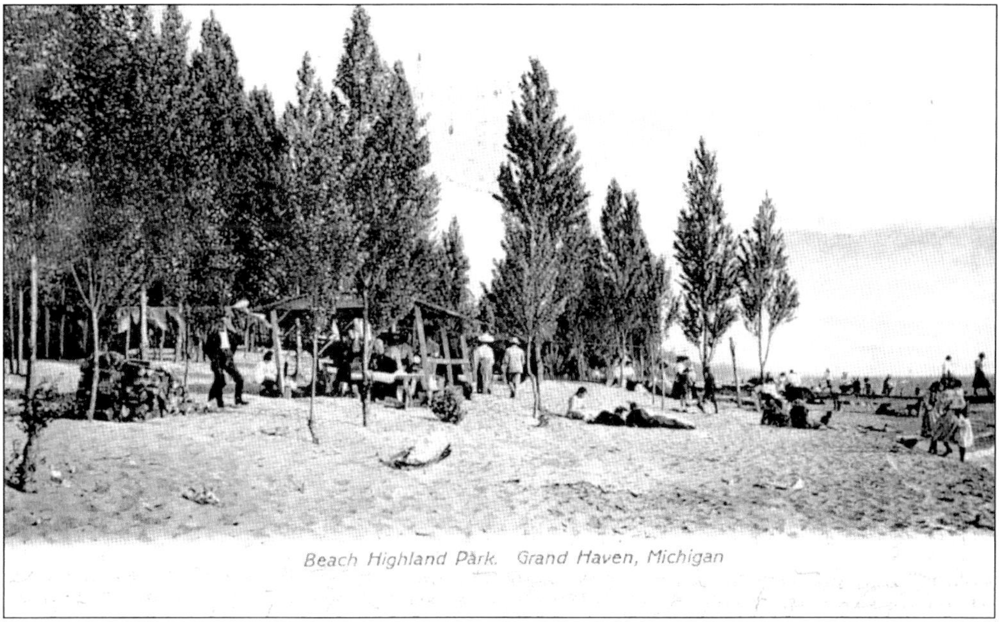

The grove of poplar trees makes the beach at Highland Park look much different than it does today, but its use has not changed much. This 1907 card shows campers and bathers in the accepted beachwear of the day enjoying an outing near the water's edge. Boseker's pier is at the far right edge of the card.

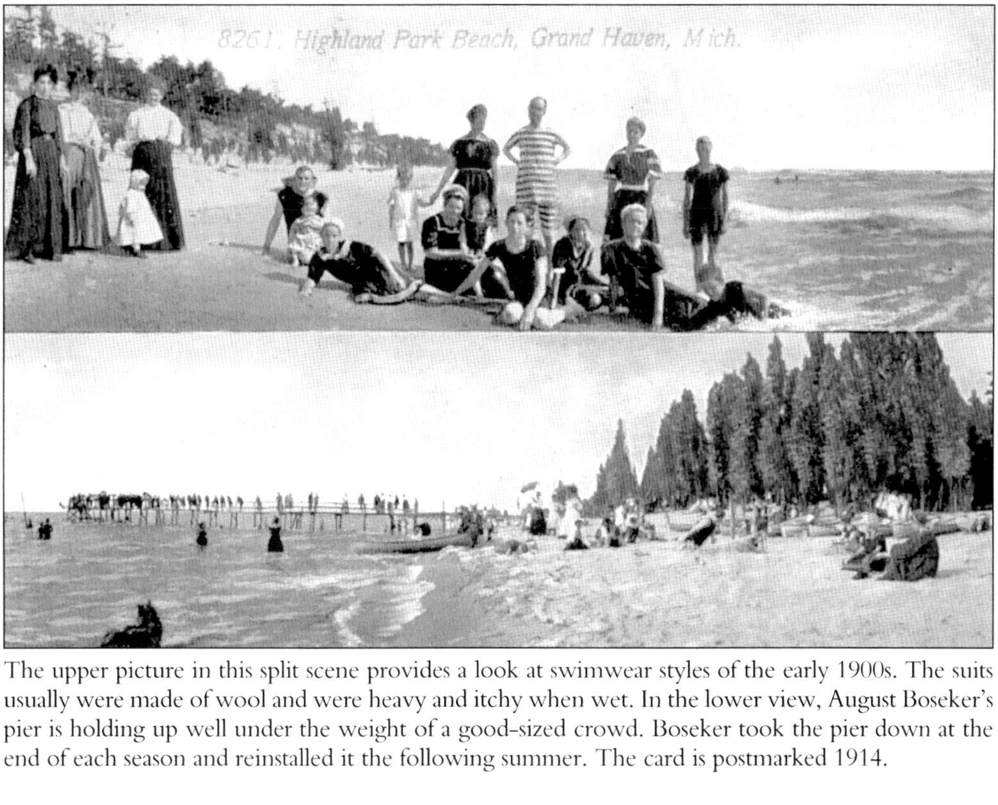

The upper picture in this split scene provides a look at swimwear styles of the early 1900s. The suits usually were made of wool and were heavy and itchy when wet. In the lower view, August Boseker's pier is holding up well under the weight of a good-sized crowd. Boseker took the pier down at the end of each season and reinstalled it the following summer. The card is postmarked 1914.

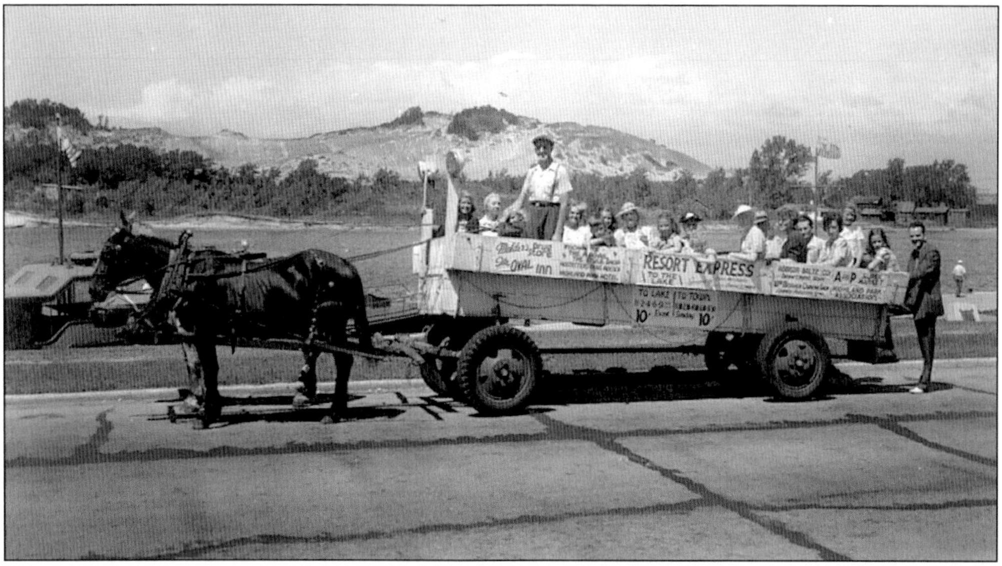

In the 1940s this horse-drawn "Resort Express" provided transportation between downtown Grand Haven and the beach for just 10 cents. Signs on the side of the wagon advertise Mulder's Drug Store, Oval Inn, Reichardt's, Hostetter's, Addison-Baltz Department Store, William Mosher Camera Shop, A & P Supermarket, and Highland Park Hotel. Fishing shanties line the riverbank on the opposite shore.

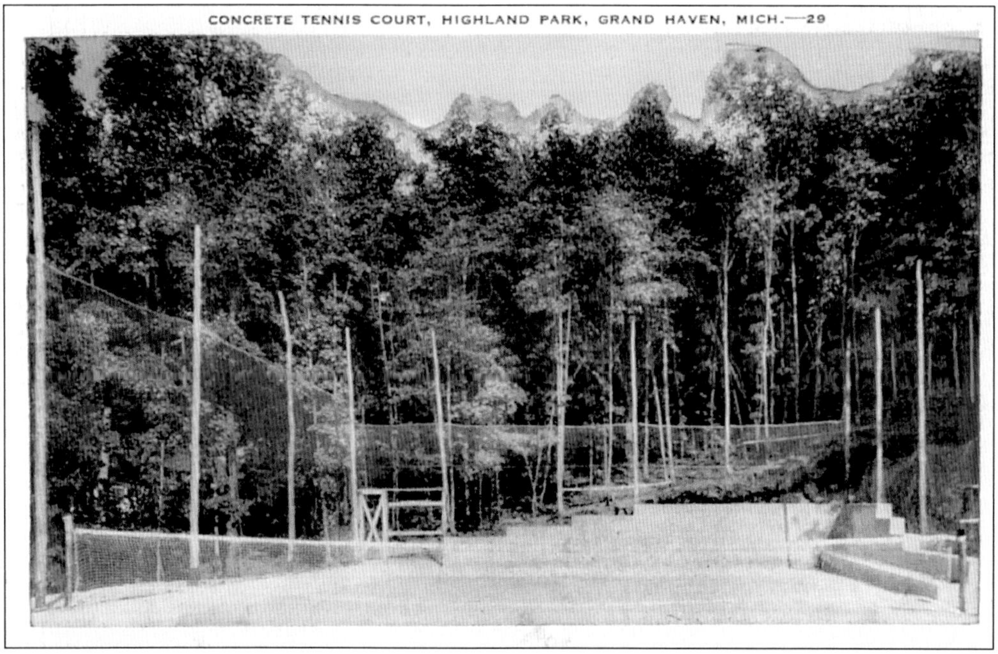

Chicago resident Thomas F. Otley formed the Highland Park Tennis Association in 1920 and ran it until his death in 1938. Nestled in the dunes, the first court was built in 1922, the second in 1927. The National Junior Boys Tennis Tournament was held here in the 1930s, and the Otley Cup awarded to the champion. This undated postcard shows the courts after they had been converted to a hard surface

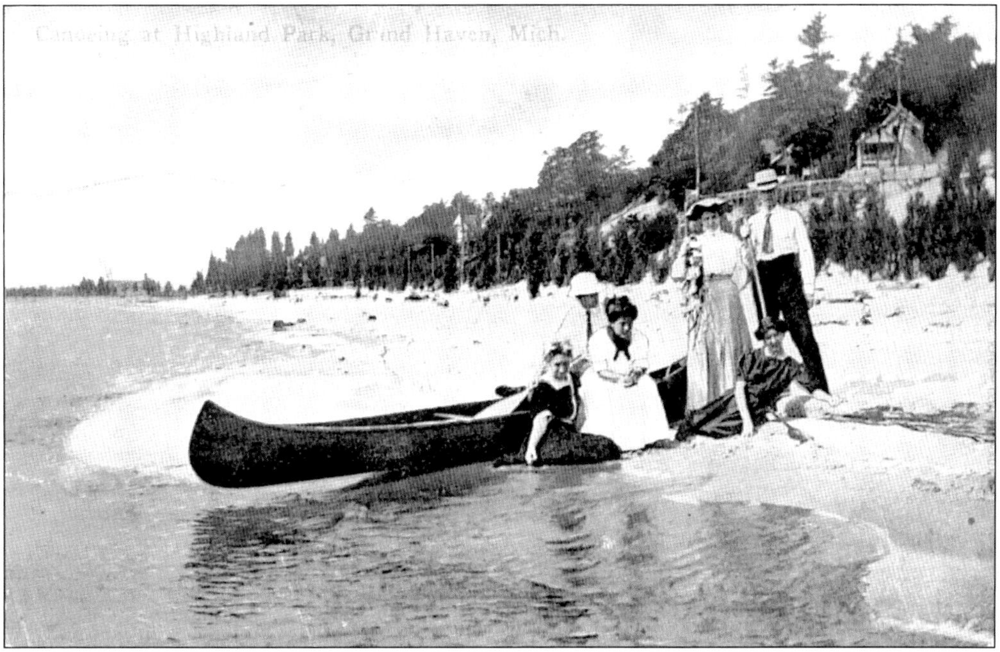

In the early 1900s people dressed well even to go canoeing! This picture was taken where Grand Avenue now makes its bend north toward the State Park. The message, addressed to a party in Chicago, says, "Nothing to do but have a good time. This sure is some town." The card is postmarked 1917.

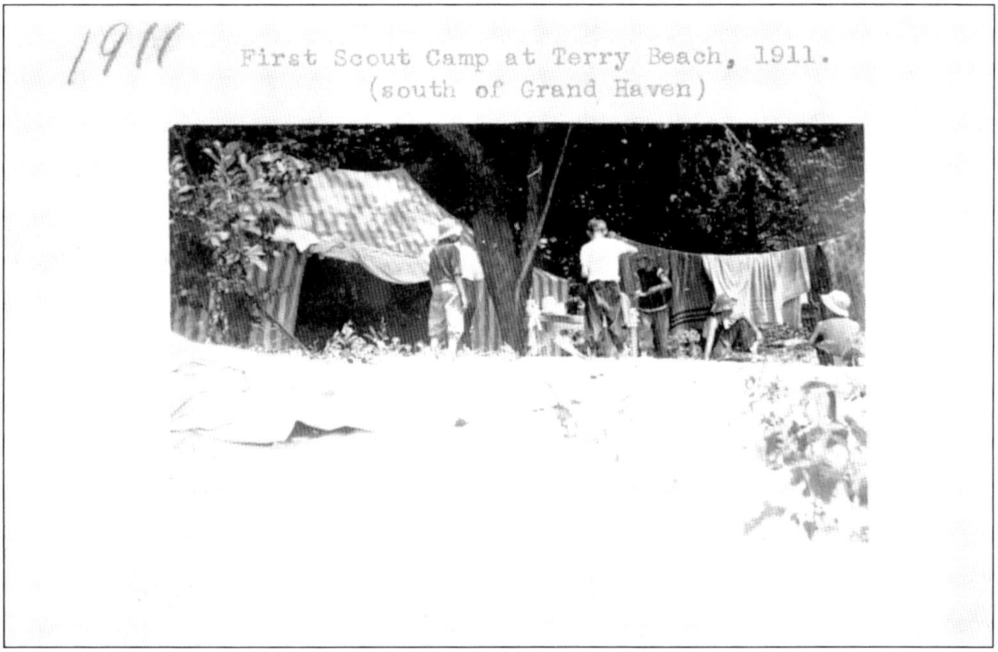

The Terry family owned considerable lakefront acreage just south of the City of Grand Haven. This view, dated 1911, shows the "First Boy Scout Camp at Terry Beach." The area today is known as Terry Trails. Evidently it was time for the scouts to air out their blankets!

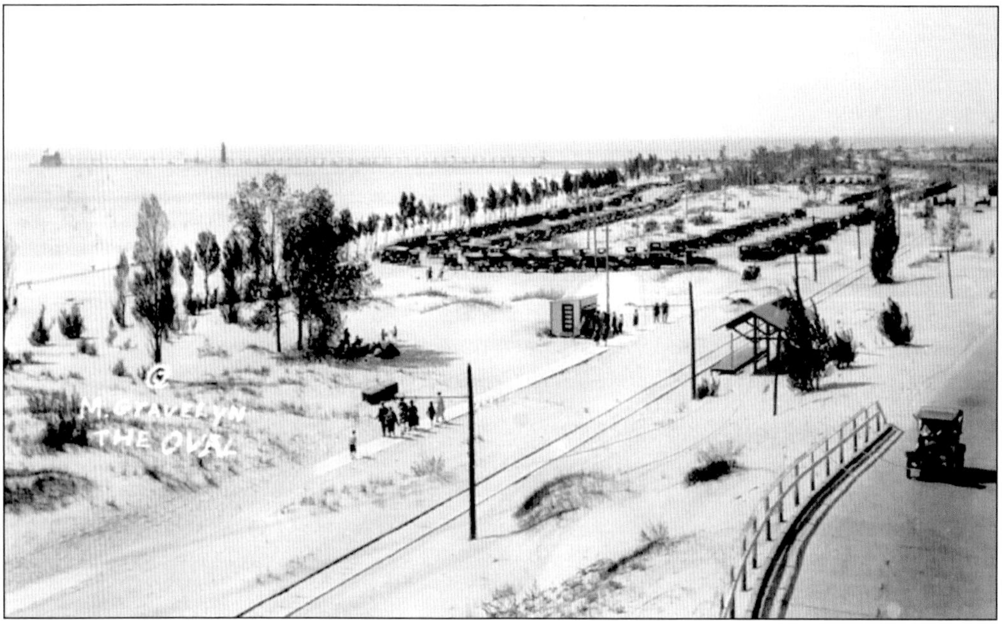

In the early 1920s people could get to the Oval by car, by Interurban, or by foot. This real photo view shows all three modes, and it appeared to be a busy day at the newly-opened State Park. By the time this photograph was taken, Lake Avenue had been extended to connect with Harbor Drive, but the Interurban tracks were still in use. The open structure near the center is the Interurban stop, and across from it is a busy concession stand.

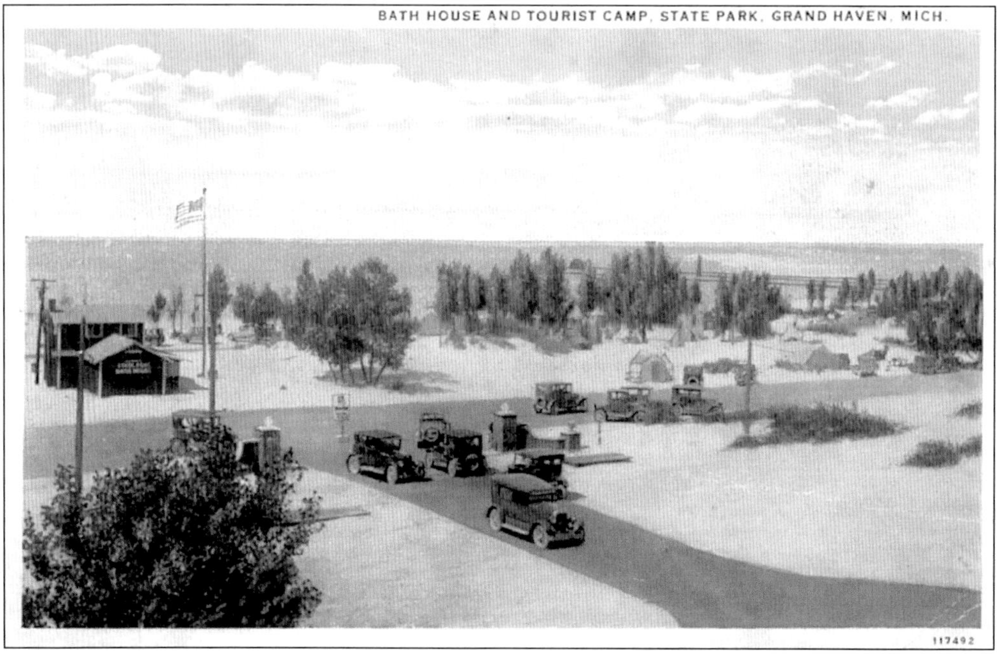

This undated postcard shows the entrance to the Oval when it was opposite the Oval Inn. The building near the left edge of the card was the State Park Bath House, which was in use from 1923 to 1938, the year it was replaced by the current pavilion.

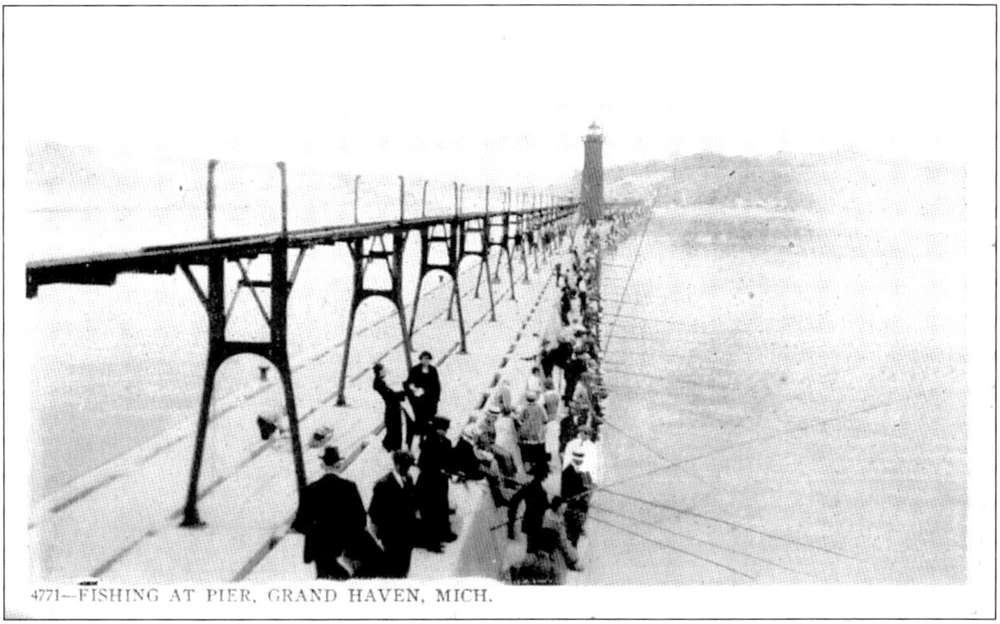

As long as there has been a pier, there have been people trying their skill—and luck—at fishing. This must have been a productive day on the Lake Michigan side of the south pier, judging from the number of anglers. Most of the men are wearing shirts, ties, jackets, and hats, and the few women present also appear to be fashionably dressed. The card was not mailed.

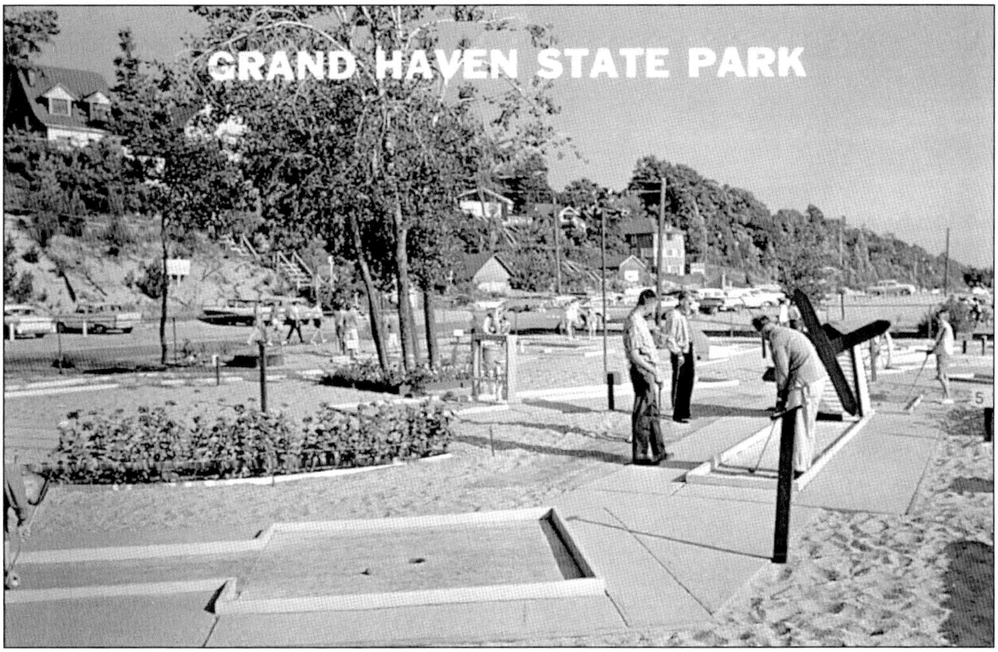

In the late 1950s a miniature golf course became a popular feature at the Grand Haven Oval. The group in the middle, playing Hole #5, is trying to make a par one through the moving blades of the windmill.

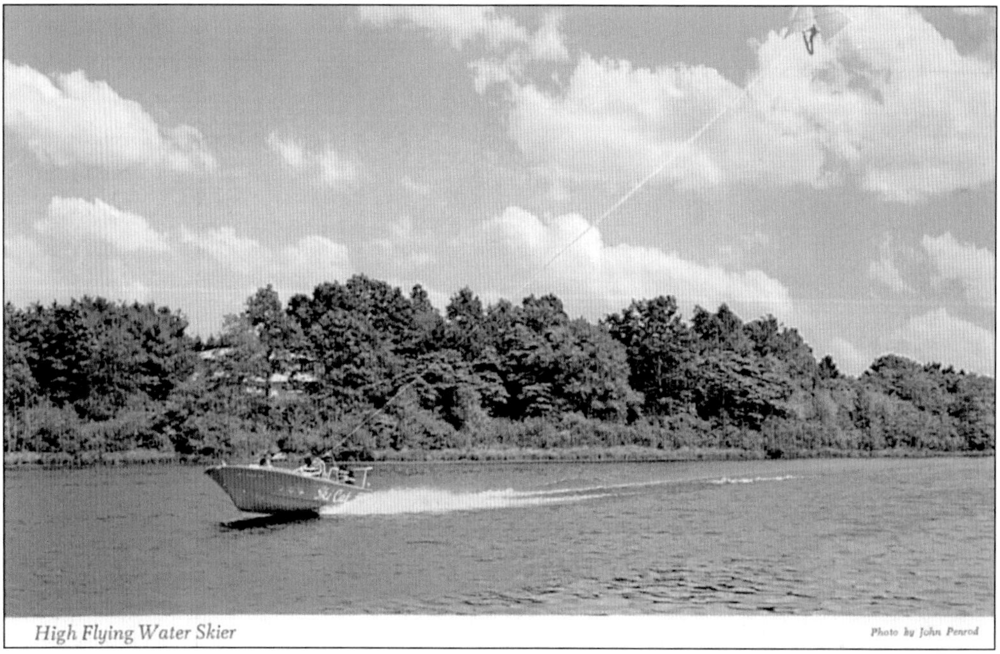

Soaring high in the air with a parasail is unidentified, but his stunt is reminiscent of Grand Haven's Water Thrill Show. During summers from 1962 to 1974, members of the troupe put on a spectacular performance at the waterfront twice a week. The boat pulling the parasail is named *Ski Cat*.

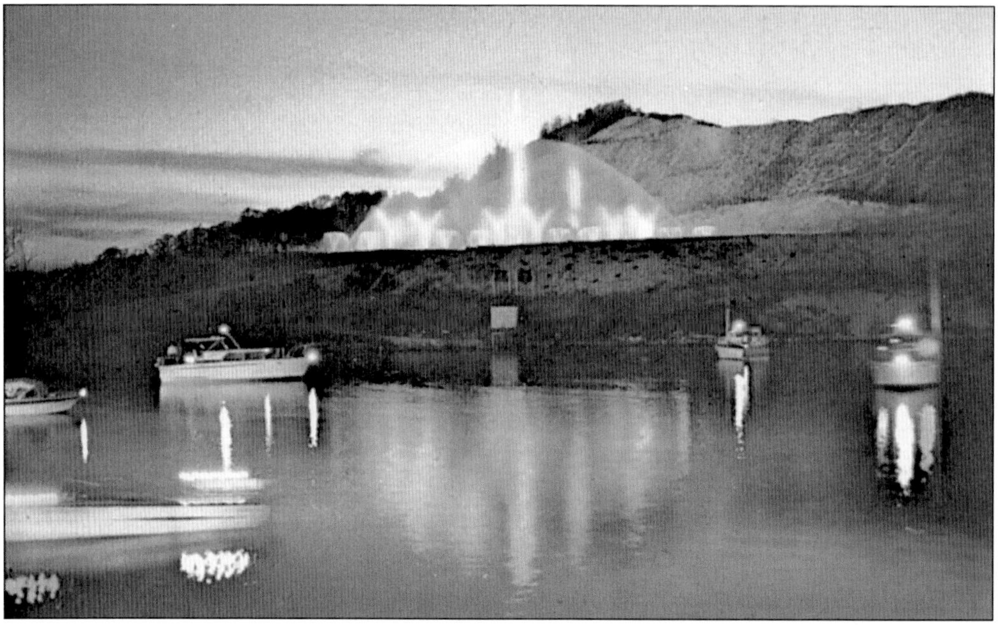

Publicized as the "world's largest musical fountain, with synchronized water, colored lights, and music," this spectacular sight was put on public display for the first time in 1962. Developed under the leadership of Dr. Bill Creason, the fountain continues to attract local residents and tourists to its nightly shows from Memorial Day through Labor Day. Dewey Hill provides a dramatic backdrop.

Five

Highways, Byways, and Railways

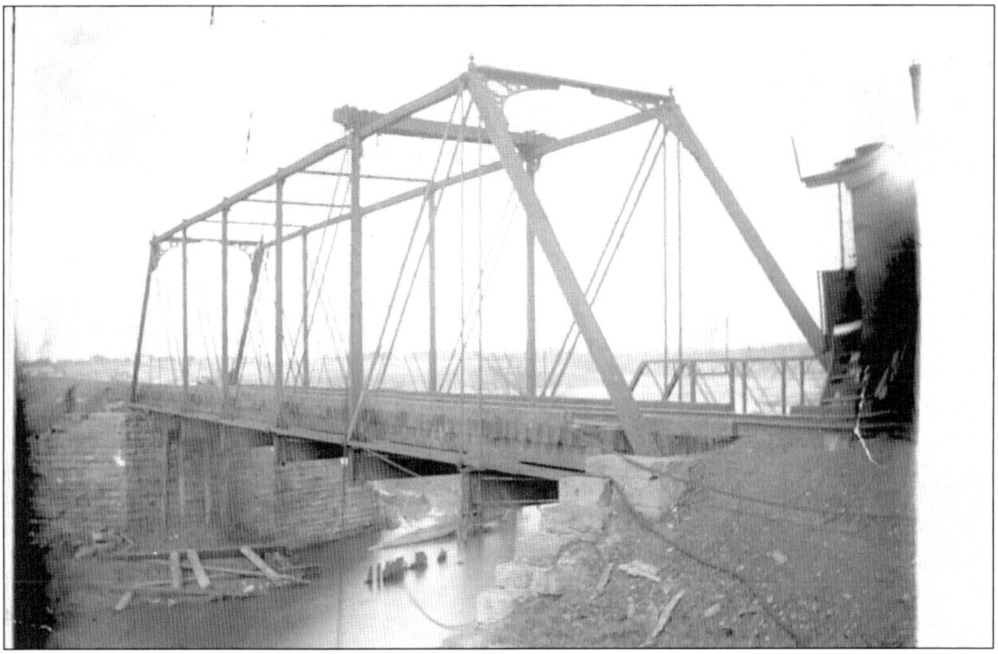

With so many waterways in the region, bridges were a necessary consideration. This early card shows the railroad bridge spanning Crockery Creek near Nunica. It was originally built for the Detroit, Grand Haven & Milwaukee Railroad. Lying in the water are the remains of an earlier wooden bridge, indicating this metal trestle span was a successor. The caboose is on its way out of the picture.

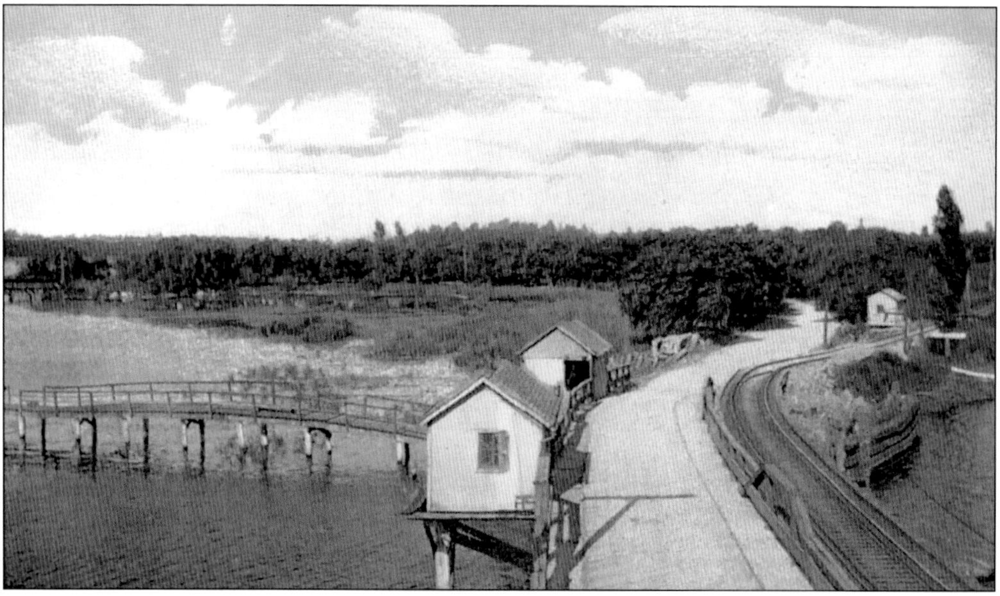

In 1866 a toll bridge was built to span the Grand River between Grand Haven and Spring Lake Village. For those traveling between Grand Haven and Ferrysburg, it was necessary to cross three bridges: one over the South Channel, another over the Grand River, and finally the bridge over Spring Lake Channel. The span pictured in this undated postcard crossed the Grand River. On the north side, the road turned west and connected with the Ferrysburg Bridge, just visible at the left edge, while the Interurban tracks headed southeast to connect with Savidge and continue their eastern route.

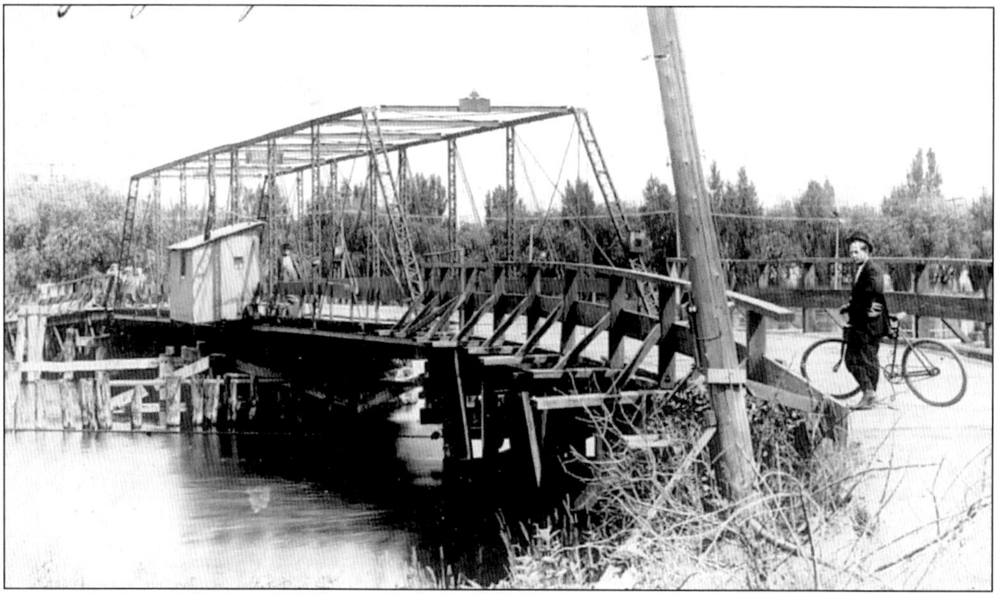

This undated card shows the swing bridge that connected the Villages of Spring Lake and Ferrysburg. The post and beam construction was augmented by a steel superstructure. A railroad bridge ran parallel to this one just a little bit to the north. The camera is looking toward Spring Lake. The swing bridge was replaced by a jack-knife span in 1924.

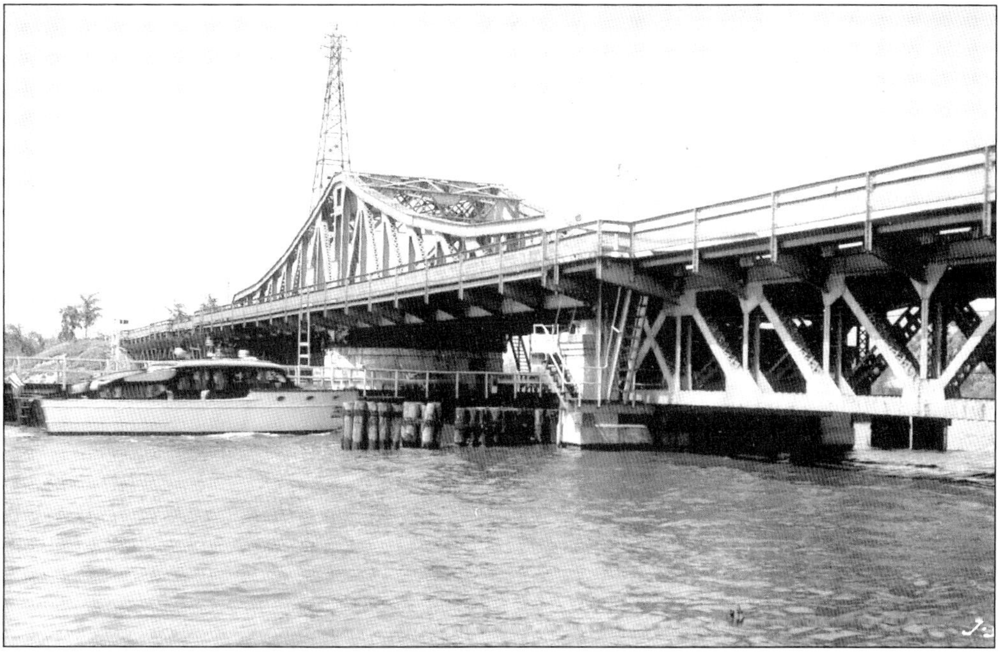

Featured in this unmailed real photo postcard is the first vehicular bridge to provide a direct link between Grand Haven and Ferrysburg. Known as the Swing Bridge, it was dedicated on November 11, 1923 and carried U.S. 31 traffic for more than 30 years before it was replaced by the current drawbridge.

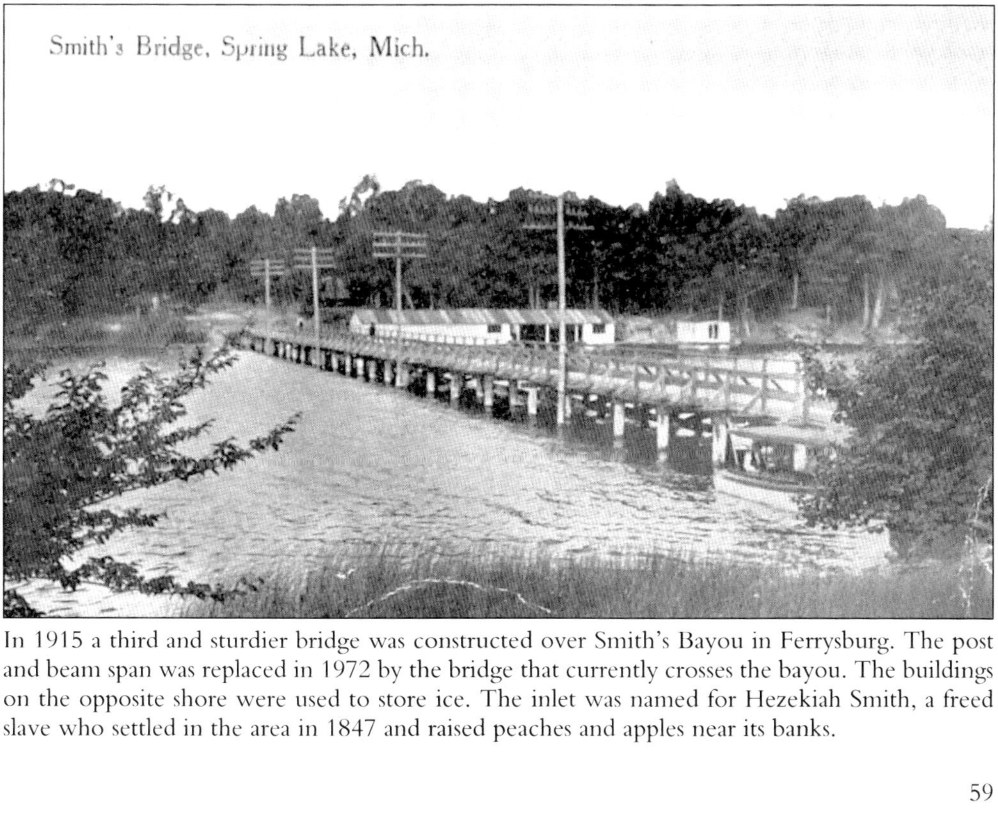

In 1915 a third and sturdier bridge was constructed over Smith's Bayou in Ferrysburg. The post and beam span was replaced in 1972 by the bridge that currently crosses the bayou. The buildings on the opposite shore were used to store ice. The inlet was named for Hezekiah Smith, a freed slave who settled in the area in 1847 and raised peaches and apples near its banks.

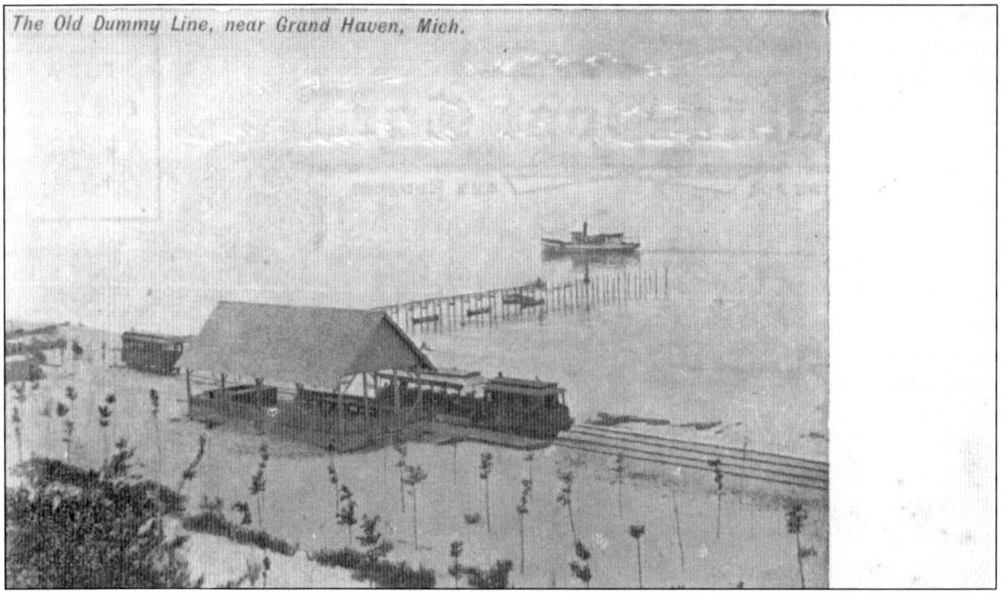

The Grand Haven Street Railway Company was organized in 1895 to provide transportation from downtown to the lakeshore. One of the steam-powered engines is shown in this postcard pulling into the station at Highland Park. The service earned the nickname "Dummy Line" because the engines didn't generate their own power, but picked up charges of steam along the way. Highland Park residents preferred to call it the "Dinky." In 1902 the company merged with another line and became part of the Interurban service between Grand Rapids, Muskegon, and Grand Haven. The card was printed before 1907.

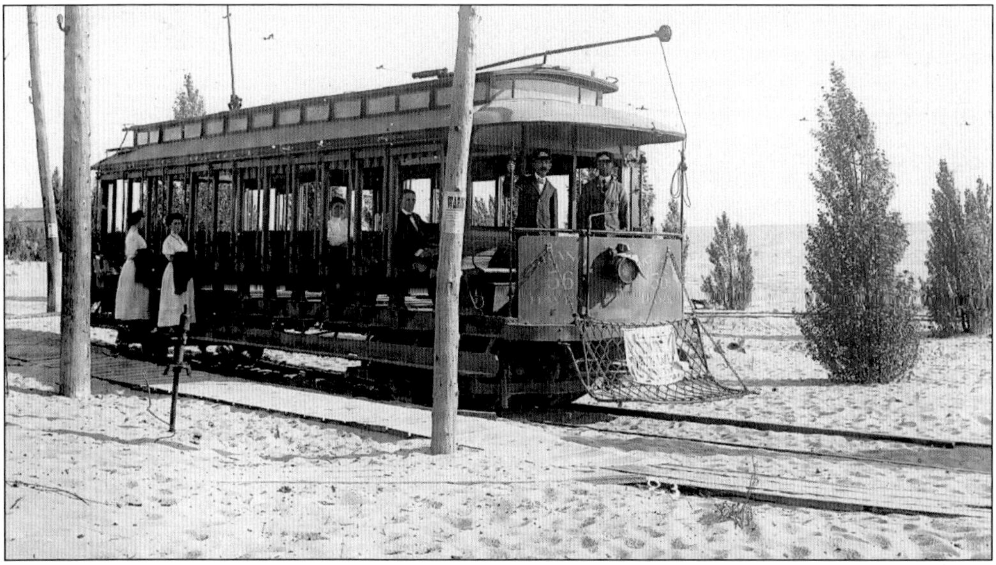

All aboard! The Grand Haven Interurban car, shown here near Indian Village at the south end of its run, is ready for the return trip to downtown and on to Spring Lake, Fruitport, and Grand Rapids. The track made a loop at this point on the beach so that the "Dummy Line" that originally made the run could reverse direction. The electric cars continued to use the loop. The passengers and two conductors seem aware there was a camera nearby. The card is postmarked 1908.

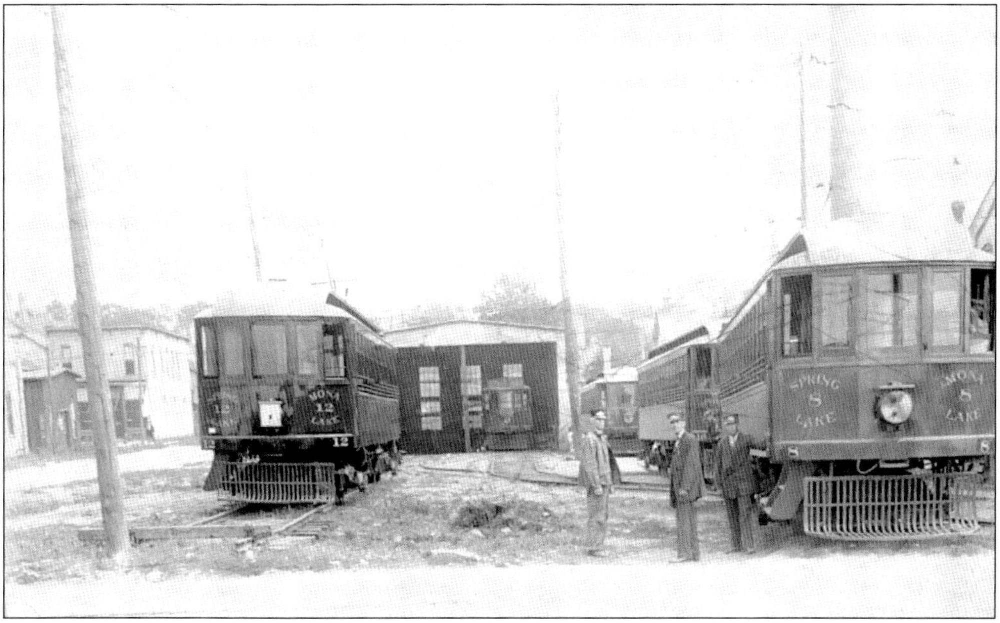

The Interurban, also called the "Electric," offered inexpensive transportation between Grand Rapids, Muskegon, Spring Lake, and Grand Haven. Passengers could transfer at the main depot in Fruitport to complete their journey to one destination or the other. Shown in this undated postcard is the Interurban car barn at Fruitport. All these cars are labeled Spring Lake and Mona Lake.

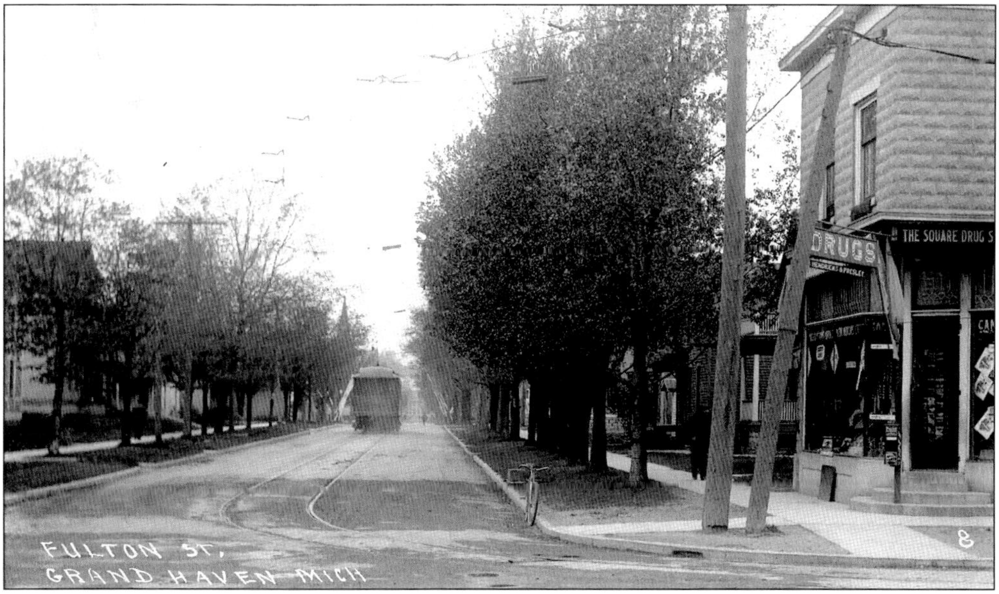

In the early years of the 20th century, the corner drugstore was as common as the neighborhood grocery. Square Drug Store at the junction of Seventh and Fulton Streets was one of the popular places. Raymond Presley and Ora Hendricks opened the store around 1912. It was still doing business as a drugstore in the late 1950s, when it was known as Voss's. The Interurban car has just made its turn onto Fulton from Seventh Street. Presley later owned a drugstore with his name at the corner of Seventh and Washington. This real photo card is postmarked 1913.

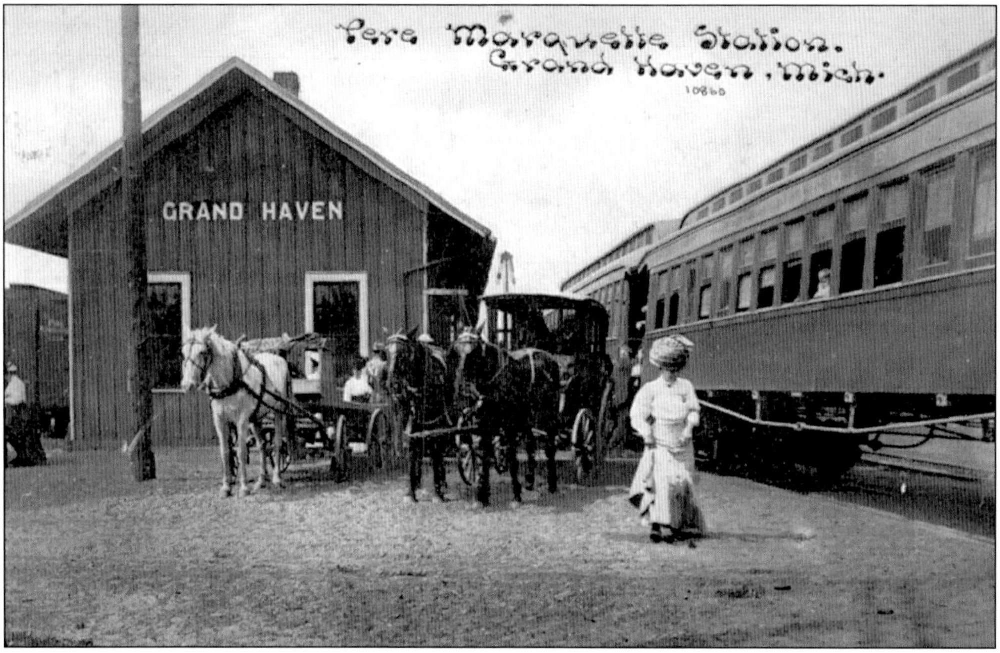

The Pere Marquette Railway Station, pictured in this 1912 postcard, was located on Jackson Street near Fourth. The frame structure was destroyed by fire in 1926 and was replaced by a brick building that today houses dental offices. The Pere Marquette line offered train service primarily north and south from Grand Haven.

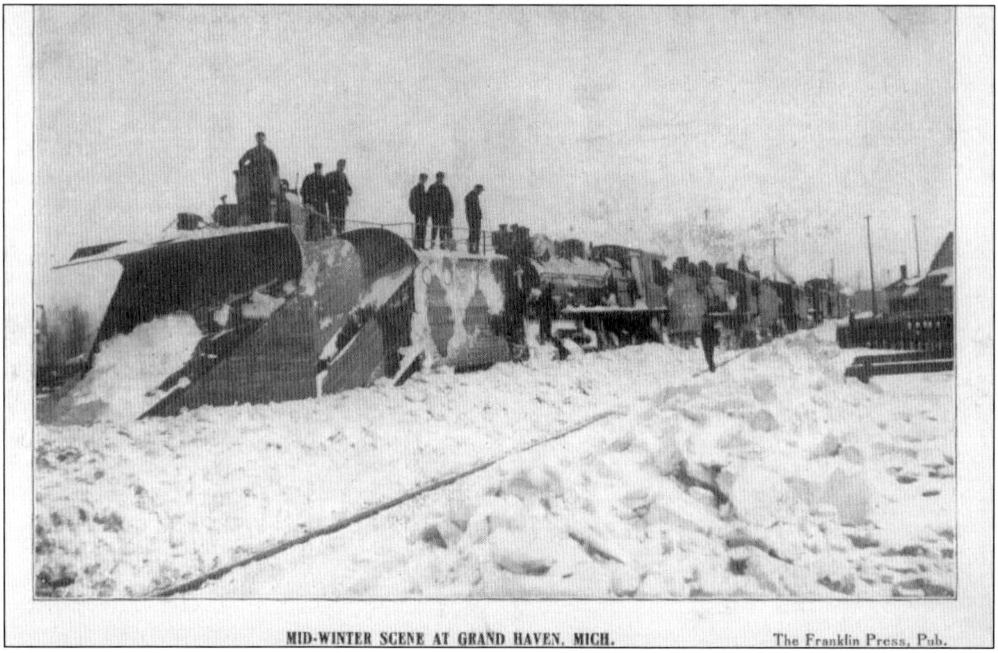

The crew of Engine 350 is ready for a camera break after freeing the railroad tracks of snow, as shown in this "Mid-Winter Scene at Grand Haven." The scene appears to be near the Pere Marquette Depot on Jackson Street. The card was unmailed, but predates 1907.

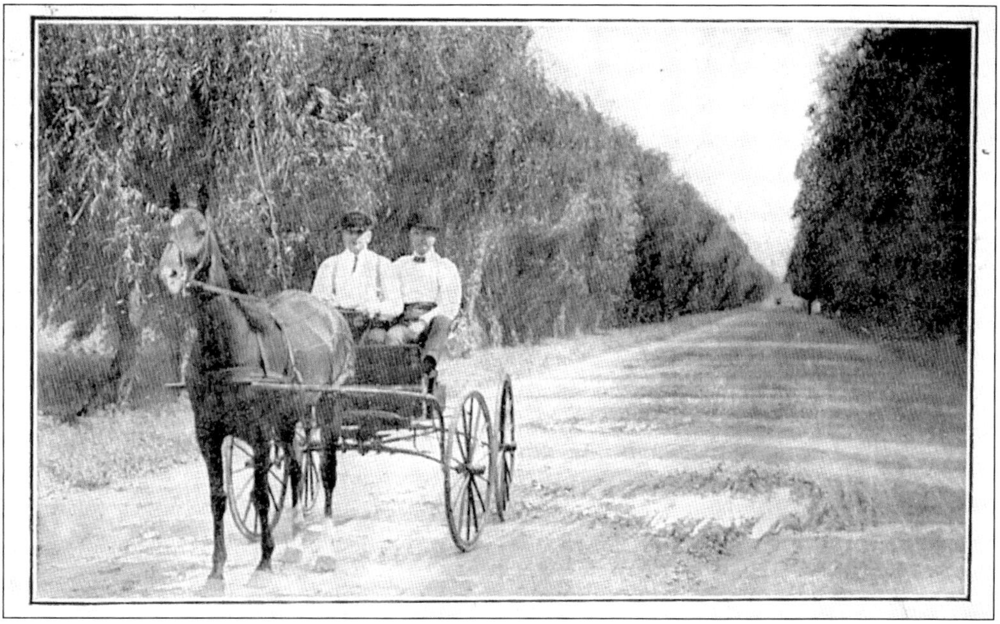

In this 1911 postcard, two well-dressed gentlemen are out for a leisurely drive with their horse and buggy on Willow Drive, between Spring Lake and Ferrysburg. The postcard caption refers to the road as a "Boulevard." The vehicle in the distance is too far away to tell if it is horse-drawn or motorized.

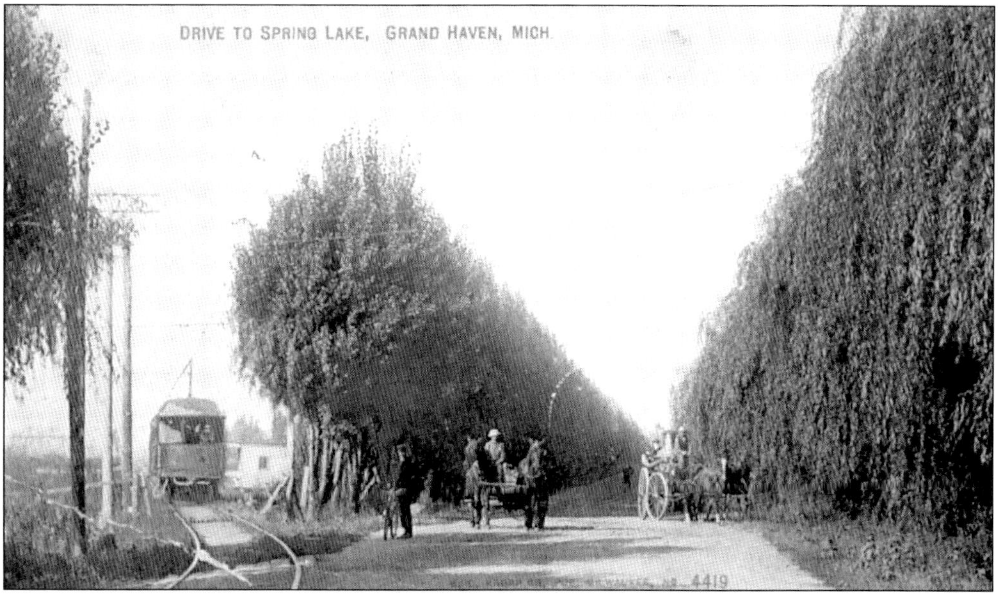

Thomas Savidge is credited with planting willow trees on each side of the road connecting Spring Lake Village with Grand Haven and Ferrysburg. Now known as Savidge Street, for many years it was called Willow Drive in recognition of the graceful trees and the wonderful shade they provided. This 1909 card shows an Interurban car about to merge with the road, while a biker, a horse-drawn cart, and a fire engine pumper wait in the tree-lined drive. As new businesses developed, the willows eventually all fell to the axe.

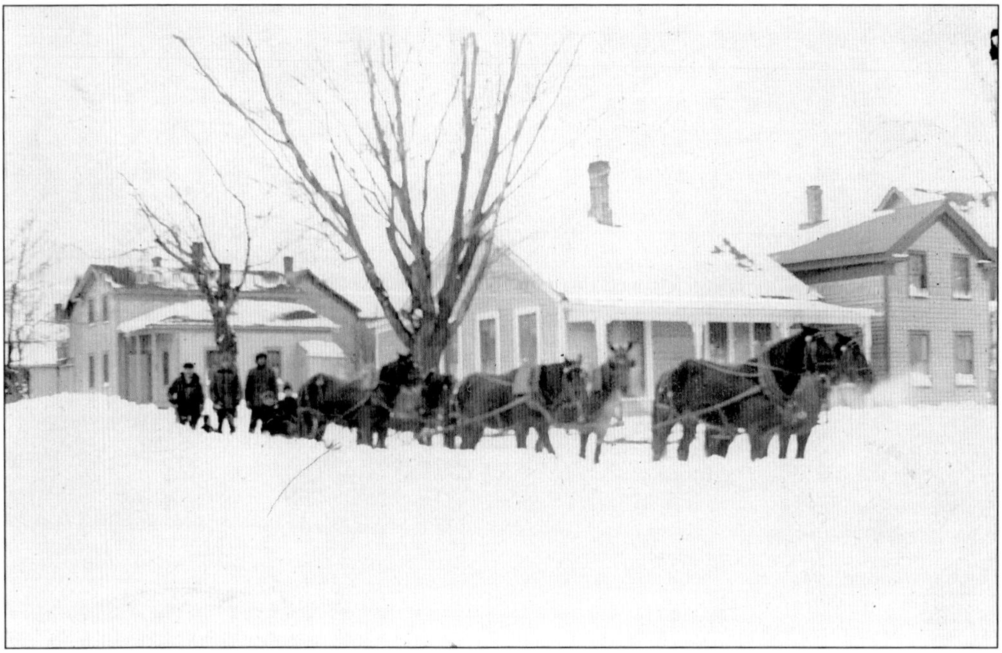

The Grand Haven area has experienced numerous severe snowstorms, including this one during the winter of 1917. Before mechanized snowplows became common, teams of horses were used to help clear the streets. The people and neighborhood are unidentified.

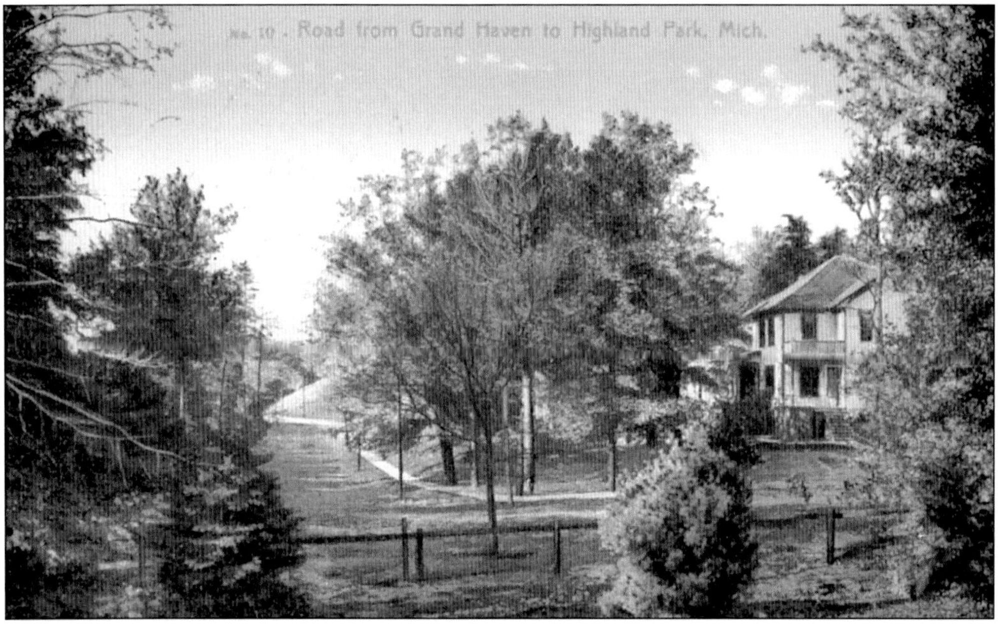

To save it from the lumberman's saw, early in the lumber era Robert Duncan purchased 50 acres of virgin timber outside the city limits. This picturesque scene shows Lake Avenue where it turns west toward Highland Park and the lake. The two-story Duncan residence is on the right. Robert Duncan died in 1903 and ten years later Martha, his widow, donated the 50 acres to the City of Grand Haven. Today the wooded land is known as Duncan Park. The card is postmarked 1911.

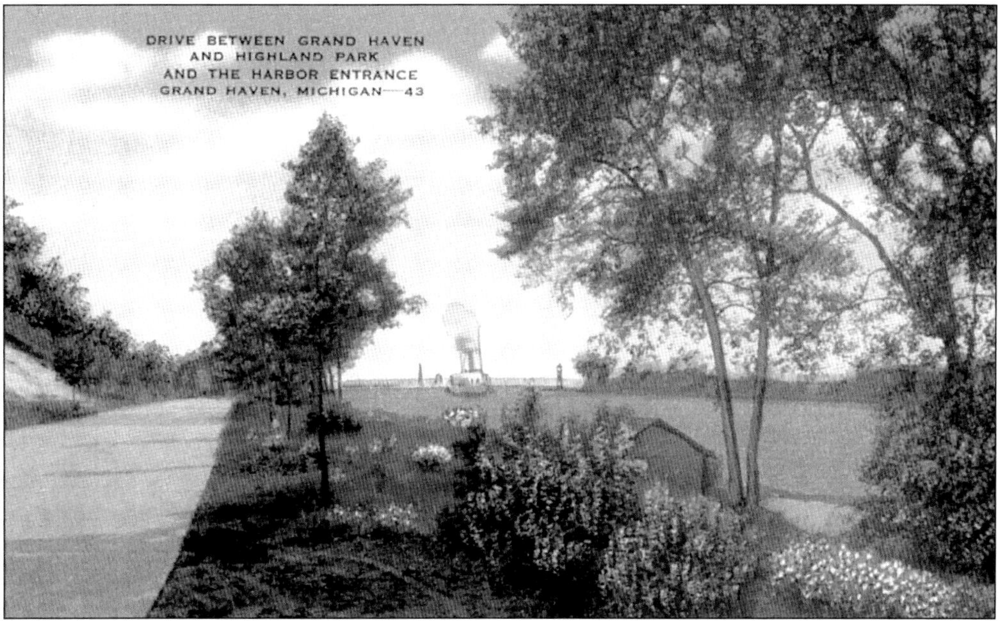

Although looking more like a lovely country lane than the road we are familiar with today, this view shows Harbor Drive looking west toward the pier. The card probably was touched up to "improve" the scene. Even the Coast Guard Station has been removed. The dune on the left now shelters Boardwalk Condominiums. The postcard was never mailed and is undated.

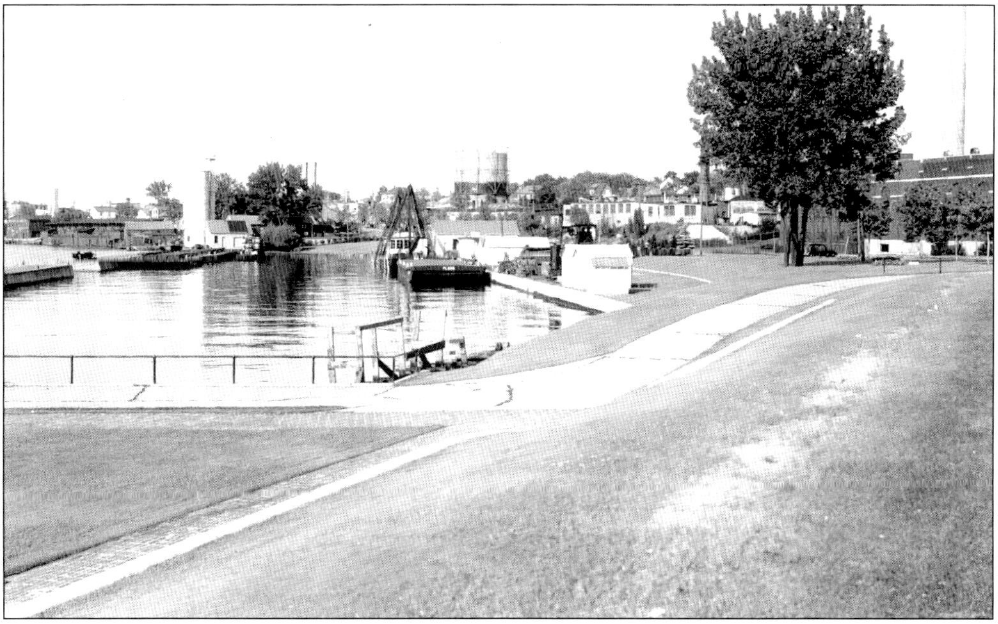

The Barn, a favorite place for young people to skate and dance, can barely be seen in the distance, near the left edge of this real photo postcard. A storage tank dominates the center horizon. Just below it is Michigan Brass, now the site of Sandpiper Condominiums, and the Board of Light and Power generating plant is at the far right. Group Commander Headquarters of the U.S. Coast Guard now sits on the edge of Government Pond.

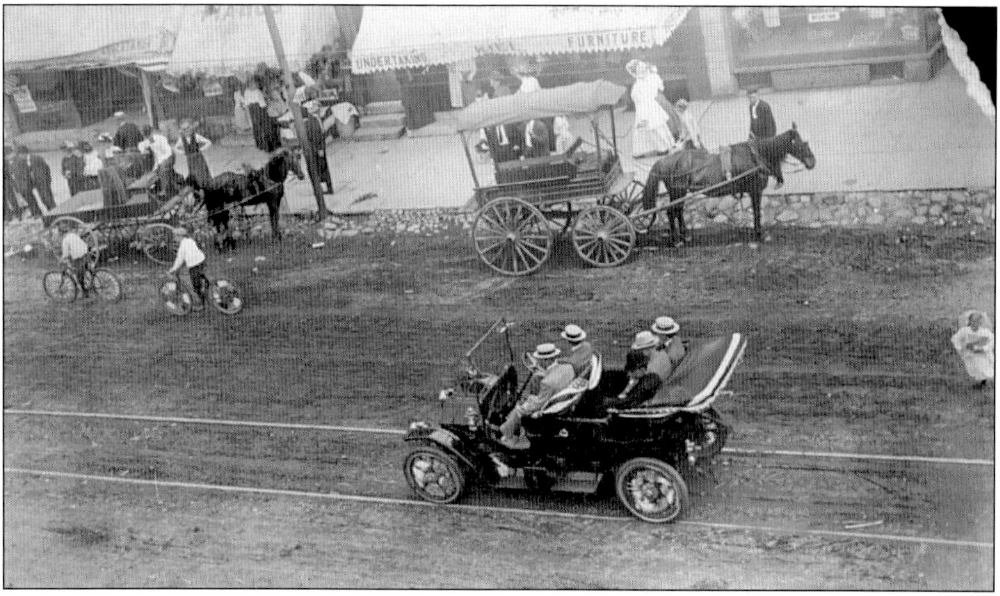

In the touring car motoring down the Interurban tracks in the 100 block of Washington Street, the straw-hatted gentlemen appear to be part of a patriotic parade, judging from the small crowd huddled near Kiel's Furniture and Undertaking business. The crepe paper arranged in the wheels of both bicycles and the automobile indicate they were participants in the parade. Washington Street was paved in 1910, two years after this card was printed. Stone was used for curbing prior to the paving, and the sidewalks appear to be made of concrete.

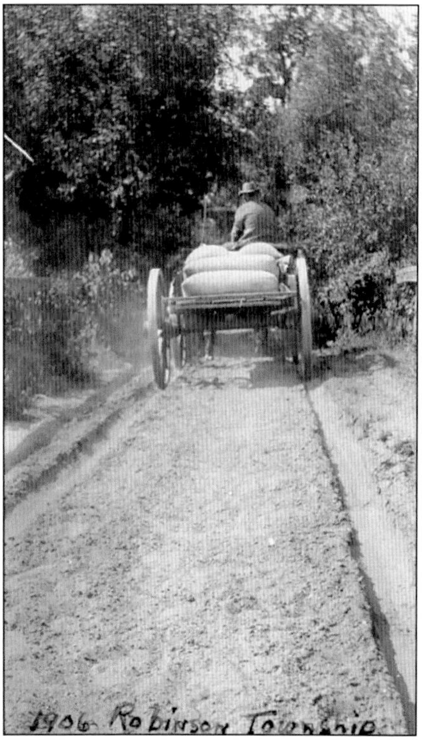

The road is unnamed, but this real photo postcard is dated 1906. It shows a miller carrying large burlap sacks of grain as he wends his way along a narrow, two-track road from Robinson Township to Grand Haven, where he will find a market for his goods.

Six

Open for Business

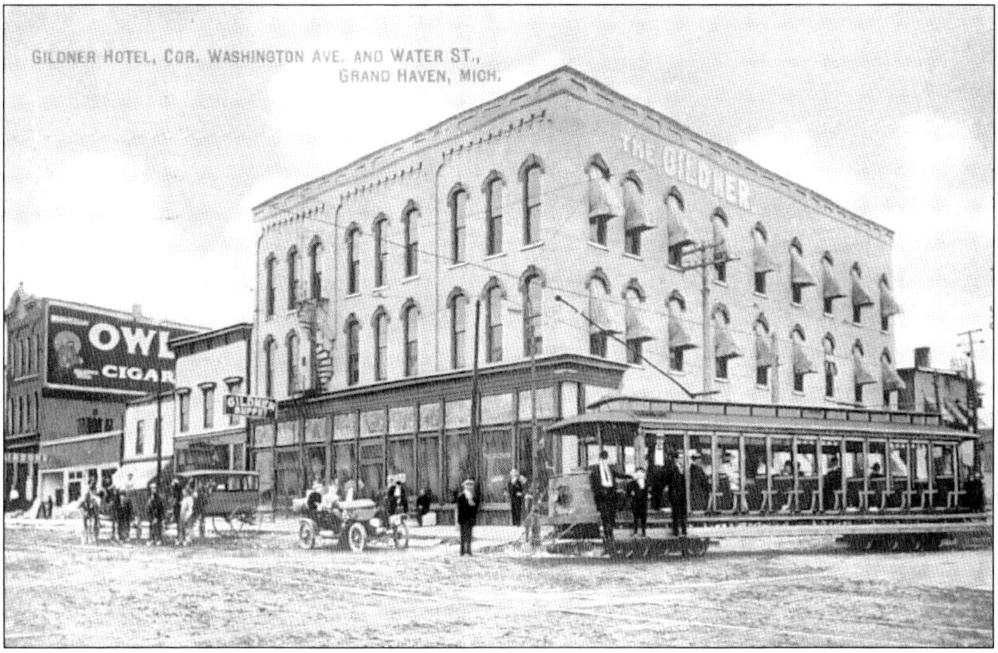

An unknown photographer carefully staged this 1913 photograph at the corner of Washington and Harbor Drive. Displayed are three modes of transportation current at that time: a horse-drawn carriage, an automobile, and the Interurban car. The Gildner Hotel in the background was built in 1873 as the Kirby House, and today, with the third floor removed, it is the site of Kirby Grill. The three-story Grey Block to the left, built in 1871, also remains in use, but the advertisement for Owl cigars has long since disappeared.

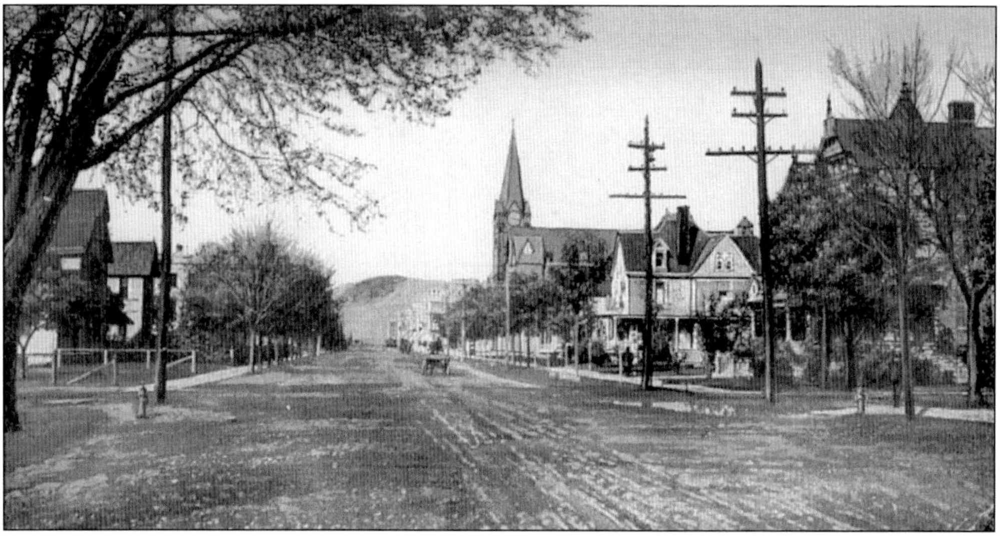

This 1909 postcard shows the residential block along Washington, just east of downtown Grand Haven. Enough of Captain William Loutit's mansion can be seen through the mature trees shading the imposing residence to recognize its grandeur. It was razed in 1959 to make room for a gas station. Just beyond it is Willard C. Sheldon's residence, built in 1890 and recently restored to its original design by new owners. One-half block farther, the steeple of the First Reformed Church with the town clock juts into the air.

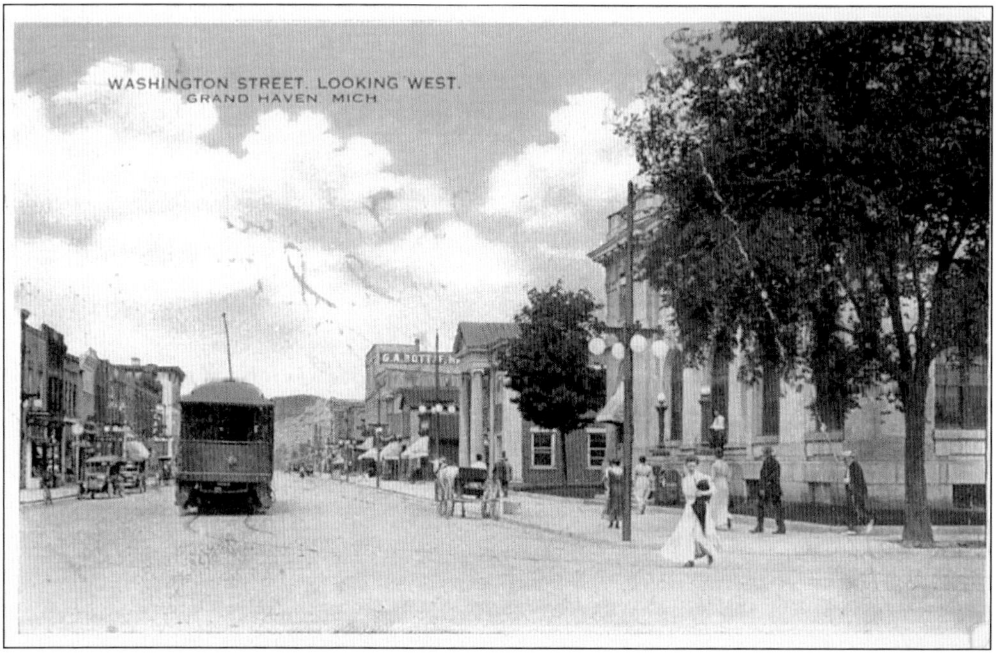

This view of downtown Grand Haven was taken at the intersection of Third and Washington Streets before the Robinhood Theater was constructed in 1916. An Interurban car has just made the turn from Third Street to Washington, while a horse and buggy wait in front of the post office. The tall brick building near the center of the card was home to Gerrit Bottje's Hardware Store, in business from 1887 until about 1920.

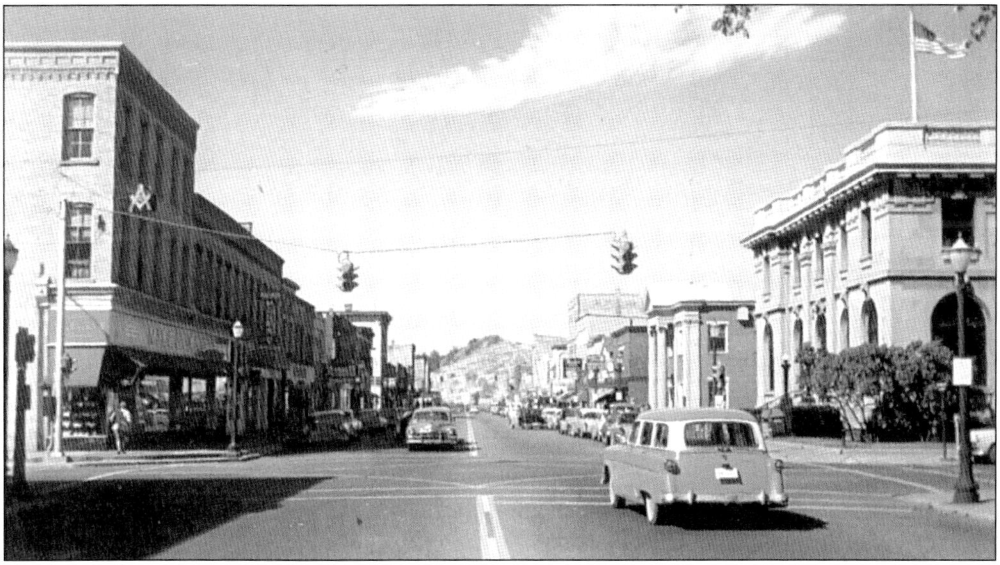

By 1957, the date of this unmailed postcard, the buildings along Washington Street looked much as they had 50 years earlier, although the vehicles are newer, the Interurban tracks are gone, and the brick street was blacktopped. McLellan's Five and Dime Store is on the left, across from the post office. McLellan's was in operation from 1940 to 1973.

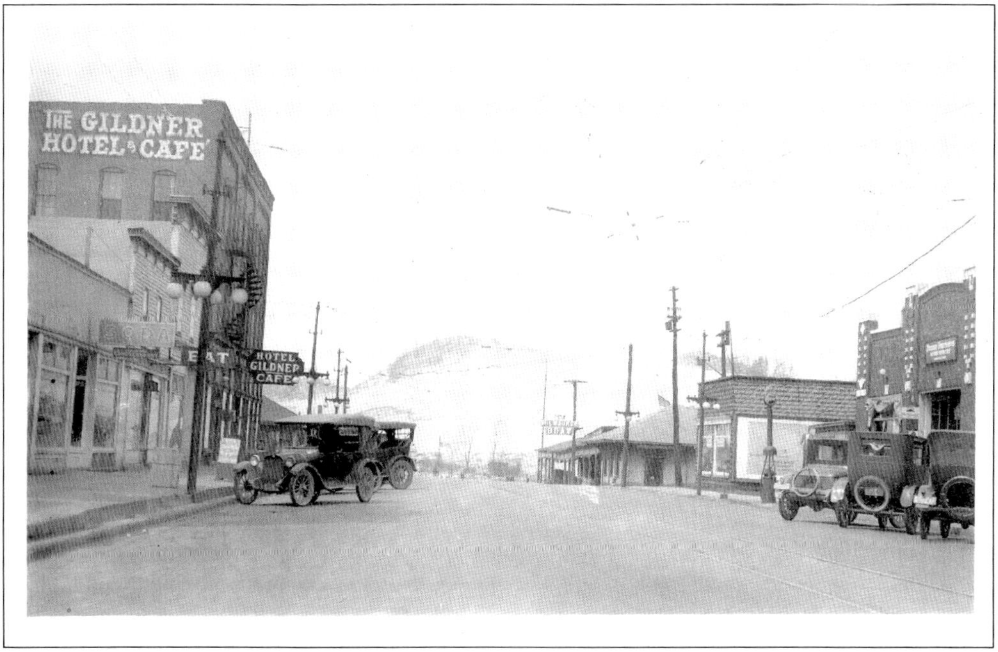

By the 1910s, automobiles were a common sight in downtown Grand Haven. This photo provides a clear view of the block on Washington between First Street and Harbor Drive. The Grand Trunk Station can be seen on the far right with the Crosby steamship office just beyond it. The concrete block building this side of the depot once housed a saloon. The Washington Garage on the right provided automobile repair and storage. The sign over the door advertises "Dodge Brothers Motor Vehicles."

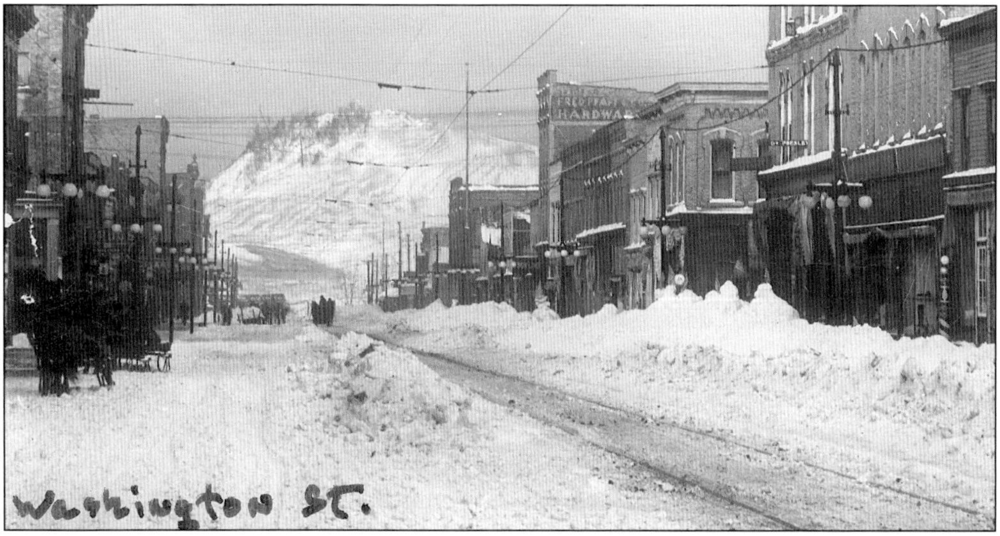

Dewey Hill in the background is reminiscent of Mt. Everest in this winter scene. The horse-drawn plow can be seen in the distance, clearing the snow off the Interurban tracks that ran down the middle of Washington Street. In this undated card, the tall brick building with the painted advertisement at the top was Fred Pfaff's Hardware Store, and the building that has housed Hostetter's News Agency for several decades stands at the corner of Washington and Second Streets. The barber pole for Lehman Brothers' Shop is visible at the far right. It is now the site of Glo Barber Shop.

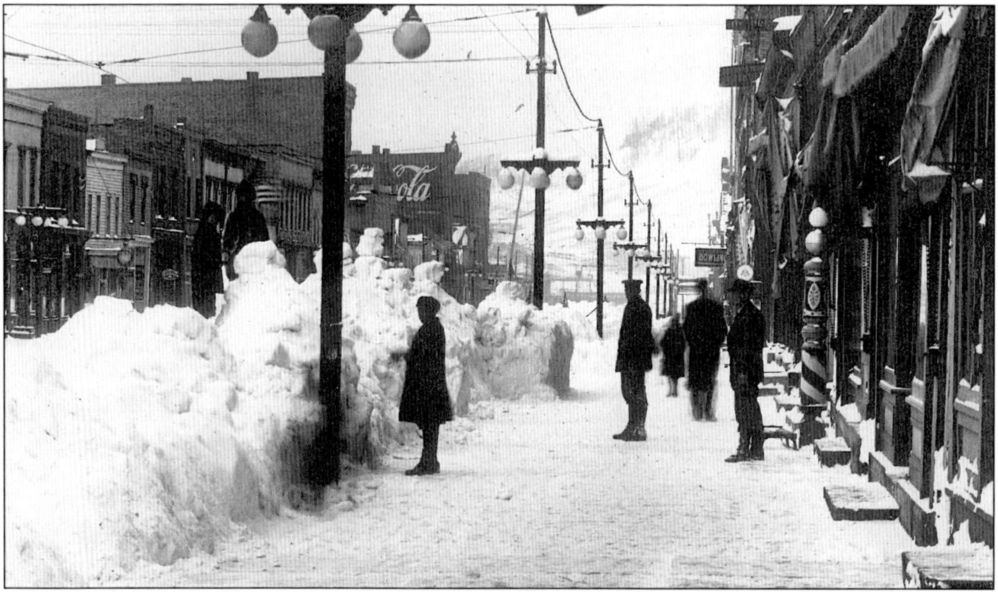

Another memorable snowstorm occurred around January 7, 1918. This view, taken in the 100 block of Washington Street, looks west toward Dewey Hill. The tall building on the left, partially obscured by a lamp post, can be identified as the old post office, now the location of the Rosebud Restaurant. A bit farther on is the Grey Block, with a large Coca Cola sign painted on its side. The Gildner Hotel is in the distance on the same side of the street. A barber shop and bowling alley are visible on the right.

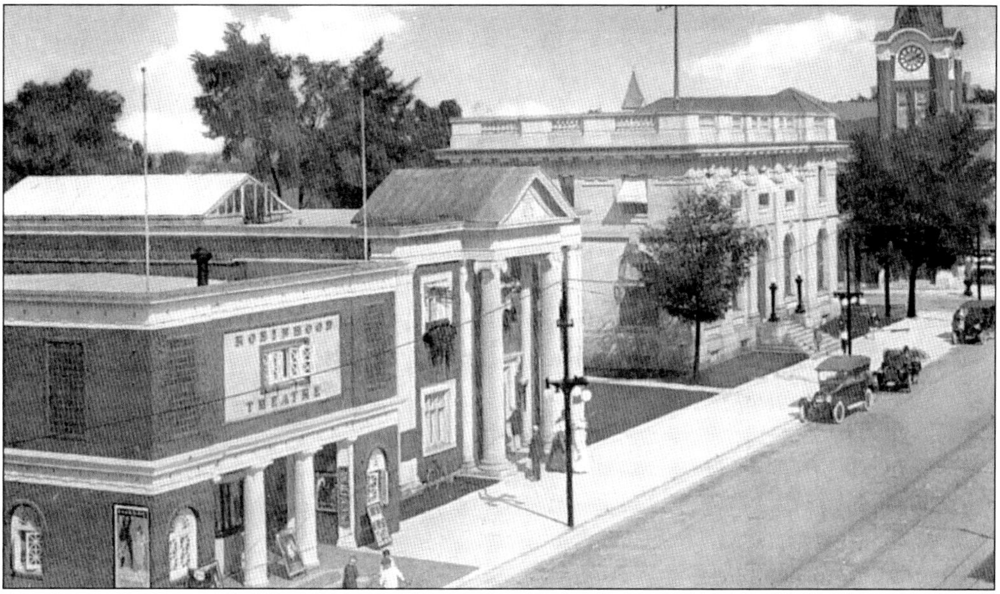

This card shows three prominent buildings erected in the 200 block of downtown Grand Haven in the early 1900s. The Robinhood Theater opened to movie lovers in 1916. The next building with the imposing pillars housed Grand Haven State Bank, which opened in 1912. The Federal Building on the corner was constructed in 1905 as headquarters for the post office and other governmental agencies. The photo was staged to show off three early automobiles.

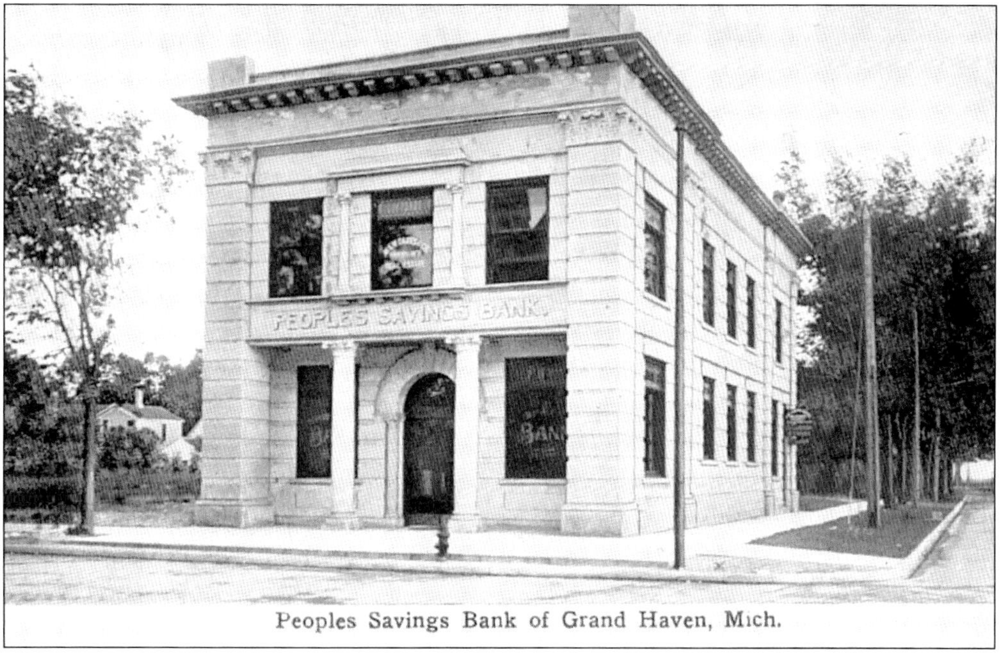

Peoples Savings Bank of Grand Haven, Mich.

The Peoples Savings Bank, now merged with Bank One, stood at the southeast corner of Third and Washington. Construction of the building began in April of 1910, and its doors opened the following February. In 1933 it was the scene of Grand Haven's only armed bank robbery. At the time this photograph was taken, James Oakes Insurance and Real Estate Office was on the second floor.

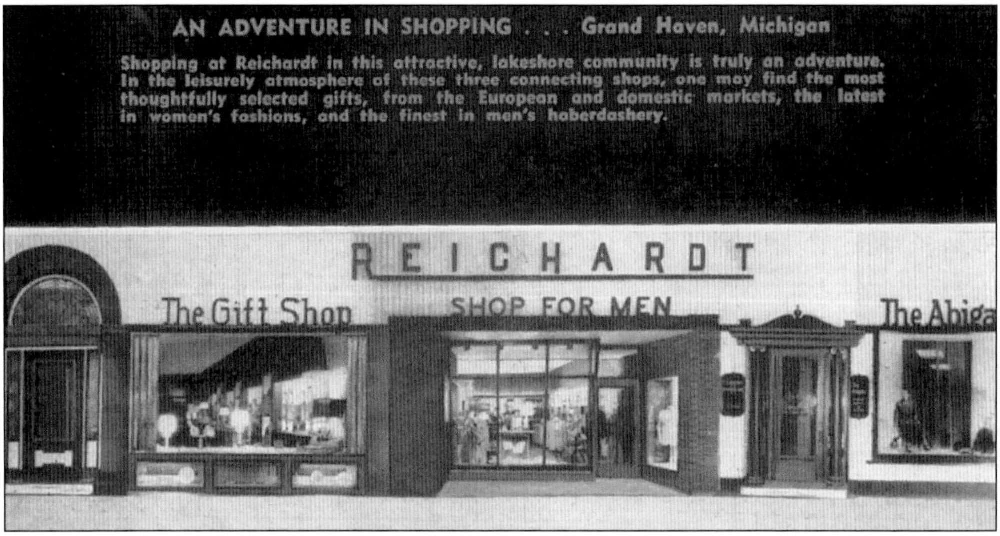

"An adventure in shopping" is the headline in this advertising card postmarked 1952. The ad goes on to say, "Shopping at Reichardt in this attractive, lakeshore community, is truly an adventure. In the leisurely atmosphere of these three connected shops, one may find the most thoughtfully selected gifts, from the European and domestic markets, the latest in women's fashions, and the finest in men's haberdashery." Reichardt was a dominant name in downtown Grand Haven for decades.

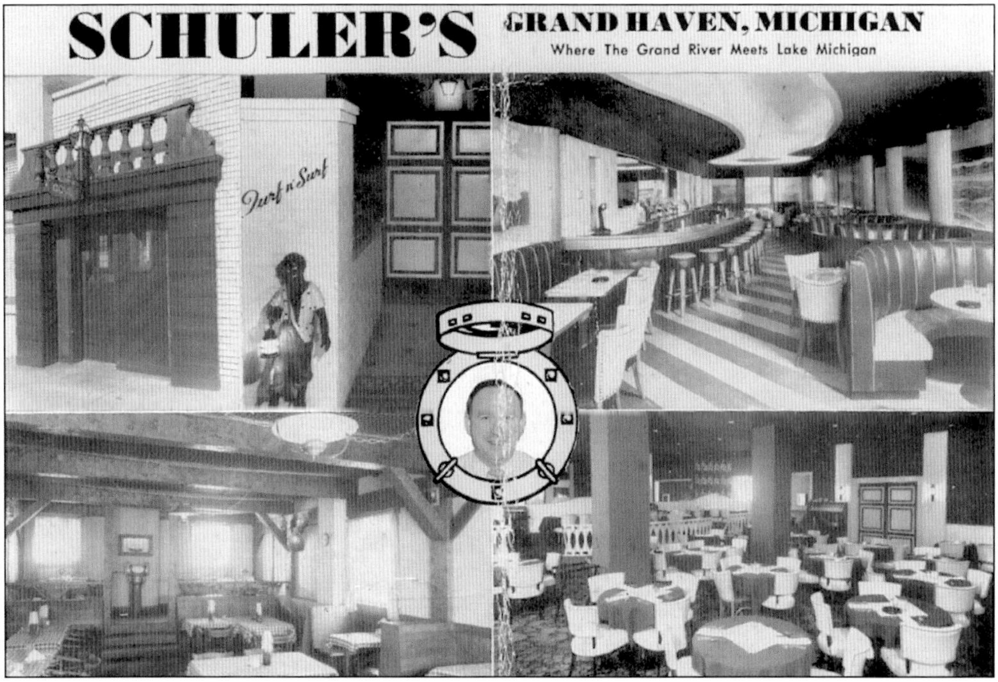

Schuler's in Grand Haven offered rooms, food, and beverages for almost three decades. The oversized postcard, with Al's picture in the center, advertises a hotel "with four outstanding and unique dining rooms." Al Schuler sold the business to his brother Win in 1962. Win removed the third floor and devoted the business entirely to food service. He sold the enterprise in 1975. Kirby Grill now occupies the site.

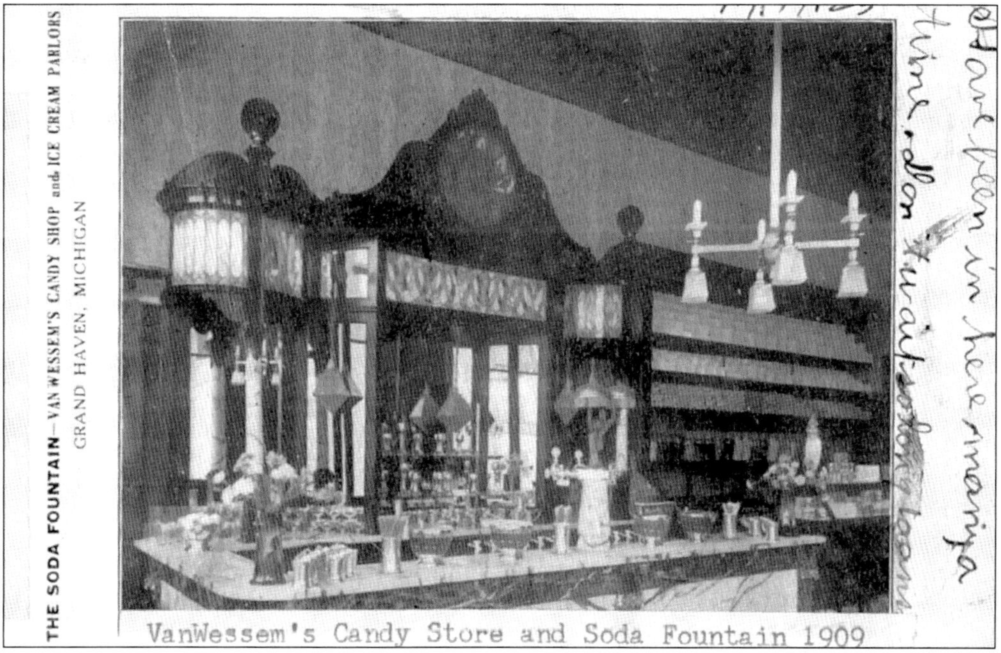

James Van Wessem owned and operated a popular "Candy Shop and Ice Cream Parlor" in the early 1900s. Located at 100 Washington, the shop offered sodas and sundaes for a nickel. The youngster who sent the 1910 postcard showing the interior of the ice cream parlor wrote, "I have been here many times." The ornate counters and fountain were fairly common in the early 1900s.

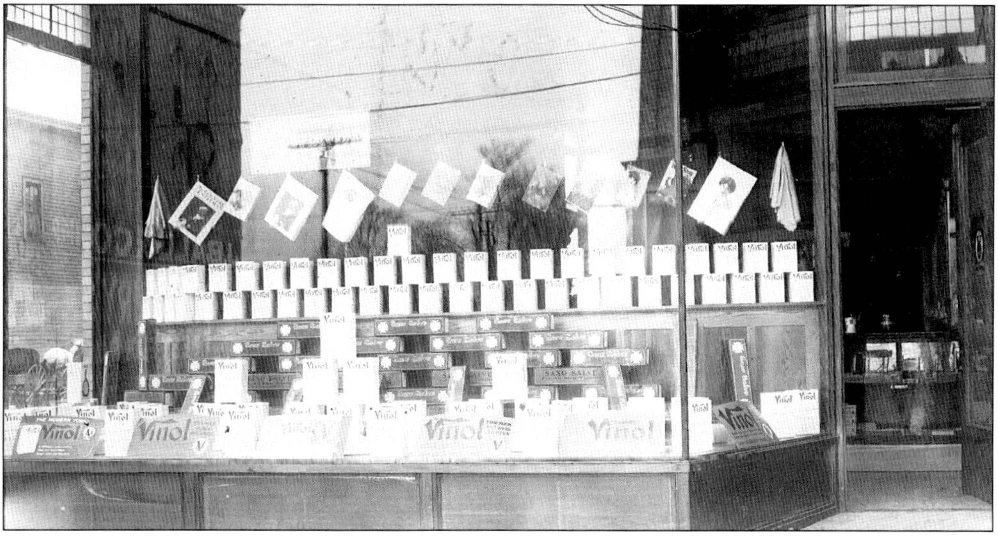

In 1873 Hunter Savidge built a three-story building at the corner of Washington and Second Streets in downtown Grand Haven. The Jacob Vander Veen Drug Company occupied the first floor from the time it opened until the 1920s. Its display window and main entrance are shown in this unmailed card. Central Drug occupied the corner spot in the 1920s and 1930s, Mulder Drug in the 1940s and 1950s, and Steiner Pharmacy from the 1960s into the 1980s. Steiner removed the top two floors of the building, and in the early 1990s, the owners of Buffalo Bob's replaced the second floor.

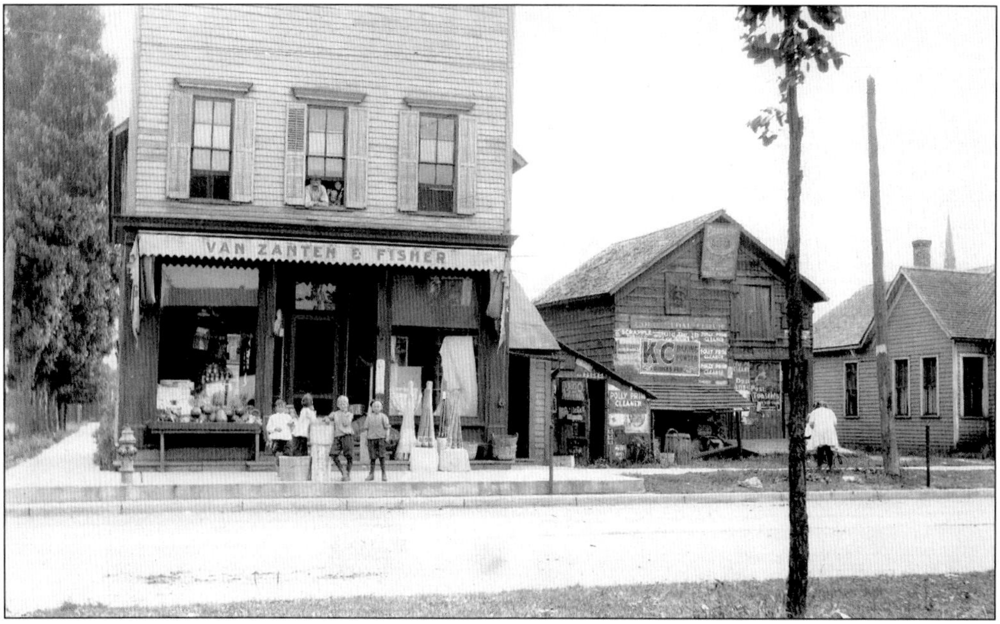

In the early 1900s, Corneil Van Zanten and Charles Fisher operated a general store at 222 North Seventh Street in Grand Haven. The store offered groceries, patent medicines, fabric, and a variety of other household items. It looks like a popular spot for the neighborhood boys, too. The old barn in the center of the undated real photo card displays several advertising posters, including one for Post Toasties and another for KC baking powder.

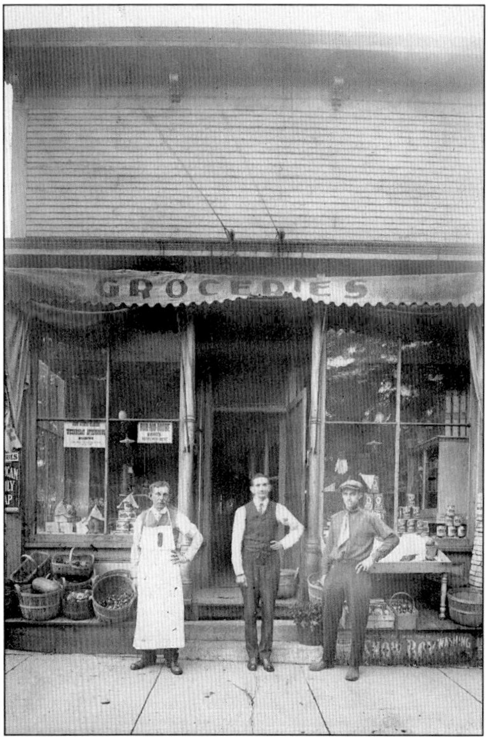

Ed Hollestelle and Gerrit Van Westrienen owned the grocery store pictured here. Located at the corner of Fifth and Franklin Streets, the store was open for business by the early 1890s and endured until Mrs. Hollestelle's death in 1943. This unmailed card is hand-dated 1916. The men are identified as Ed Hollestelle, Pete Hollestelle, and Harold Van Westrienen. In 1955, Dr. David Seibold erected a small brick building for his dental practice at this site.

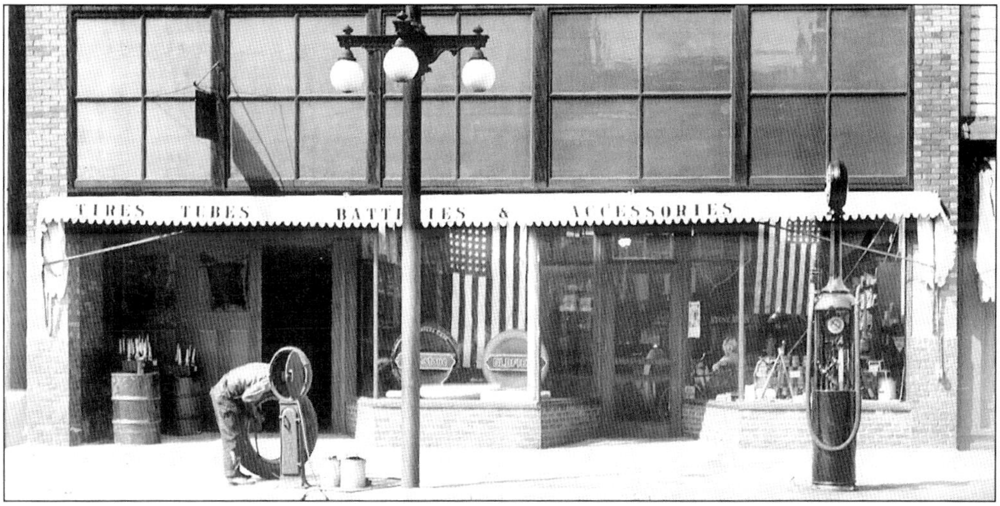

In the early 1900s, topping off the gas tank was as easy as driving up to the curb at 705 Washington. This tires, tubes, batteries, and accessories outlet was owned by brothers Jacob and William Poel. The gas pump is at the right and a man is inflating a tire at the left. Among the many items displayed in the windows are Goodyear and Oldfield Tires. The Poels also offered vulcanizing service, a process used to patch the inner tubes of pneumatic tires. The year 1922 is handwritten on the back of the card.

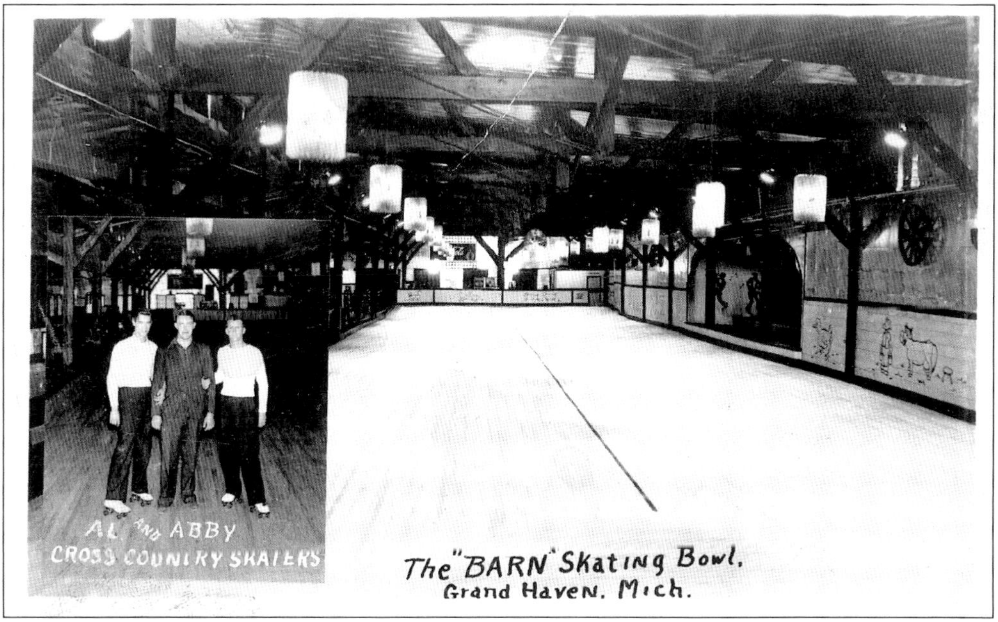

Formerly a warehouse, the Barn on South Harbor Drive became a favorite recreational spot, especially for young people. The popular dance pavilion and roller skating rink was first owned by Nat Robbins, who sold it to Joe Davis in 1934. The three men in the inset are Al Fisher and Abby (Chuck) Aborgast, the cross-country skaters, with Joe Davis in the middle. "Mom and Pop" Davis maintained the Barn as a reputable gathering place for teenagers by keeping out the "roughnecks." The Barn burned to the ground in a spectacular blaze in the spring of 1946. The unmailed card is hand-dated 1937.

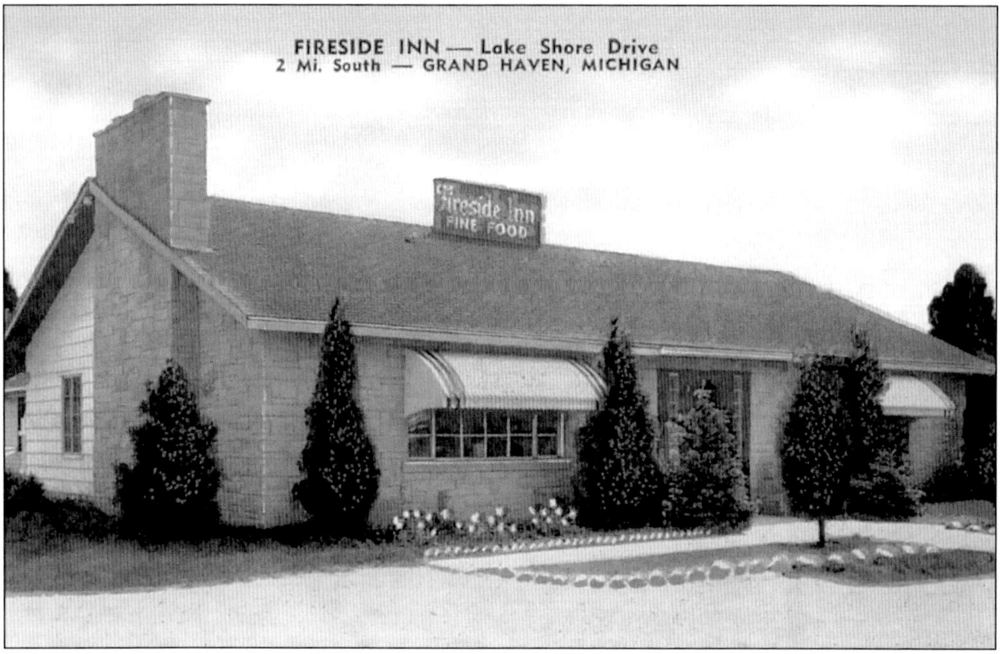

During the 1950s, the Fireside Inn opened on Lakeshore Drive, about a mile south of Robbins Road. The restaurant in the stone and frame building advertised "Just Good Food." After the Inn closed, the building was expanded and converted to the apartment building that is in use today.

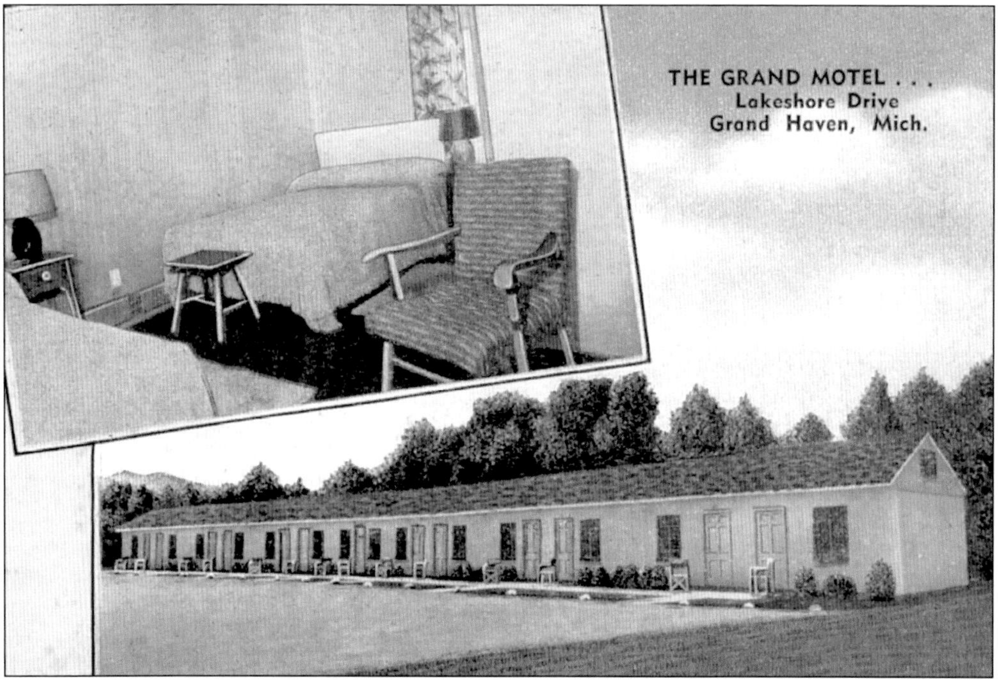

Across the street from the Fireside Inn on Lakeshore Drive was the Grand Motel, owned by J. Fred Hieftje. The 12 units later were converted to small apartments, primarily for transient workers. The units are still rented out today.

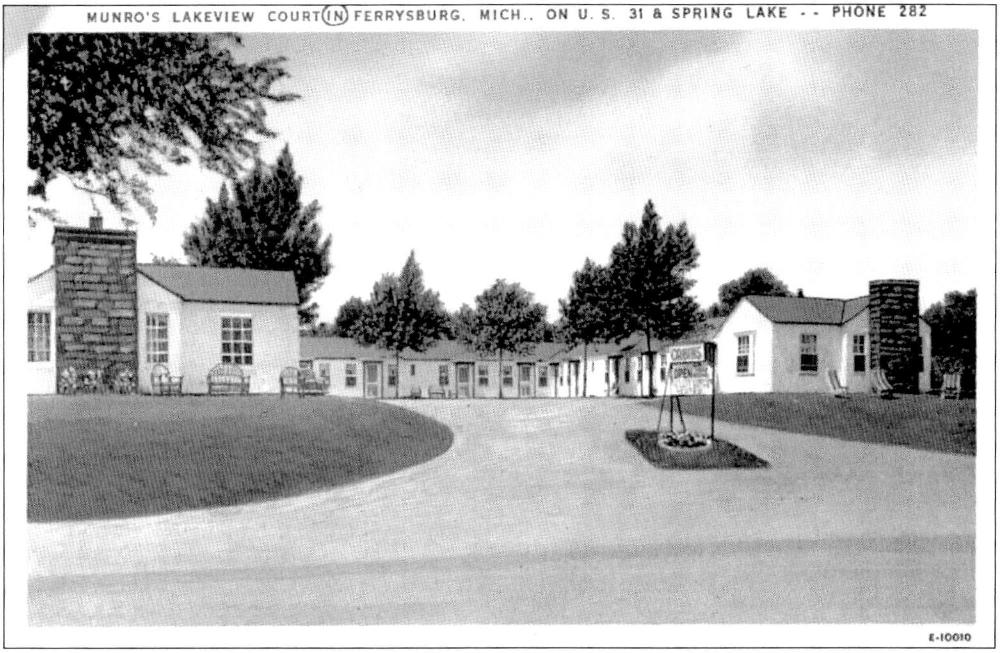

Pine Street in Ferrysburg was once the route for U.S. 31 between Grand Haven and Muskegon. As early as 1940 Dexter Munro offered year-round accommodations at Munro's Lakeview Court, and it was still operating in the late 1950s. The units are now available for short term housing. Spring Lake is in easy viewing distance. The postcard is undated.

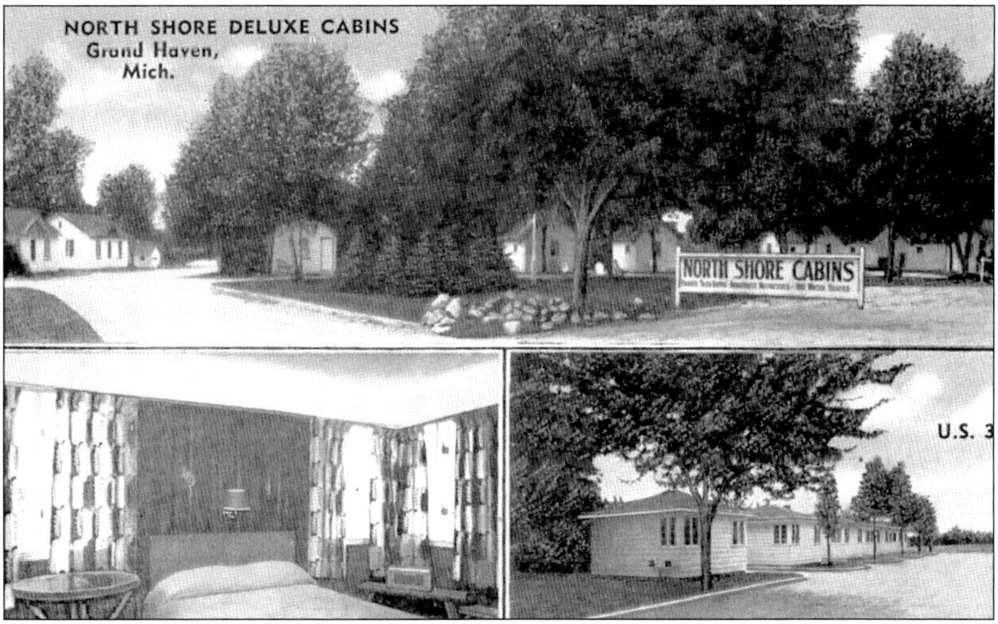

Art and Hanna Vander Sys opened the North Shore Motel in Ferrysburg on old U.S. 31, many years before the route was moved to its present location as a divided highway in the late 1950s. The 15-unit motel continues to offer temporary quarters today. The card was never mailed and has no date, but the lack of a zip code indicates it was printed prior to 1963.

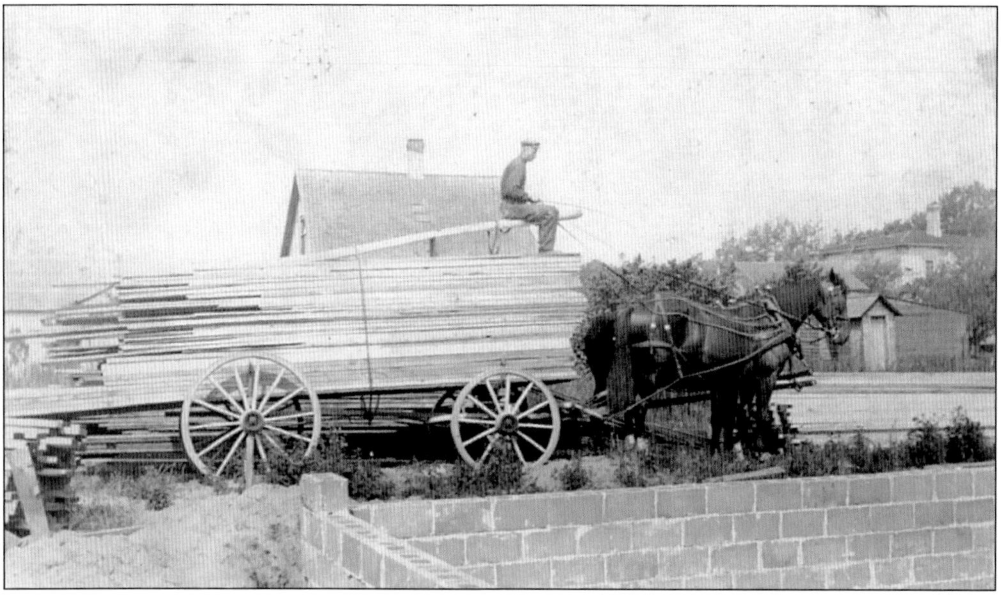

Peter Van Zylen's lumberyard provided supplies for many buildings throughout the Grand Haven area. This heavy load, brought by horse-drawn cart, was ready to be unloaded and put to use, but not until the shallow concrete block foundation was finished. Horse power was used to excavate basements until machines were developed for that purpose and could dig deeper holes. Barney Wilthof is identified as the driver.

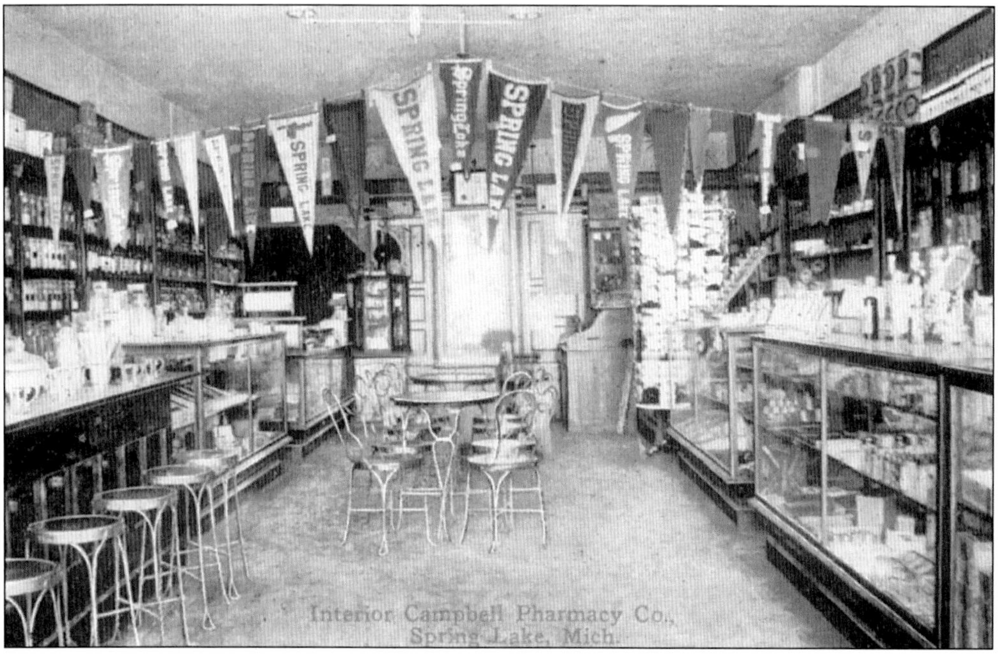

This interior view of Leon Campbell's drugstore on Savidge Street shows a soda fountain typical of those found in drugstores in the first half of the 20th century, along with the usual small round tables and wire-back chairs. The pennants hanging from the line near the ceiling all have "Spring Lake" printed on them. The card appears to date to around 1930.

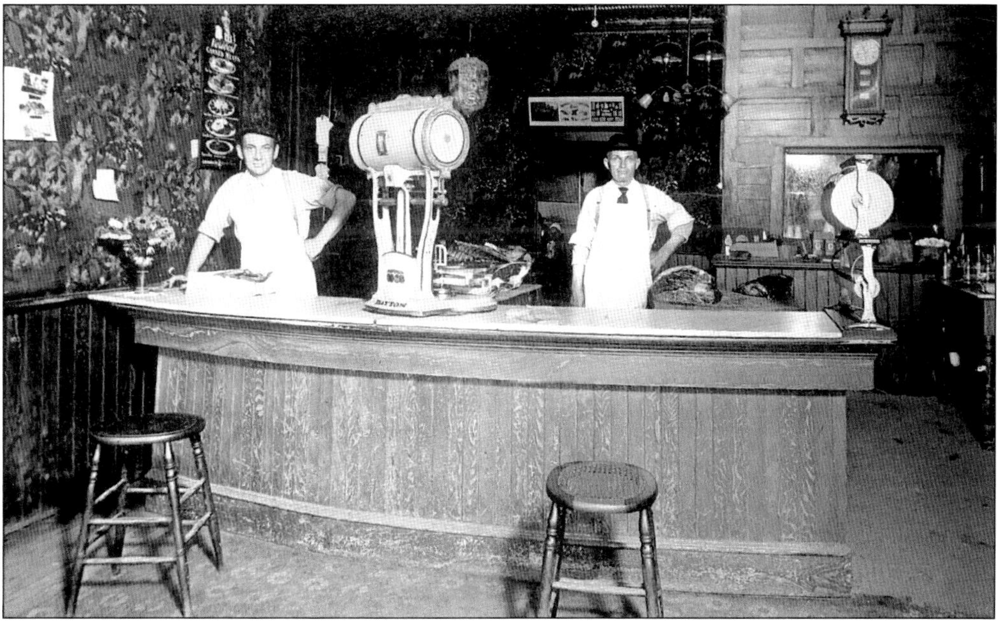

Brothers Ed, Abraham, and Peter De Vries owned and managed the De Vries City Meat Market at 215 West Savidge. Their father started the business in 1877. Ed is standing to the right and Peter to the left. By 1905 Peter was the sole owner. The card is undated, but the photograph must have been taken before 1905.

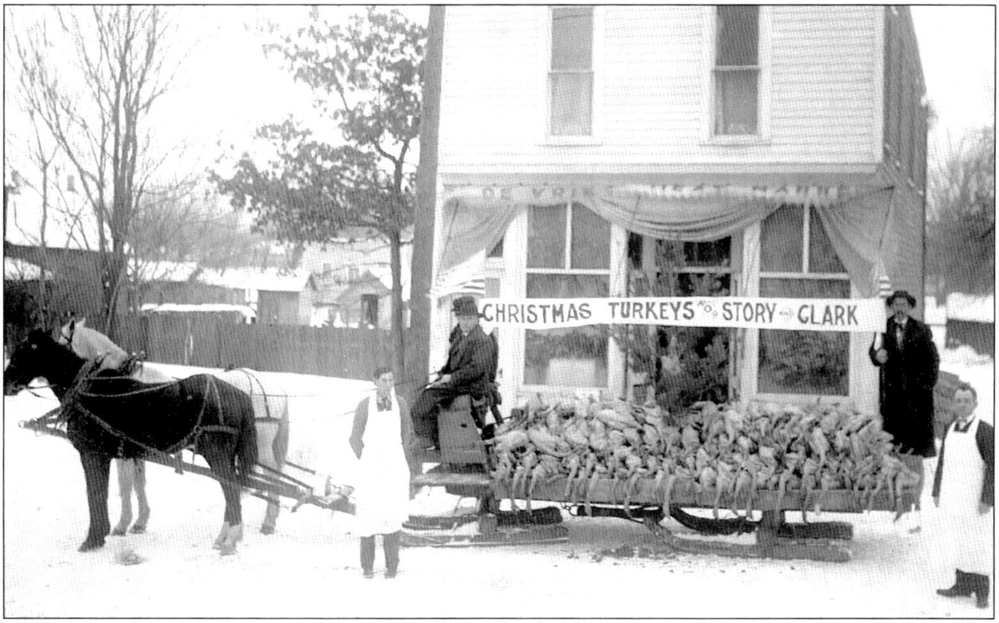

With some fanfare, including an impressive banner, the De Vries Meat Market is ready to deliver a huge cartload of Christmas turkeys to employees of the Story & Clark Piano Company. This undated real photo card was sent to Ruby Barrett, a Spring Lake resident, while she was visiting St. Louis, Missouri. The writer identified the driver as Ed De Vries and one of the men standing nearby as his brother Peter.

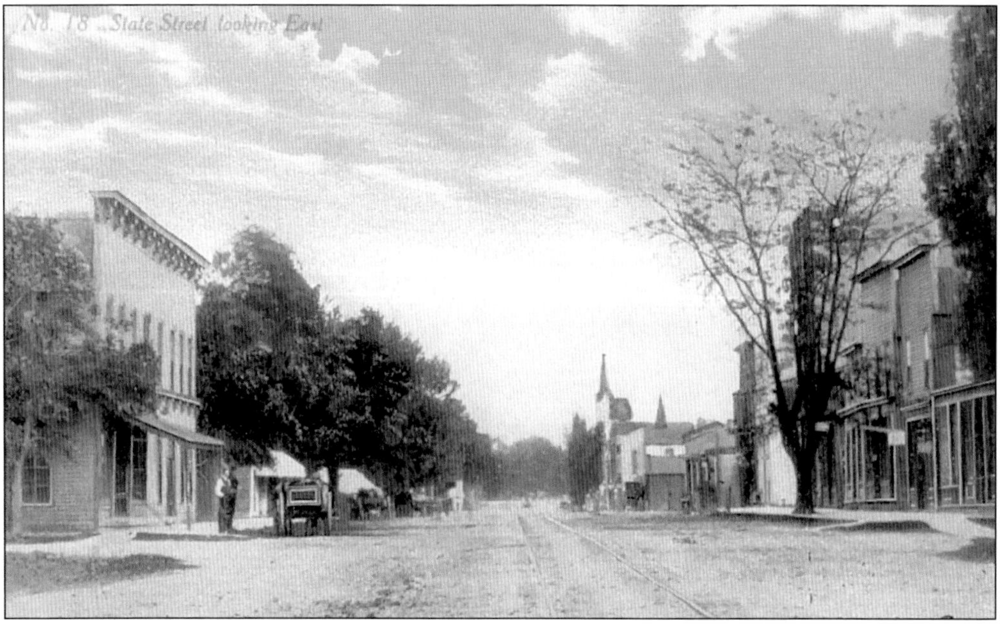

Titled "State Street looking East," this 1913 card looks down the Interurban tracks near the junction with Division Street in Spring Lake. The main thoroughfare through the Village was later renamed Savidge Street, in honor of the family that contributed so much to the community. The building with the canopy at the far left was the Central House Hotel. The three-story brick building on the right side of the street housed Loren Perham's Drug Store and the post office.

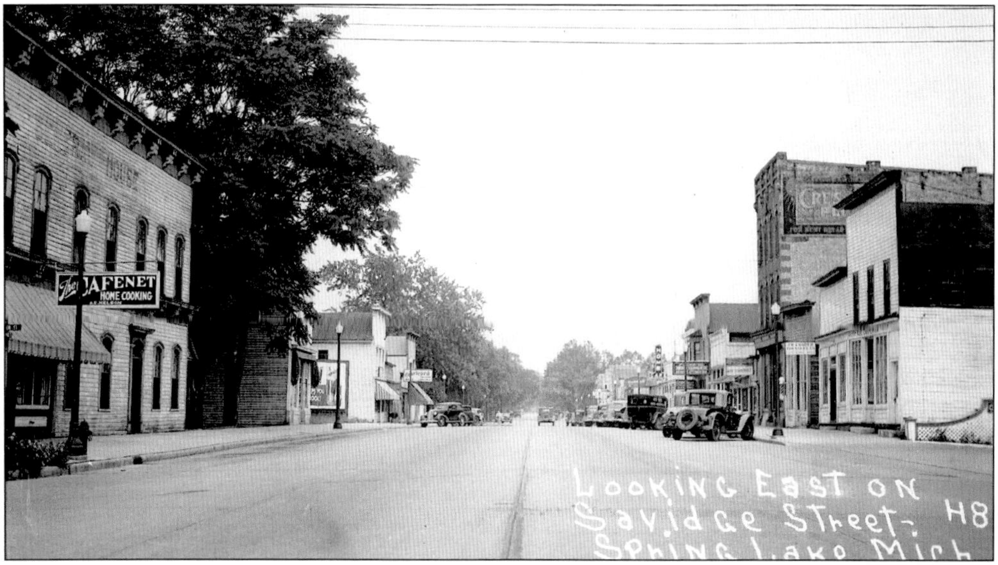

Taken some 20 years or more after the 1913 card pictured above, this real photo card shows the Central House Hotel still standing at the corner of Division and Savidge Streets in Spring Lake Village, but at the time the building was home to the Cafénet. A block or two up the street is the Courtyard Tavern, and across from it stands the Spring Lake State Bank. The three-story building that housed Perham's drugstore has a sign advertising Crescent Flour painted on its west side. The card is undated.

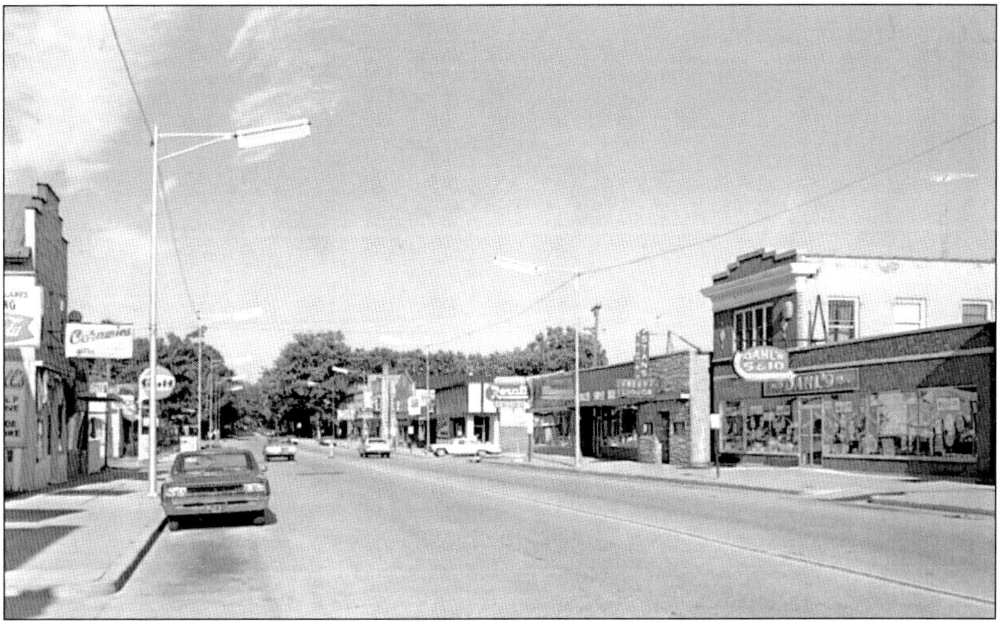

After Spring Lake State Bank moved from 210 West Savidge in 1954, the space was occupied by Dahl's Five and Ten Cent Store. Russell Dahl enlarged his store to include 212 Savidge. Just east of his shop was Stan's Bar, which opened in the late 1940s and remains in business today. The postcard is undated, but was printed after 1963.

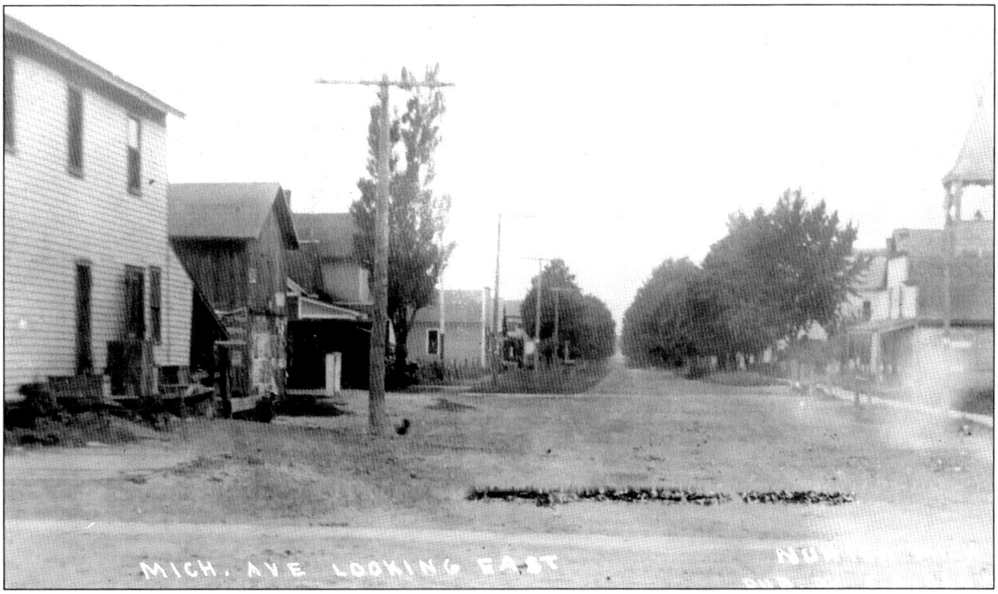

The Village of Nunica named its main thoroughfare Michigan Avenue. This view, looking east, shows some of the buildings that lined the unpaved street in the early 1900s. The town's name was derived from the Ottawa word "menonica," which referred to the clay found in abundance in the area. The Native Americans made pottery, or crockery, from the substance, and that provided a name for the township as well as the river that courses past the Village. This real photo card is postmarked 1910.

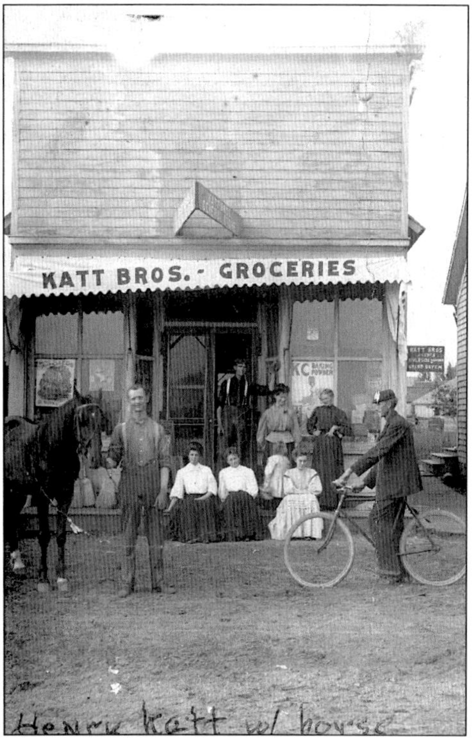

In 1894 John Katt of Ferrysburg opened a general store on the northeast corner of Third and Beech Streets. Many members of the Katt family posed for this old but undated postcard picture: Henry Katt, holding the horse; Claus Katt on the bicycle; Hilda, Tena, and Hannah, all seated; John J. Katt (the owner's son); Mrs. Harry Katt and her daughter, Stina; and Mrs. John Katt standing near the door. The Katt Feed Store was next door to the left. The General Store burned down in 1931.

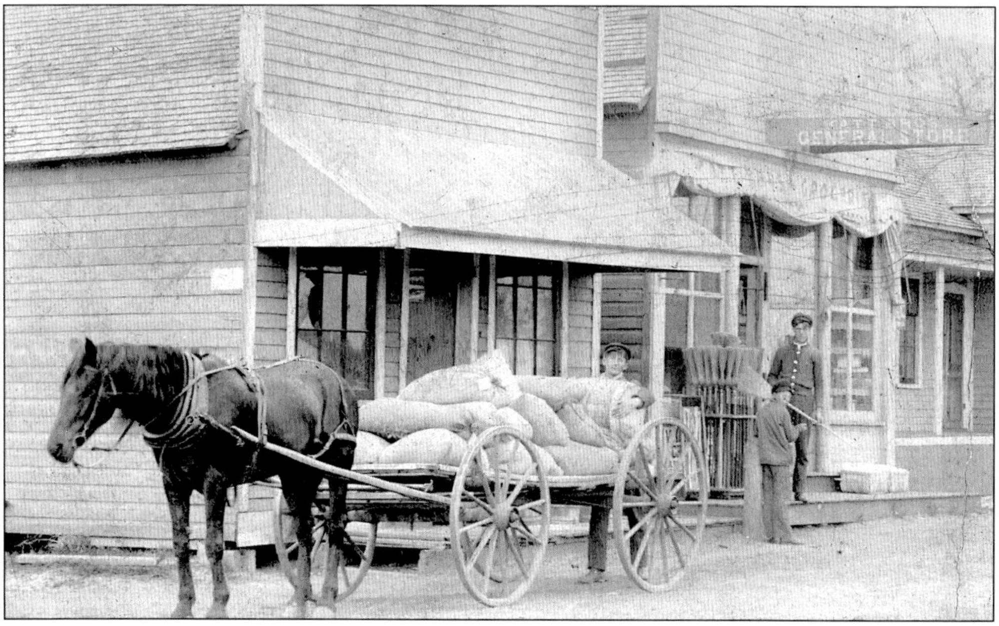

The feed store started by John Katt in 1894 was adjacent to his general store in Ferrysburg. The retail establishments were later managed by his sons, and the name changed to Katt Brothers. Here one of John's sons, Henry, is unloading feed for the store, while next door his brother John J. stands guard at the entrance to the general store. The boy with the broom is not identified and the card is not dated.

Seven

MADE FOR THE U.S.A.

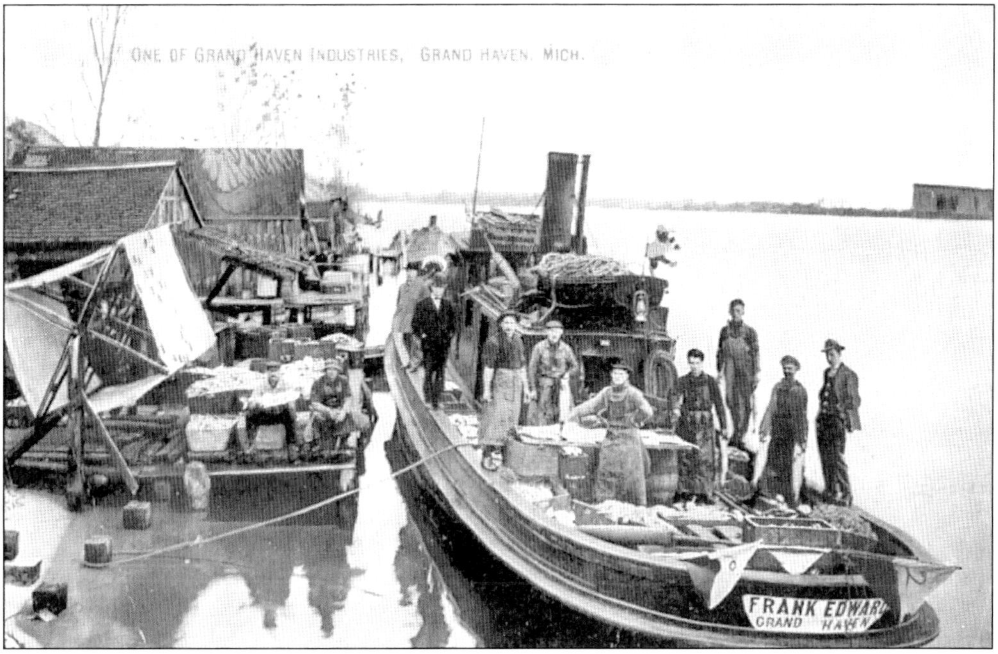

The fishing tug *Frank Edward*, built in Grand Haven by the Robertson Shipyard in 1890, was owned by John Zietlow. Zietlow died two years later and his fishing business was carried on by his sons, Edward and Frank. The fish shown in this picture look large and plentiful. The figure on top of the cabin was probably a weather vane.

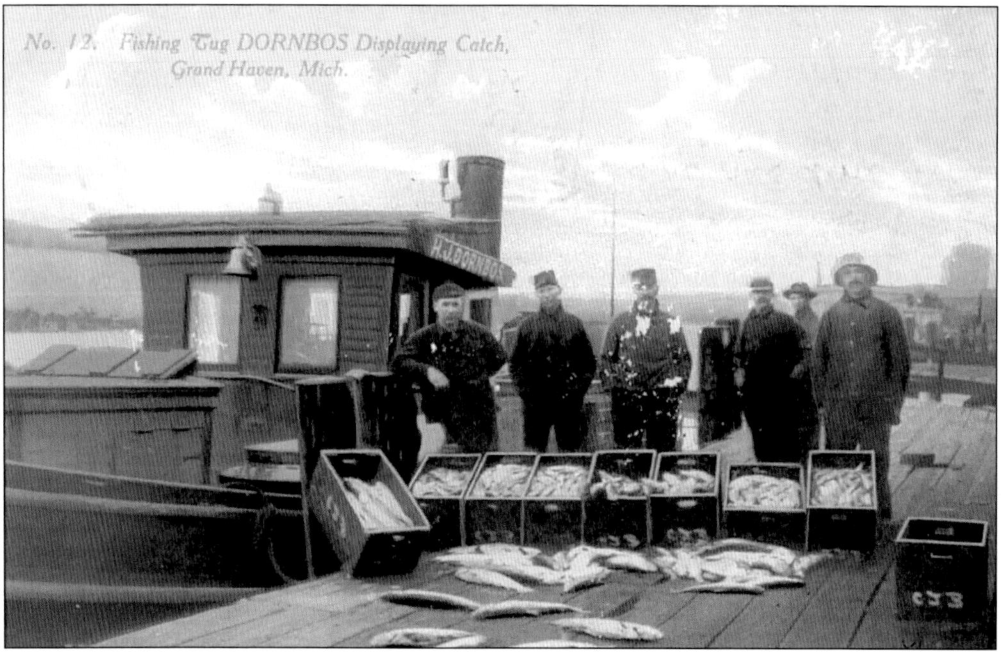

Commercial fishing was a major industry in the Grand Haven area beginning in 1856 and continuing for nearly a century. The men in this 1911 postcard proudly display their day's netting aboard the Ver Duin fishing tug *H.J. Dornbos*. Although not in the business of bringing in the fish, the Henry J. Dornbos Company played a large role in processing and marketing the fishermen's catch from 1889 to 1966.

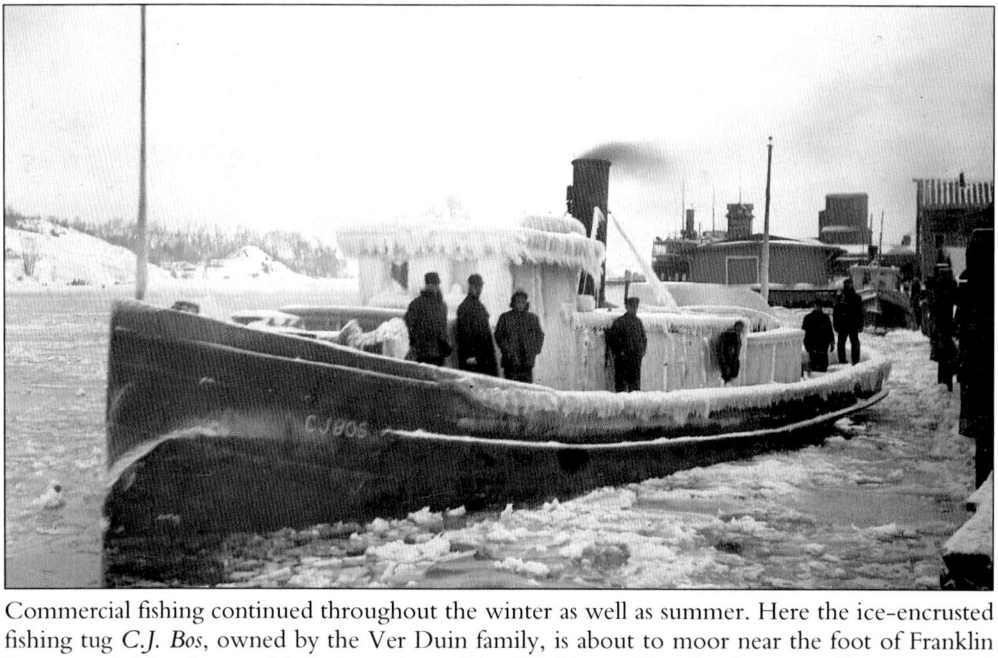

Commercial fishing continued throughout the winter as well as summer. Here the ice-encrusted fishing tug *C.J. Bos*, owned by the Ver Duin family, is about to moor near the foot of Franklin Street, probably after a cold day's work on Lake Michigan. The Crosby Line office tower and grain elevator are in the background. The card is undated.

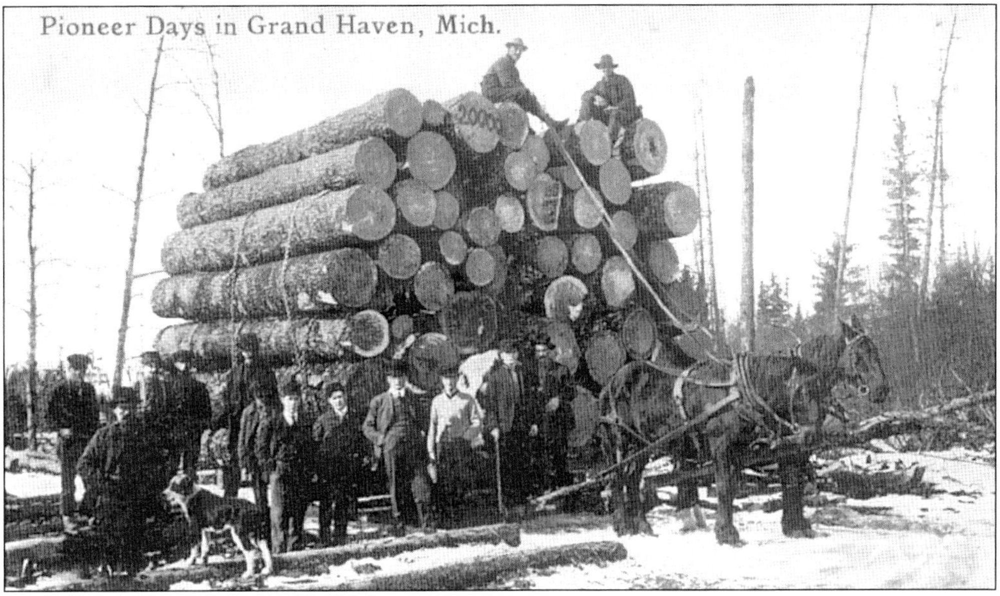

Labeled "Pioneer Days in Grand Haven, Mich.," this picture shows a very large load of freshly-cut timber being hauled to the river by a team of two horses, where the logs would then be rafted to a sawmill. Painted across the butt-end of one log is the number "20,000," possibly a reference to the board-feet contained in this single load. The card, published by Reichardt's Book Store, was mailed from Nunica in 1914. Lumbering was the main commercial venture in the Grand Haven area between 1840 and 1890.

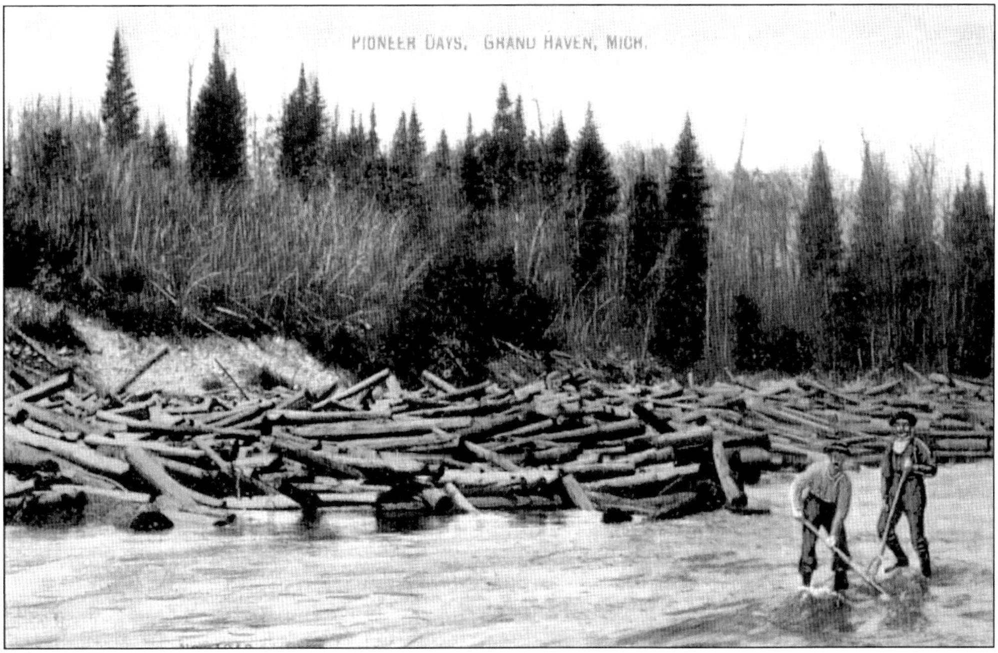

Also titled "Pioneer Days in Grand Haven" and from the same era, this undated card illustrates the next step in the lumbering process: combining the logs into rafts to be floated downstream to a sawmill.

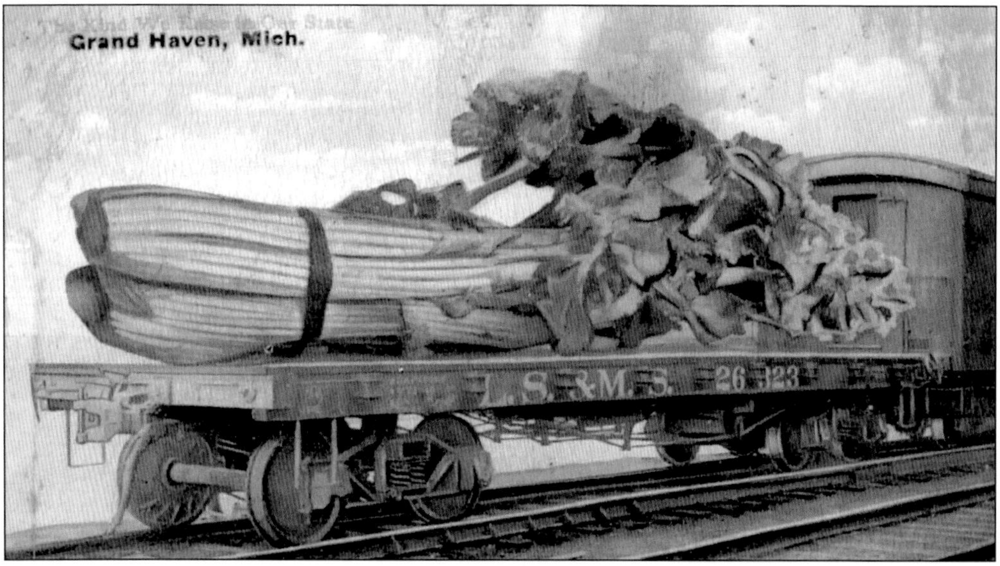

By the late 1800s, celery was an important product for export in the Grand Haven area. Although the celery fields flourished, the vegetable probably never grew to quite the size pictured here! George Hancock was one of the major growers in Grand Haven, but many smaller celery farms could be found along Fulton Street and today's Beacon Boulevard—wherever river bottom had left its rich, nourishing muck. The caption reads, "The Kind We Raise in Our State." The card has a copyright date of 1912.

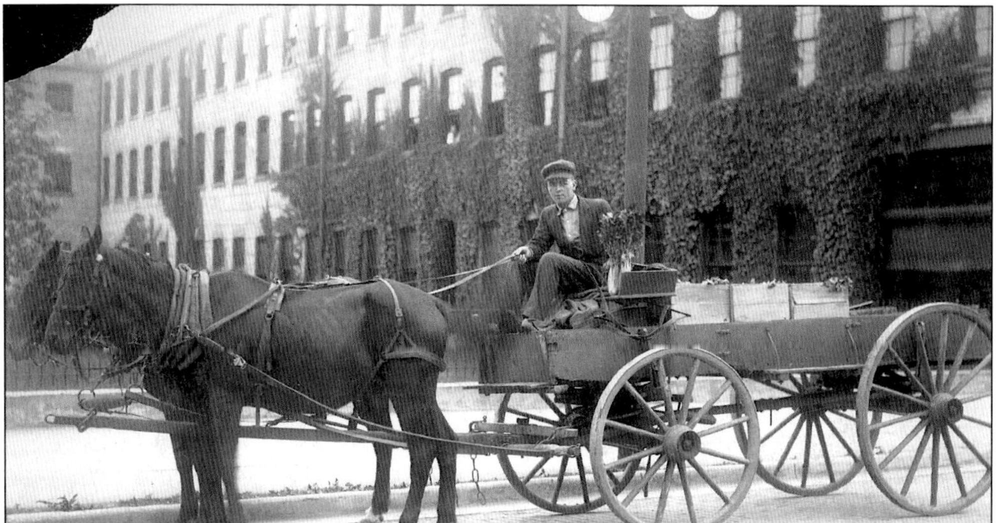

This is a more realistic view of locally-grown celery being taken to market. The driver is identified on the back of the card as Henry Ritsema. He is posing with his team of horses near the Story & Clark Piano building, a bouquet of celery stalks in hand. The curbing and brick pavement indicate the photograph was taken after 1910.

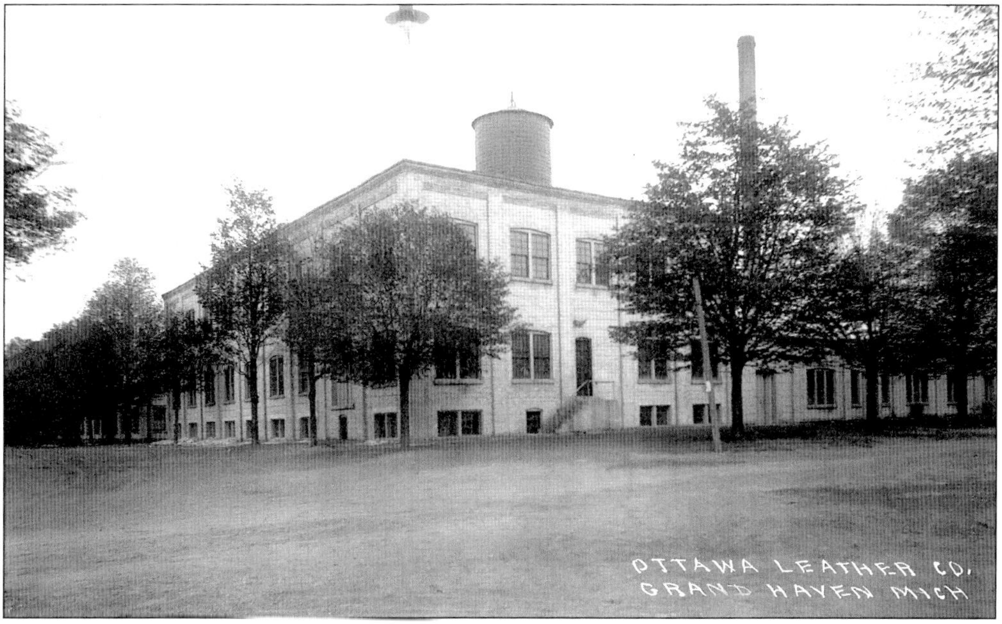

As the lumbering industry diminished, manufacturing began to flourish. This 1915 real photo postcard shows the Ottawa Leather Company plant at the intersection of Fulton and Beechtree before the streets were improved (and one year before the name "Eagle" was added to the company name). The Grand Haven firm, which remains in business today, can trace its history back to 1865. At one time its leather upholstery could be found in President Coolidge's Cadillac and Charles Lindbergh's Franklin.

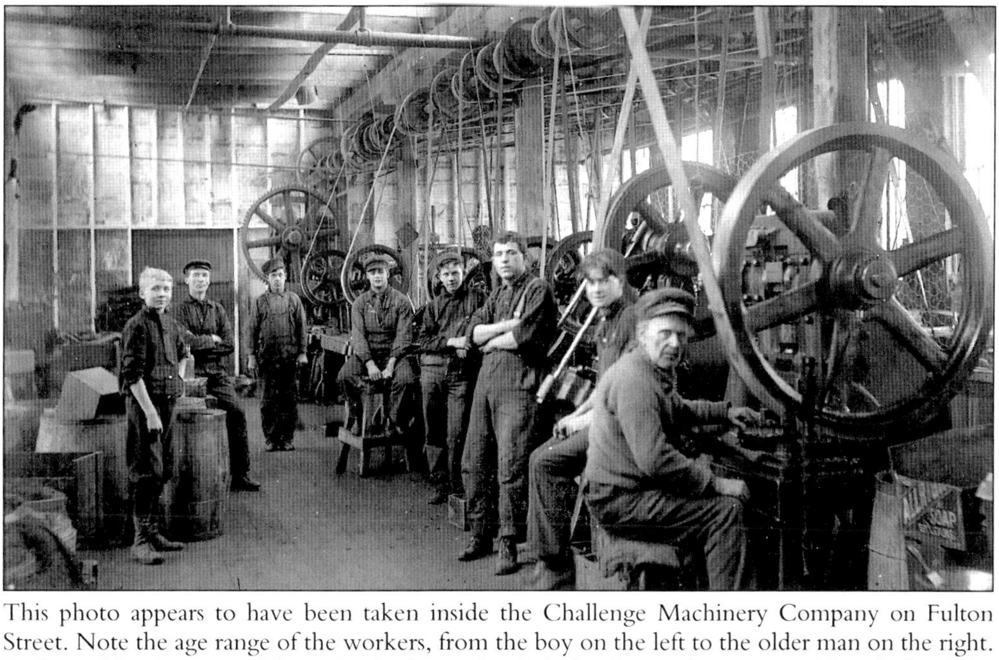

This photo appears to have been taken inside the Challenge Machinery Company on Fulton Street. Note the age range of the workers, from the boy on the left to the older man on the right. Each machine is operated from the single overhead shaft. The workers are not identified and the card is undated. Challenge Machinery started in Grand Haven in 1903.

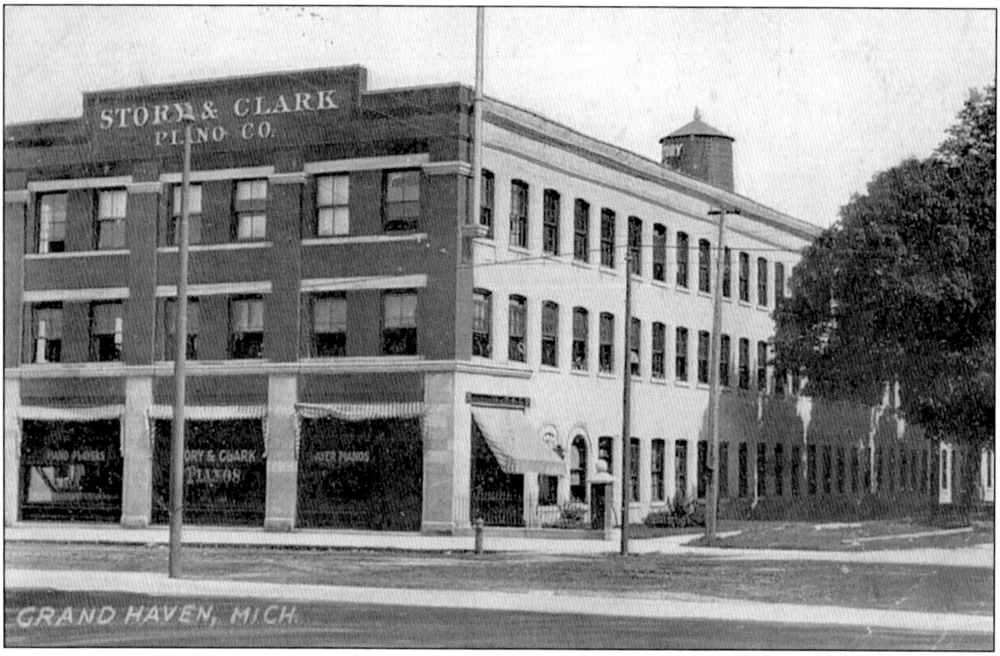

This three-story brick building was erected by the Story & Clark Piano Company in 1905. It now houses Harbourfront Place. The firm produced pianos from 1901 until 1984. The card is undated, but predates 1910, the year Washington Street was paved.

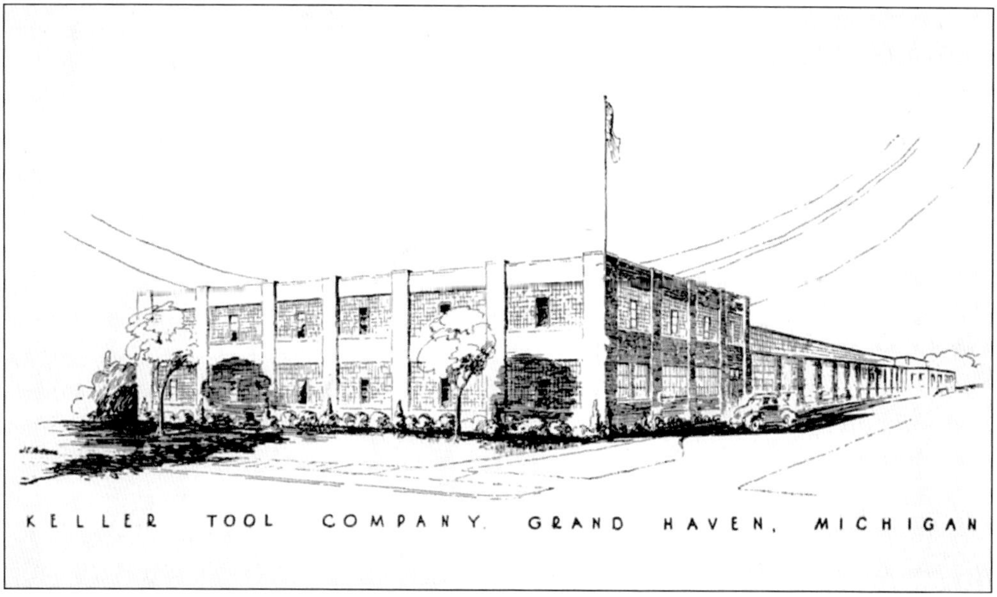

Occasionally postcards were printed from sketches rather than photographs, as in this drawing of Keller Tool Company in Grand Haven. In 1917 the Board of Trade attracted the company to Grand Haven from Fond du Lac, Wisconsin. Keller Tool, which was located at 1333 Fulton Street, merged with Gardner-Denver in 1954 and went out of business in 1982.

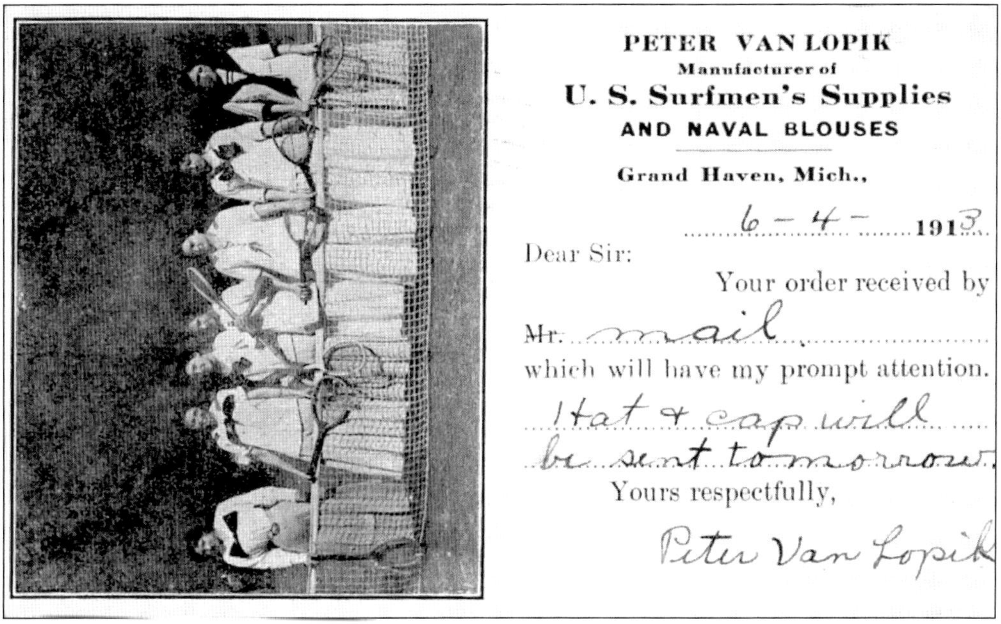

Picture postcards could be used for business purposes, too. On June 4, 1913, Peter Van Lopik sent this one to a customer to let him know that his order would be sent the next day. The young women at the tennis net may have been students at Akeley Hall. They were among Van Lopik's best customers for middy blouses. The card was mailed to a customer at the Jackson Park Life Saving Service in Chicago.

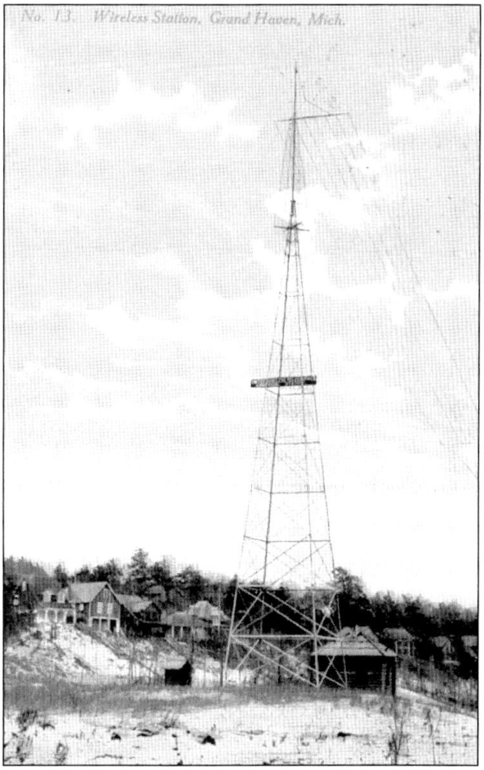

In the early 1900s a Wireless Station was erected on the beach, not far from Highland Park. The station and tower allowed two-way radio connection with ships on Lake Michigan. The sign on the tower reads, "United Wireless Telegraph Co. Commercial Station." The card is postmarked 1910.

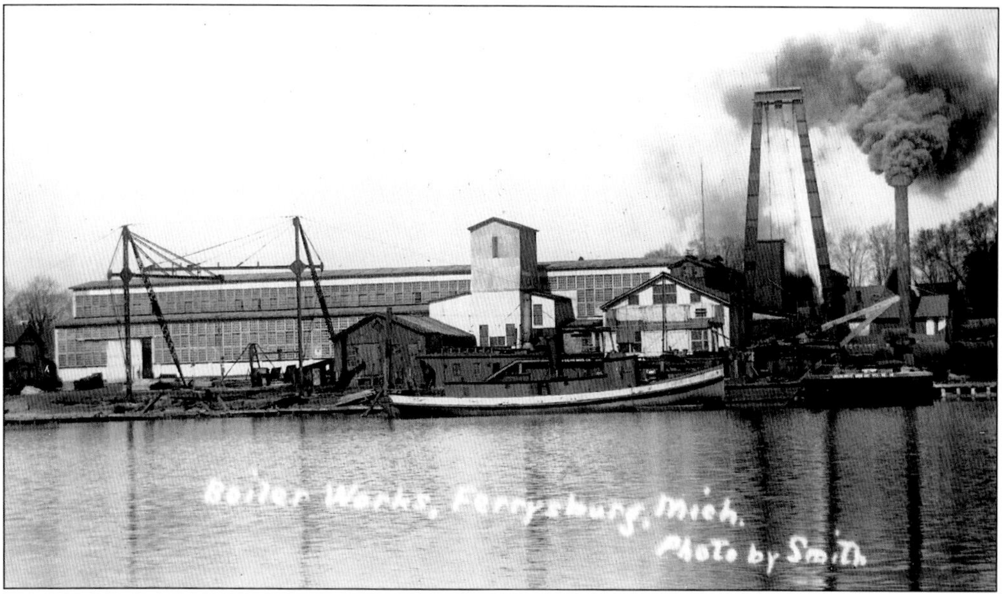

Johnston Boiler Company in Ferrysburg traces its origin to 1864. The company made ship boilers for many years, and in 1898, manufactured its first charcoal iron boat, the fish tug *C.J. Bos*. This undated real photo postcard shows the Boiler Works on the east shore of Spring Lake with thick smoke, indicating the factory was in full operation. Johnston Boiler launched 53 metal vessels before discontinuing shipbuilding in 1926.

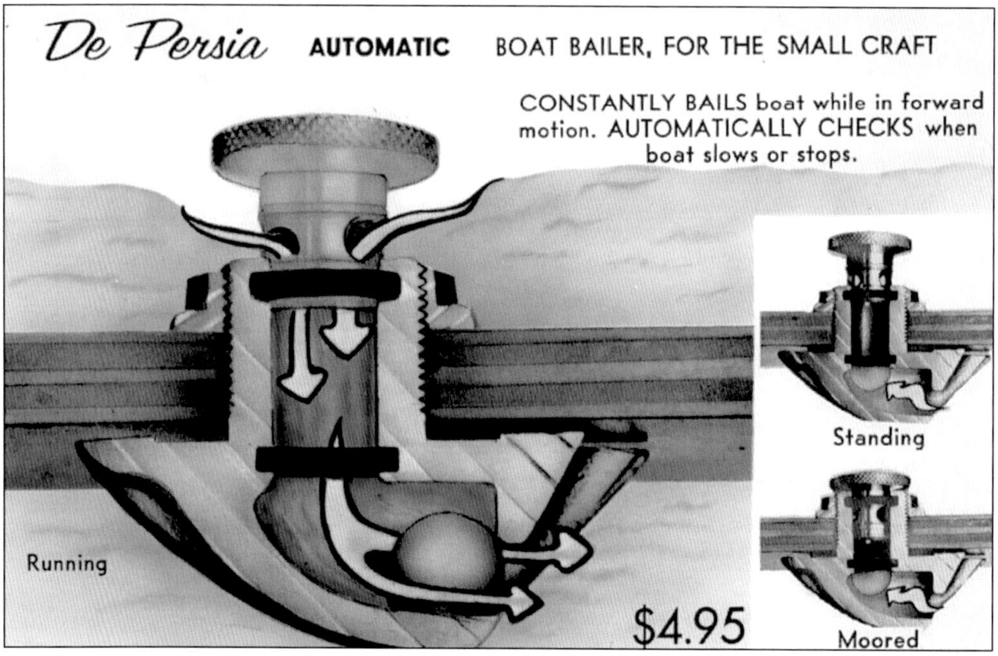

This advertising postcard is dated 1965. It was distributed by John L. De Persia, founder and owner of De Persia Automatic Bailer, first located on Friant Street in Grand Haven and later on Hayes. The bailer could be used with hulls varying from three-eighths of an inch to one-and-one-quarter inch in thickness, all at the same price of $4.95.

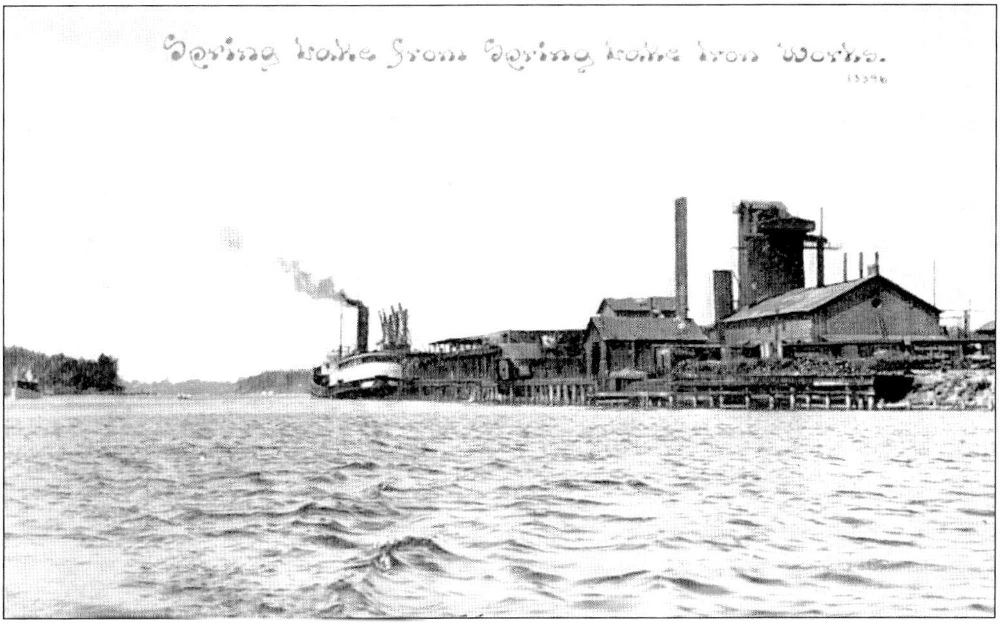

The Spring Lake Iron Works was incorporated in 1879. Located at the north end of Spring Lake, near Fruitport, it employed as many as 400 men at its busiest times. The plant consisted of a power plant, a blacksmith shop, a company store, a boarding house, and company-owned residences rented to employees. The Iron Works closed in 1912. The postcard was never mailed and has no date.

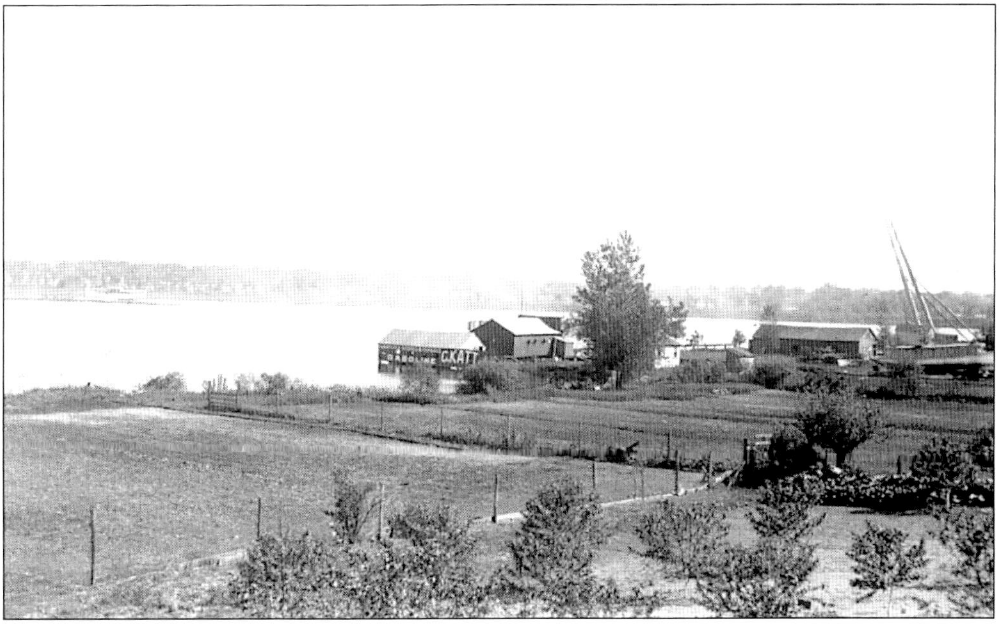

Claus Katt started a shipbuilding business in Ferrysburg in 1913. Situated not far from the Johnston Bros. Boiler Company on the western shore of Spring Lake, Katt's company produced riveted steel pleasure boats. The sign on the side of his waterfront shed reads, "LAUNCHES STORED & REPAIRED GASOLINE C. KATT."

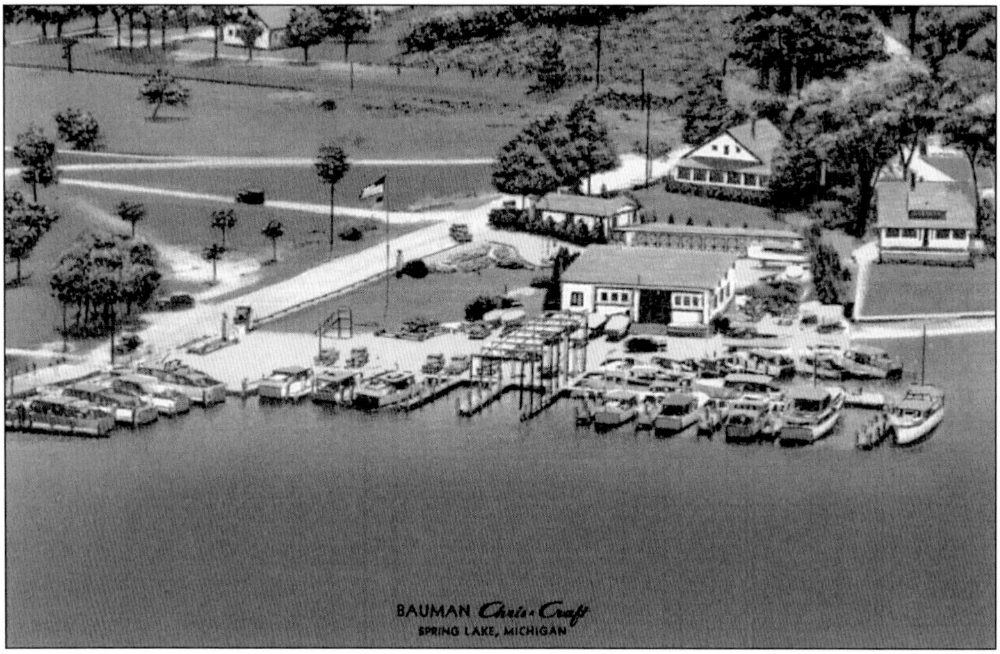

The Chris Craft Company of Algonac, Michigan was one of the early leaders in the manufacture of pleasure boats. Situated on the banks of Spring Lake at the end of Alden Street, Edward Bauman's company, shown in this aerial view, specialized in the sale of Chris Crafts and other marine products. Cote La Mer, a condominium complex, now occupies the site.

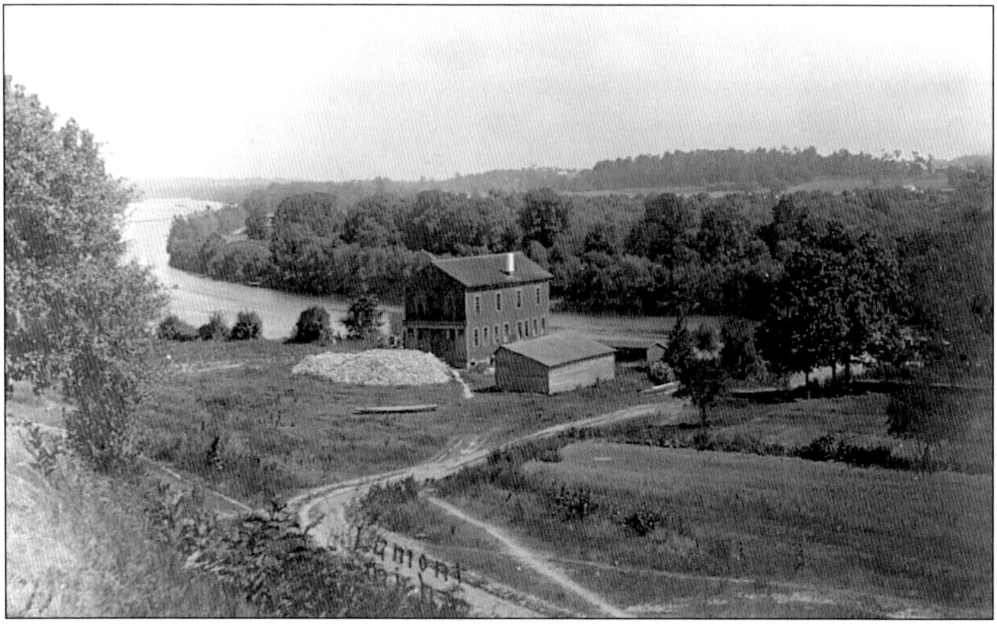

This isolated building housed the Lamont Button Factory, located on the Grand River near the Village of Lamont. Plugs were cut from thick-shelled river clams and tumbled smooth prior to being made into buttons. A pile of clamshell discards is heaped by the tall frame building. This real photo card is postmarked 1913.

Eight

PUBLIC PLACES

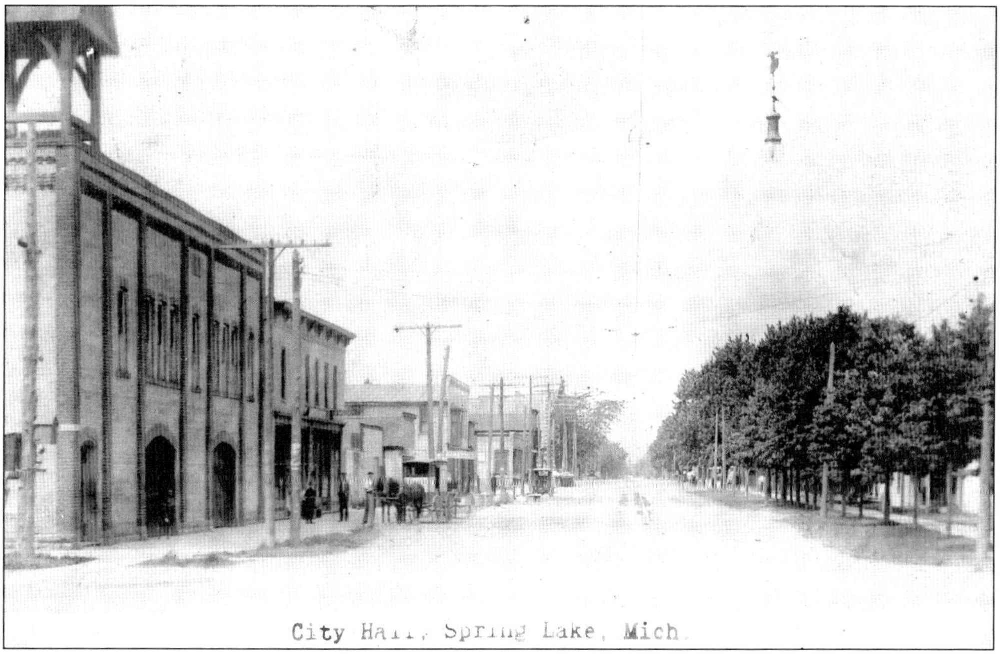

Spring Lake City Hall, pictured here on the left, was built in 1872. It survived until 1937, when the WPA erected the structure that is still in use today. In this undated scene, the camera is looking west at the junction of Savidge and Buchanan Streets. Braaks Bakery is a few buildings beyond City Hall, with a very early automobile parked nearby.

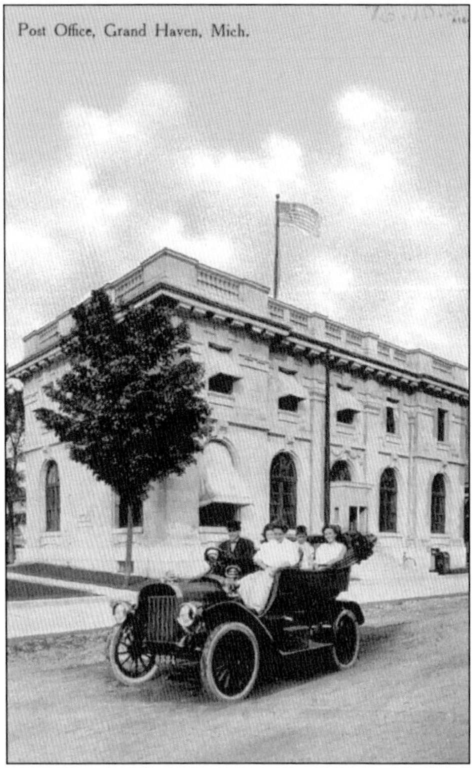

With tinted clouds and flag flowing artistically, the new Federal Building/Post Office, constructed in 1905 at the corner of Third and Washington Streets, made the perfect backdrop for this staged card, postmarked 1909. Washington Street was paved the next year. The post office was razed in 1967 to make room for bank expansion, and this corner is now the site of Fifth Third Bank.

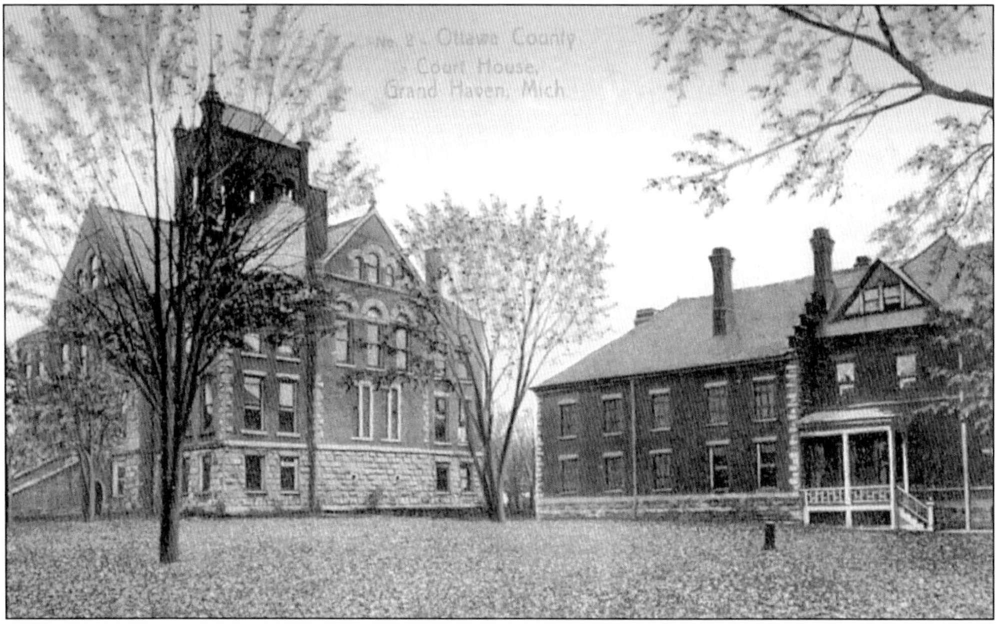

The sheriff's residence and jail, both shown in this undated postcard, stood adjacent to the old Court House, which was constructed in 1894. The jail was built in 1898 for $13,000. Like the Court House, these buildings were razed in the mid-1960s and replaced by a $350,000 jail. The sheriff's residence was not replaced.

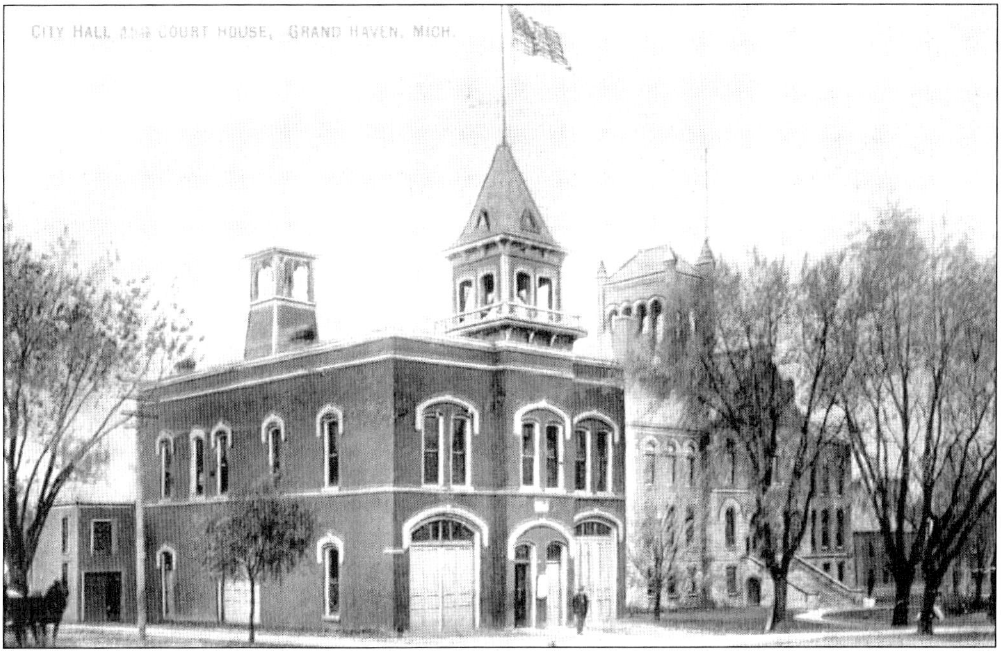

In 1878 Grand Haven built its first City Hall and Fire Station east of the County Court House. Before Grand Haven became a city in 1867, the first Council meetings were held in Hubbard Hall at 117 Washington. When that building burned down in 1872, meetings were transferred to Mayor George Parks's place of business at 16 Washington. The card is dated 1909.

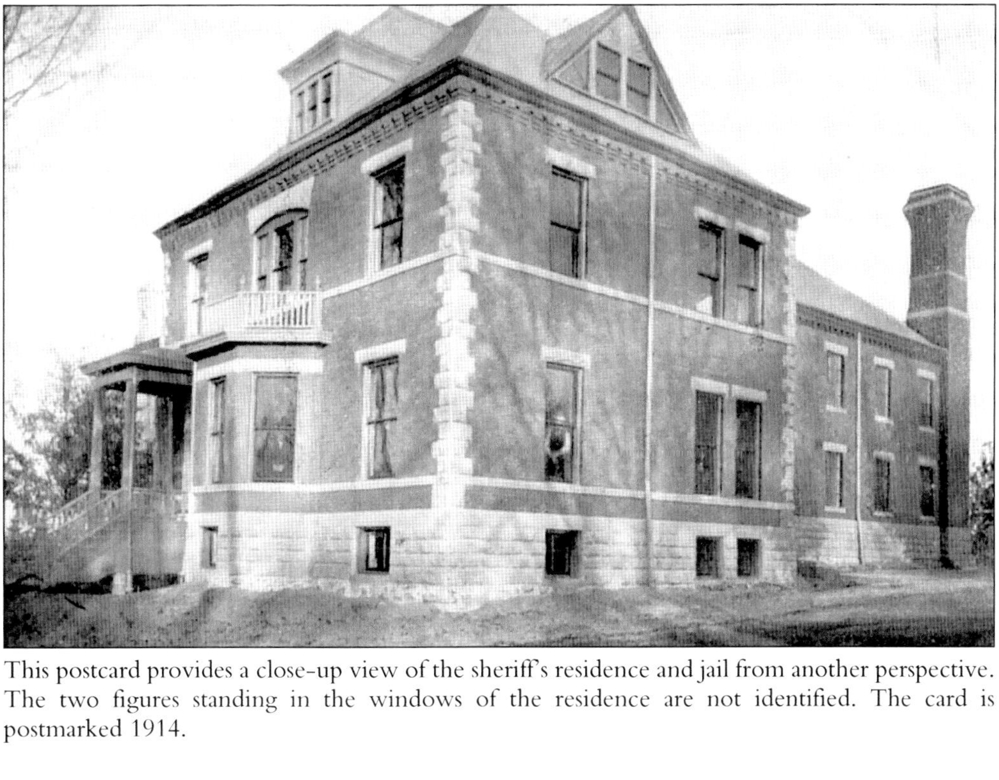

This postcard provides a close-up view of the sheriff's residence and jail from another perspective. The two figures standing in the windows of the residence are not identified. The card is postmarked 1914.

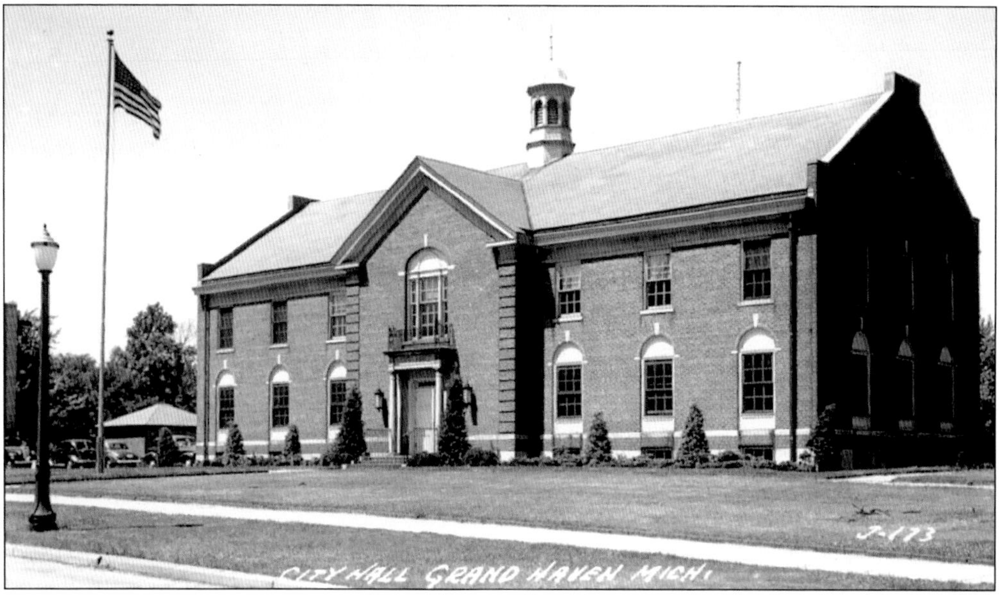

A new City Hall was built of brick by the depression-era Works Projects Administration (WPA) in 1933–1934, replacing the structure that had stood since 1878 near the Court House. With slight modifications, the building is still used by the City of Grand Haven for its administrative offices. The postcard was never mailed, but the parked cars on the left date to the mid- and late-1930s.

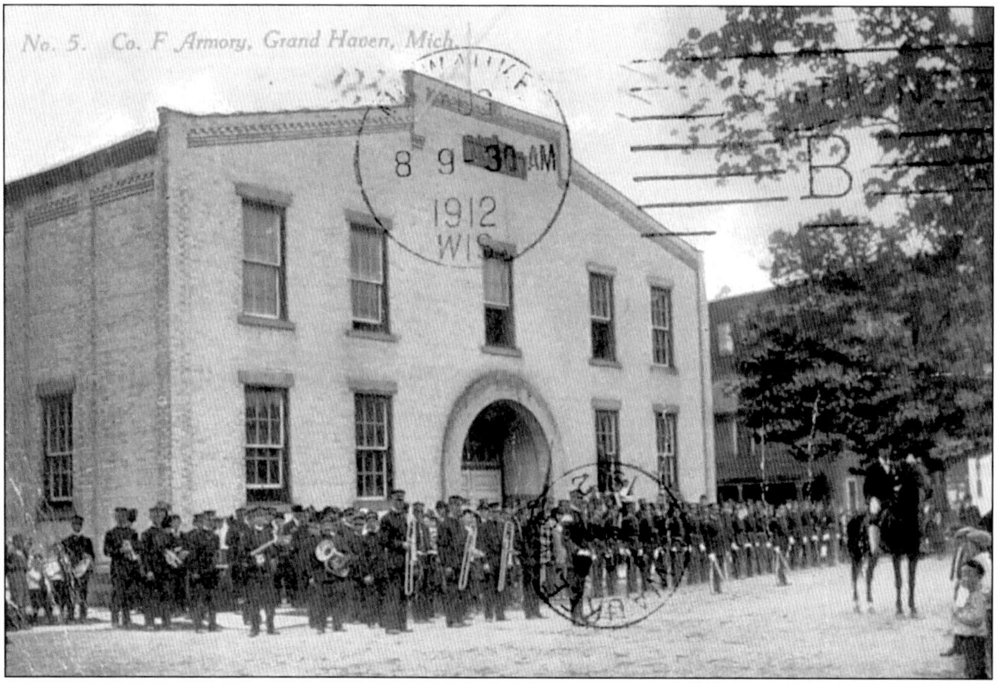

The officers and men of Company F are standing at attention with white gloves and full uniform in front of the Armory, their meeting place. The small brass band undoubtedly was ready to play patriotic songs, perhaps for a Fourth of July observance. The red brick building next to the armory housed Wiltshire Glove Company. The card is postmarked 1912.

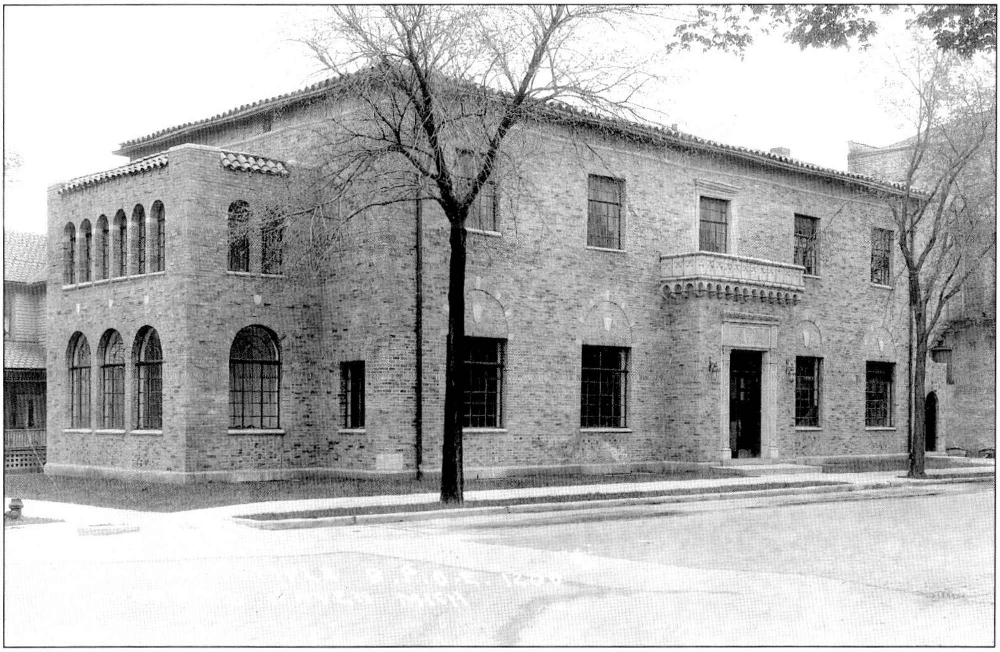

In its early years, the Benevolent and Protective Order of Elks (B.P.O.E.) met on the second floor of the former post office building at First and Washington Streets in downtown Grand Haven. In 1928, around the time this picture was taken, the members moved into this new masonry building with a tile roof, built at an estimated cost of $50,000.

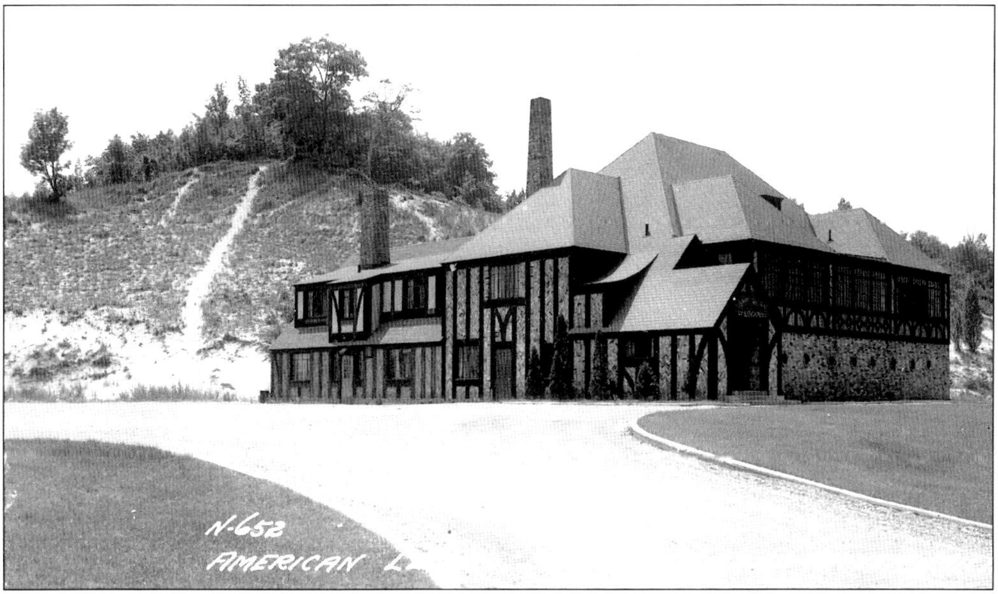

In the 1930s the American Legion in Grand Haven acquired land on Harbor Drive, across from Escanaba Park. Known as the Charles A. Conklin Post #28, the Tudor-style building shown in this undated photo postcard was constructed in 1938. Prior to moving into the new building, the Legion met above Beaudry's Department Store at the corner of Washington and Third Streets. Grand Haven resident Charles Conklin was the first serviceman to be killed in action during World War I.

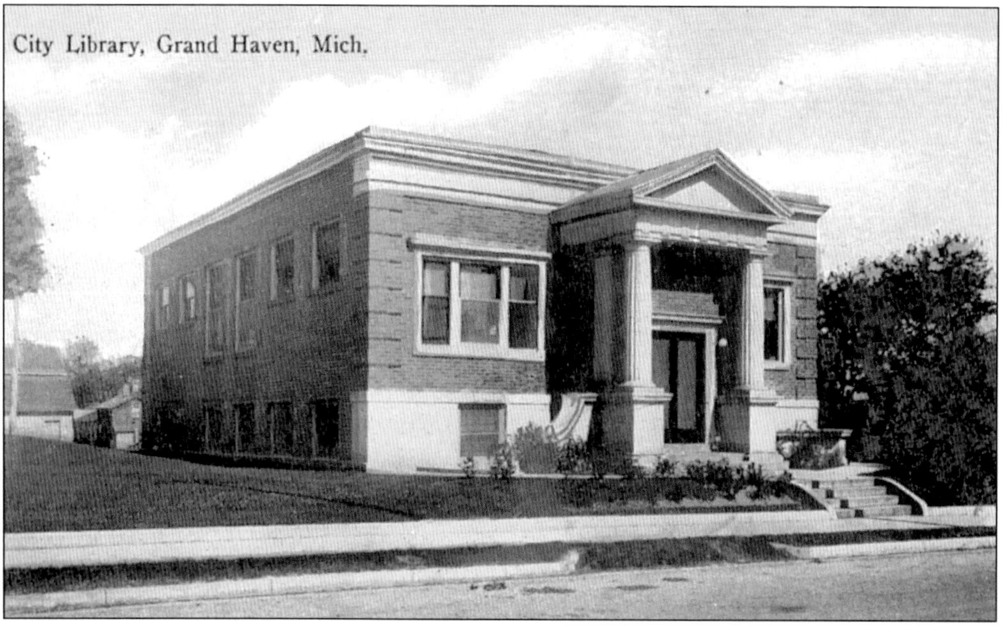

Under the leadership of Dr. Elizabeth Hofma and the Women's Club of Grand Haven, a grant of $12,500 was obtained from the Carnegie Endowment Foundation for the city's first library. With the help of additional local funds, enough money was raised to open Carnegie Public Library on North Third Street in 1914, around the time this picture was taken. The site now provides parking for customers at Fifth Third Bank.

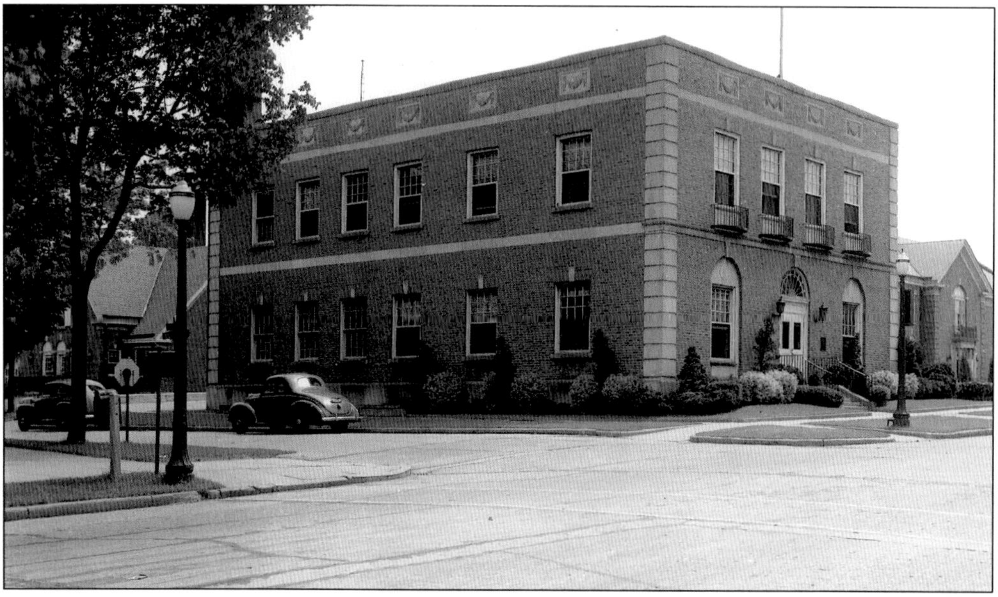

In 1929, Bell Telephone purchased the corner lot at Washington and Fifth Streets for $13,000, and the same year erected the building shown in this undated photo card. This had been the site of the magnificent Akeley Mansion, built in 1881 and later part of the Akeley Institute Campus. Grand Haven City Hall can be seen at the right. The Fire Department building at the left currently is home to the Senior Center.

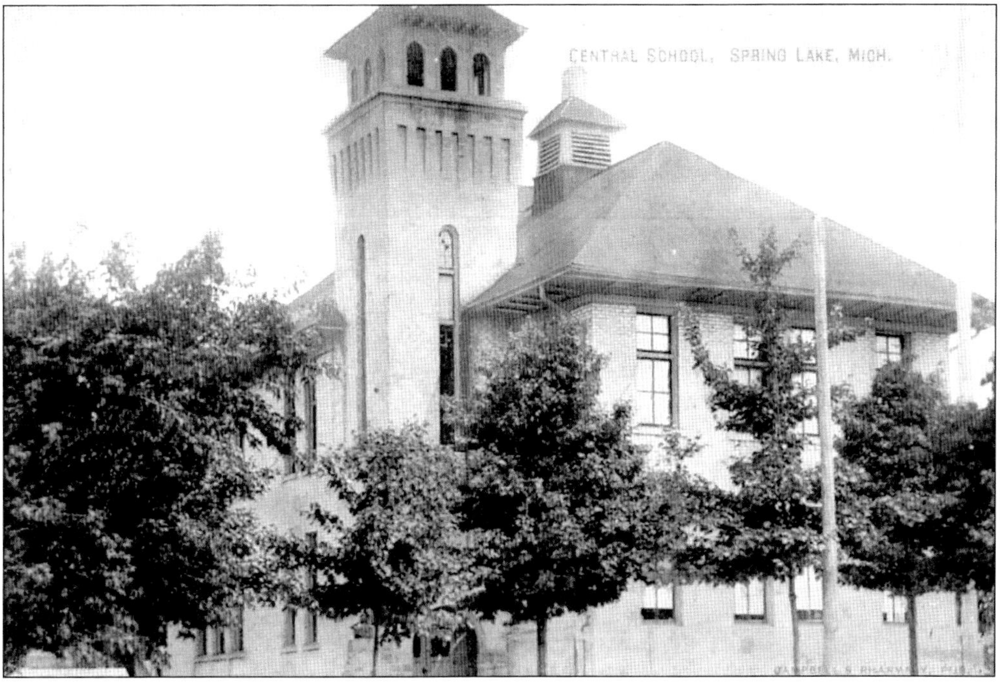

Known in Spring Lake as both Union School and Central School, this structure was erected in 1894 to replace the frame building that had been destroyed in an extensive fire the previous year. The brick building with the unique tower served students until Holmes School opened in 1951. The card is dated 1910.

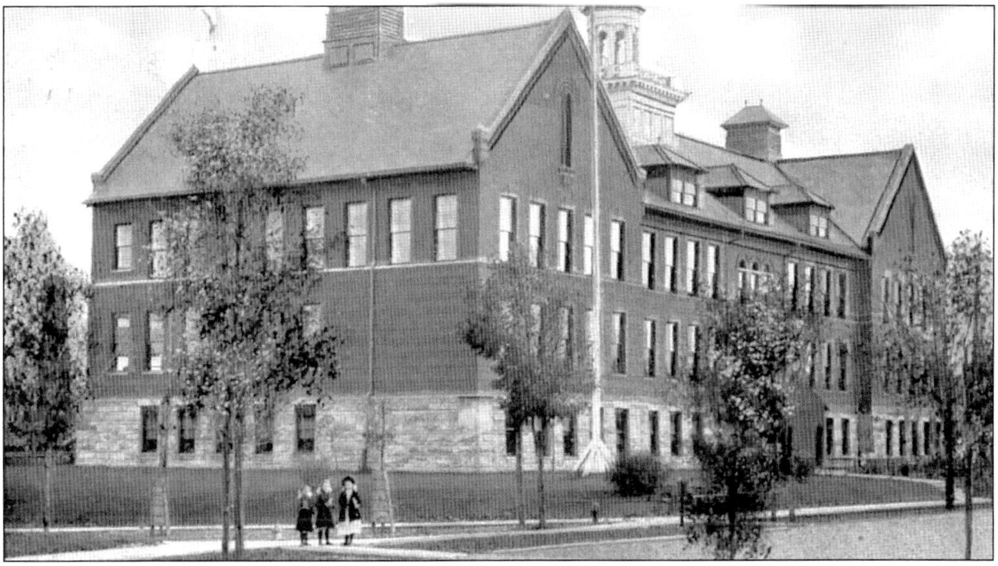

Dated 1910, this postcard shows children posing for the camera in front of Central High School on North Sixth Street. They were probably born around the time the school first opened in 1902. When the high school grades moved to a new building on Seventh Street in 1922, Central continued to be home to students from kindergarten through eighth grade. Central School burned to the ground in 1963.

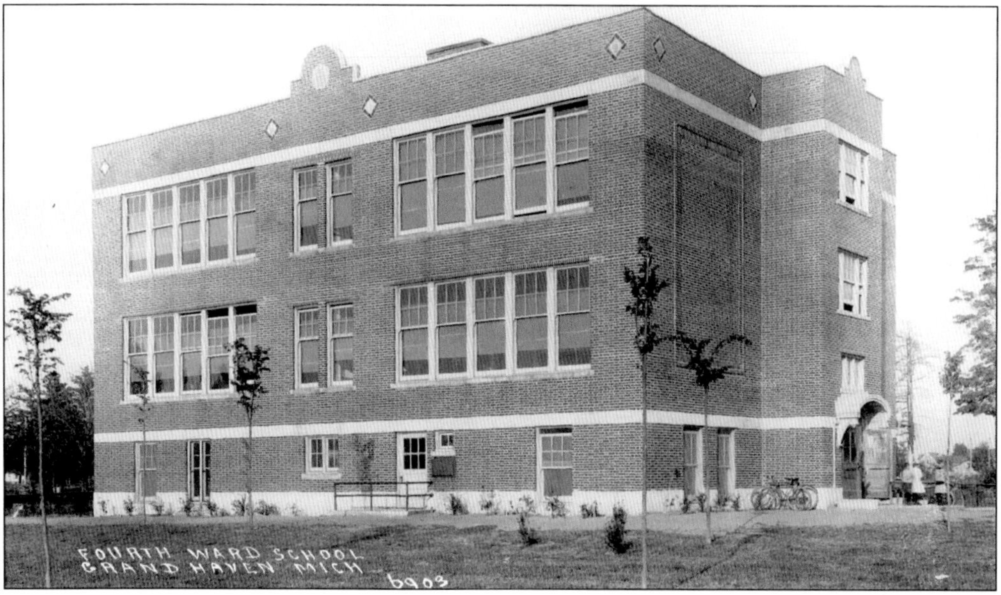

Ferry School on Pennoyer Street in Grand Haven opened its doors for the first time to elementary students in 1913. At that time it was known as the Fourth Ward School. The five-acre site had been a garden and cow pasture for Henry and Lena Bolt's farm. The name was changed to Ferry School in 1928 to honor Grand Haven's founding family.

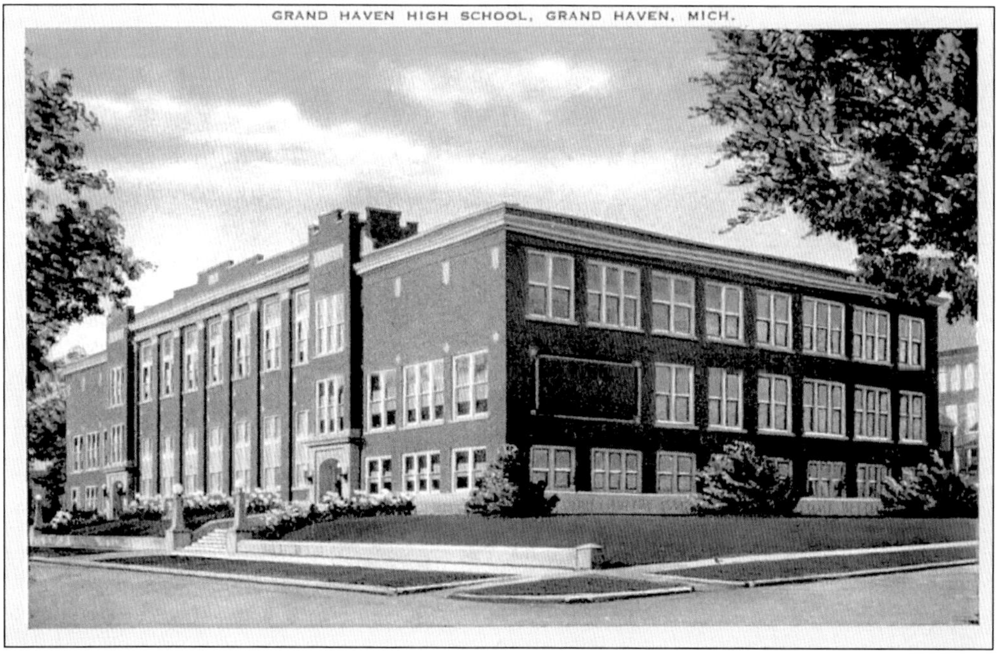

In 1922, Grand Haven High School students were moved from Central School on Sixth Street to this new brick structure on Seventh. When a new high school was built on Cutler in 1953, this building became the junior high school. Griffin Junior High opened in 1967, and the school shown here was torn down to make room for a larger playground for the elementary students attending Central. The card is postmarked 1931.

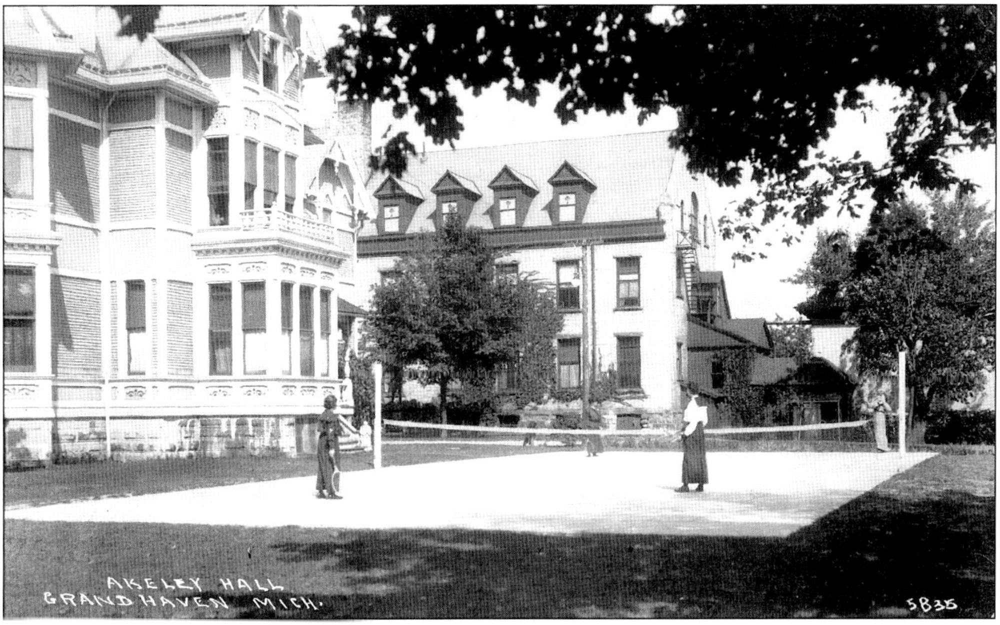

Tennis anyone? Four students from Akeley Institute answered "Yes," and met on the tennis court to play a brisk game of doubles. Two of the players are wearing middy blouses, a popular clothing item across the country in the early 1900s and chosen as the school's uniform. The court's surface was undoubtedly clay. The residence to the left was originally Healey C. Akeley's home. Gillespie Hall is behind the players.

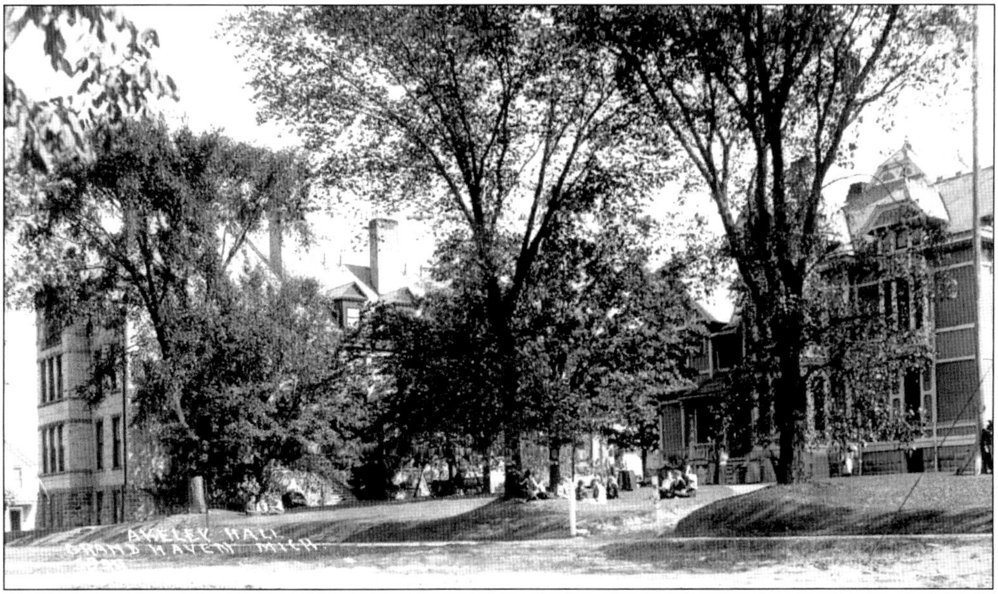

Located on the crest of the rise at Fifth Street, between Columbus and Washington, the buildings of Akeley Institute for Girls must have been an impressive sight. The house on the far right was once the home of the school's main benefactor, Healey C. Akeley. The large masonry structure at the left was dedicated as Lathrop Hall in 1891, but was more commonly known as Gillespie Hall. The school opened in 1886 and graduated its last class in June of 1928.

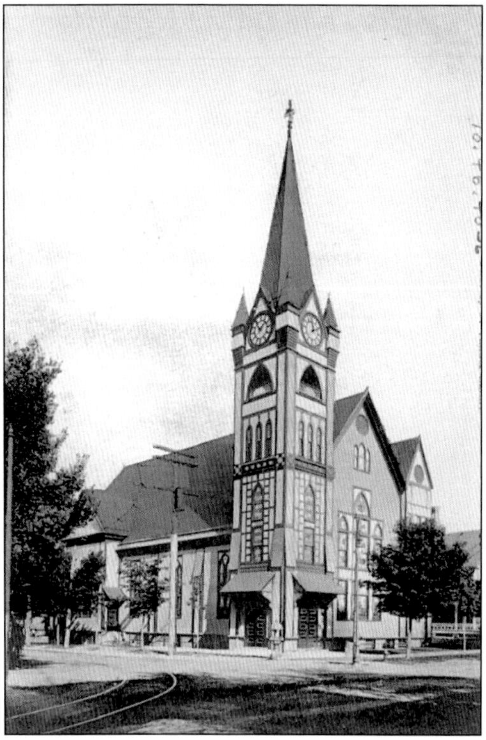

Pictured here is the First Reformed Church on the corner of Washington and Third Streets as it looked before it was destroyed by fire in 1907. The church lost three buildings to fire at the same location. This was the first of the clock towers to be replaced after each fire, including the current one that is a dominant feature in downtown Grand Haven. The church now on this corner was built in 1914. The lithographed card is remarkable for its clarity and detail

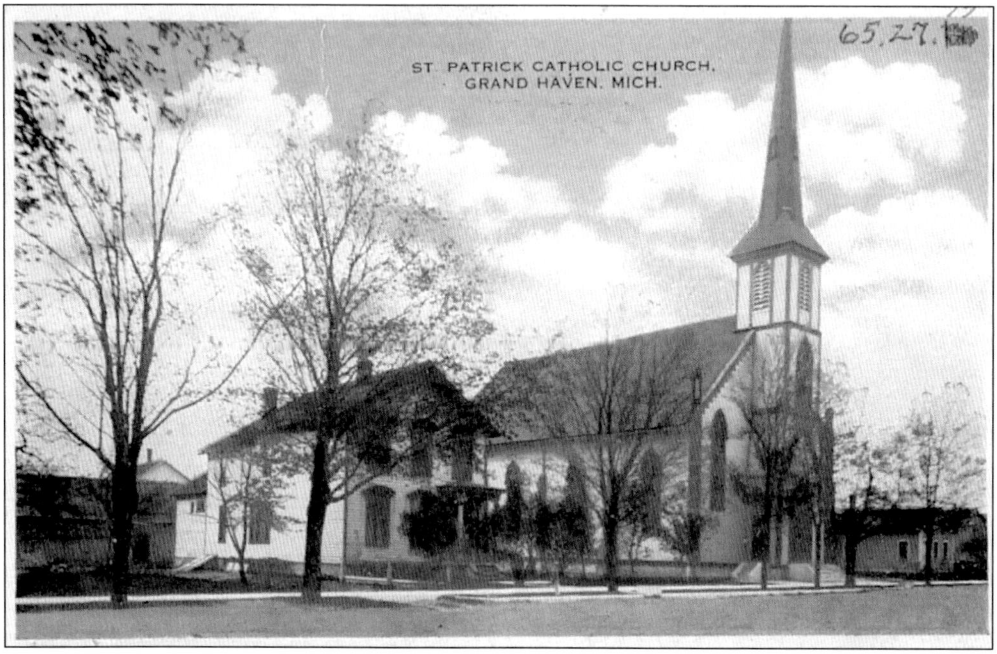

St. Patrick's Catholic Parish was organized in 1867. In 1872, this two-story frame structure with the tall steeple was built at 810 Fulton Street, and served its parishioners until U.S. 31 was rerouted down Beacon Boulevard, displacing the church in 1956. The building next door housed the church school, begun in 1919. The card is postmarked 1922.

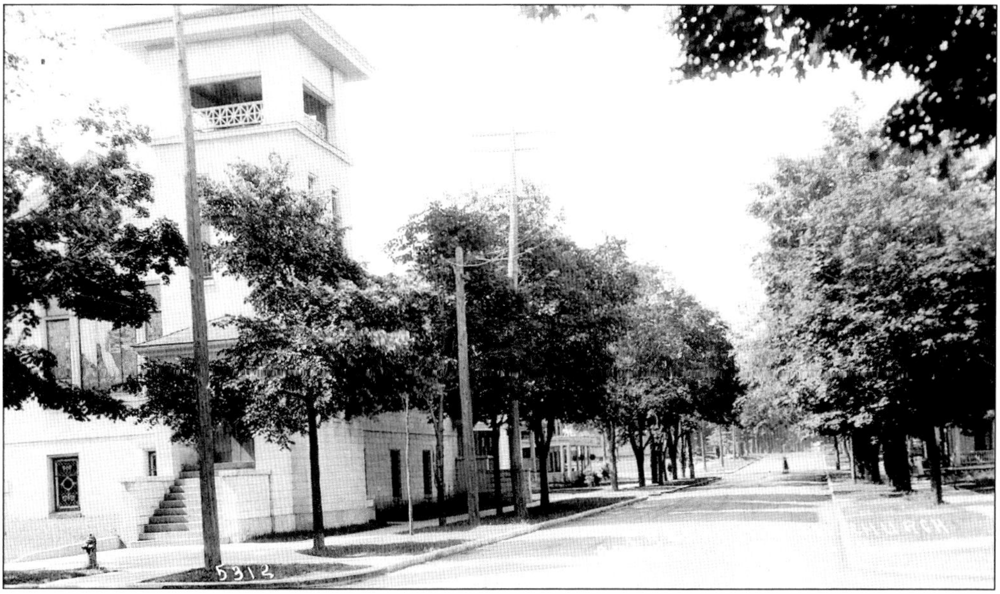

In 1885, the Presbyterian Church in Grand Haven was moved from its original location in the 200 block of Washington to this spot at the corner of Fifth and Franklin. The entryway and tower, seen in this real photo, were added when the church was remodeled in 1910. With some additional modifications, the original church served its parishioners until it was razed in 1956. The stained glass windows were saved from the wrecking ball and still may be seen today. The Armstead house, built toward the end of the 19th century, is visible just beyond the church.

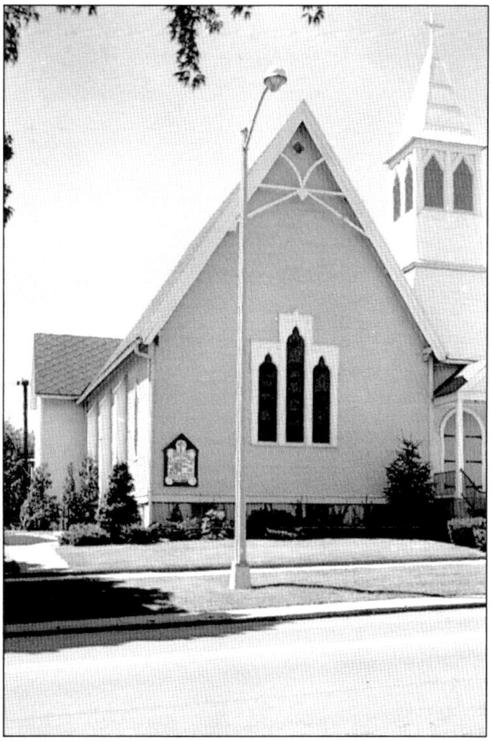

The cornerstone for St. John's Episcopal Church was laid on May 10, 1869. In its early years the church was heated by means of a wood stove. Two men tended to it Saturday night so that the building would be cozy and warm for worshippers on Sunday morning. The interior of the church has a unique "inverted ship" design. The building remains in use today, looking much as it did in the pre-1963 postcard.

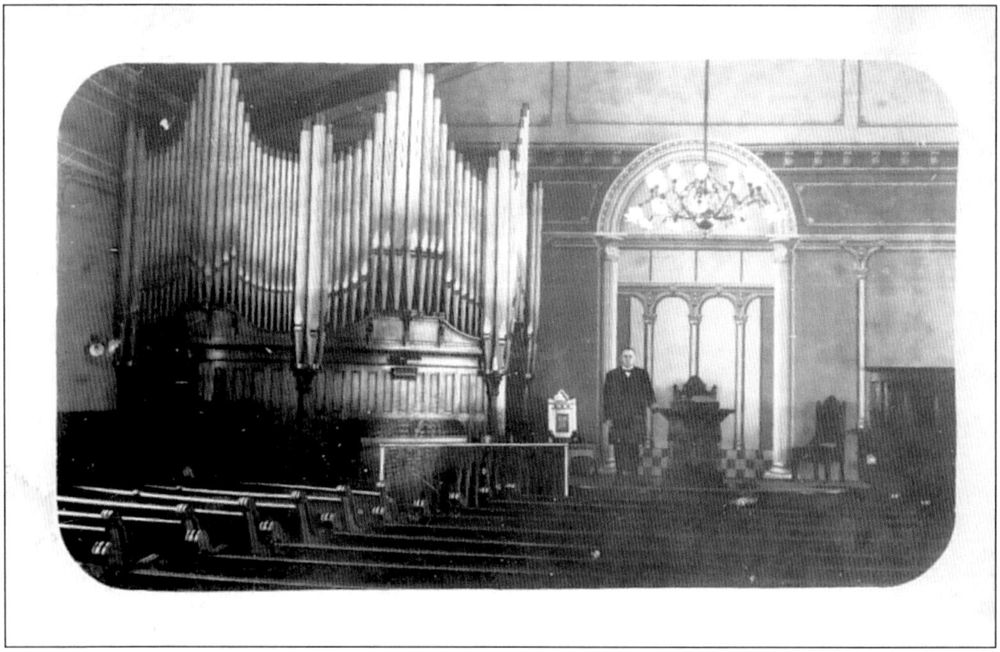

The magnificent pipe organ shown in this postcard provided music to accompany worshippers at the First Christian Reformed Church in Grand Haven. A handwritten message on the back of the real photo postcard identifies the occasion as the dedication of the church on September 2, 1915. Reverend J. Bruinooge is standing by the organ. The church was located at the corner of Fourth and Fulton Streets.

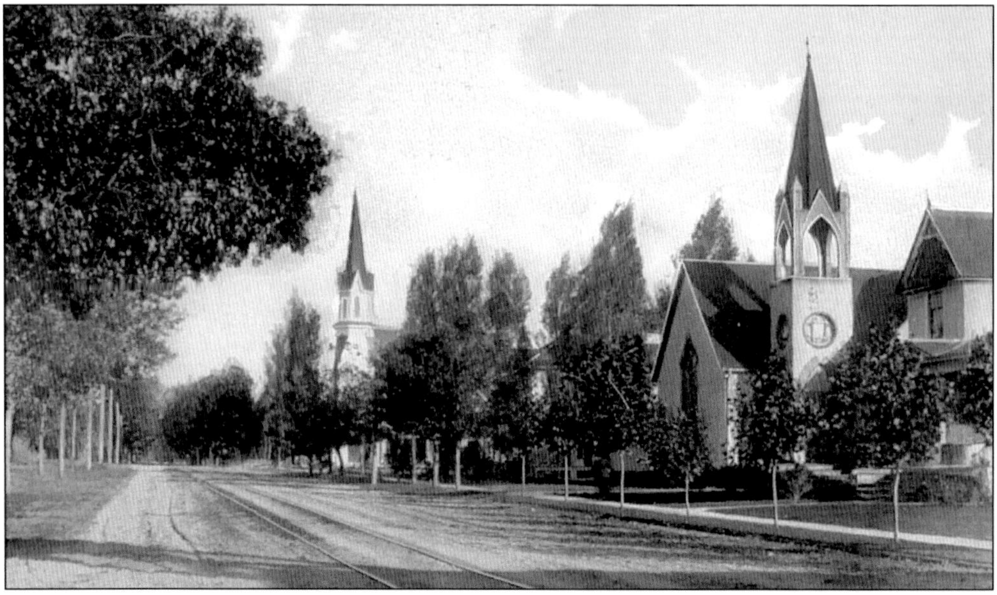

This remarkably clear and detailed view of Savidge Street looking east shows the Methodist Episcopalian Church in the foreground and the First Presbyterian Church on the next block. The Interurban tracks also are visible, and it looks as if most of the trees lining each side of Savidge had been recently planted. The card is postmarked 1912.

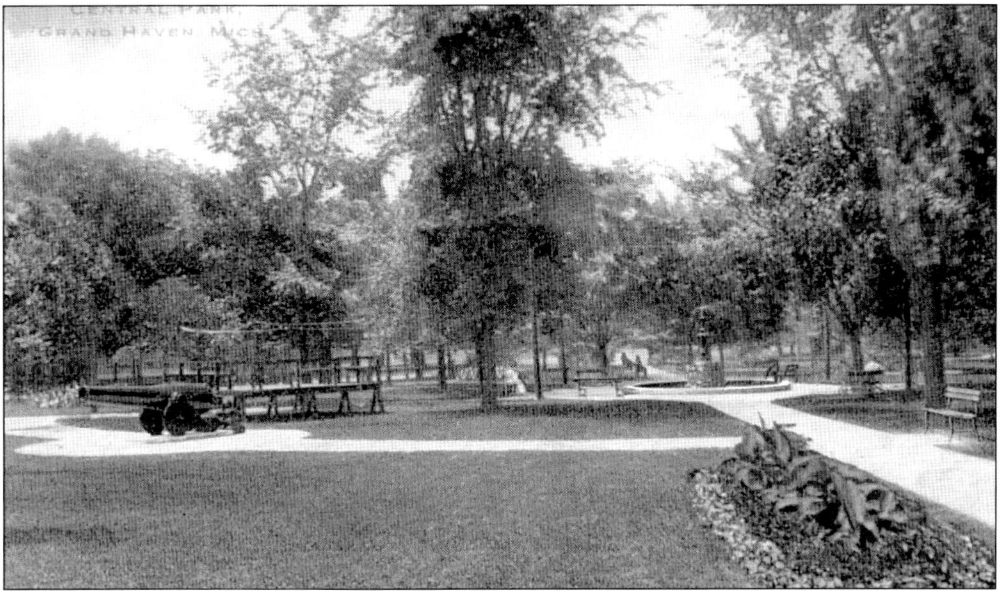

This 1914 view shows one of the two brass cannons that had been placed in Central Park six years earlier. The cannons and cannon balls were from the battleship *New Orleans*, which served in the War of 1812. The two historic guns and cannon balls were scrapped for the war effort during World War II.

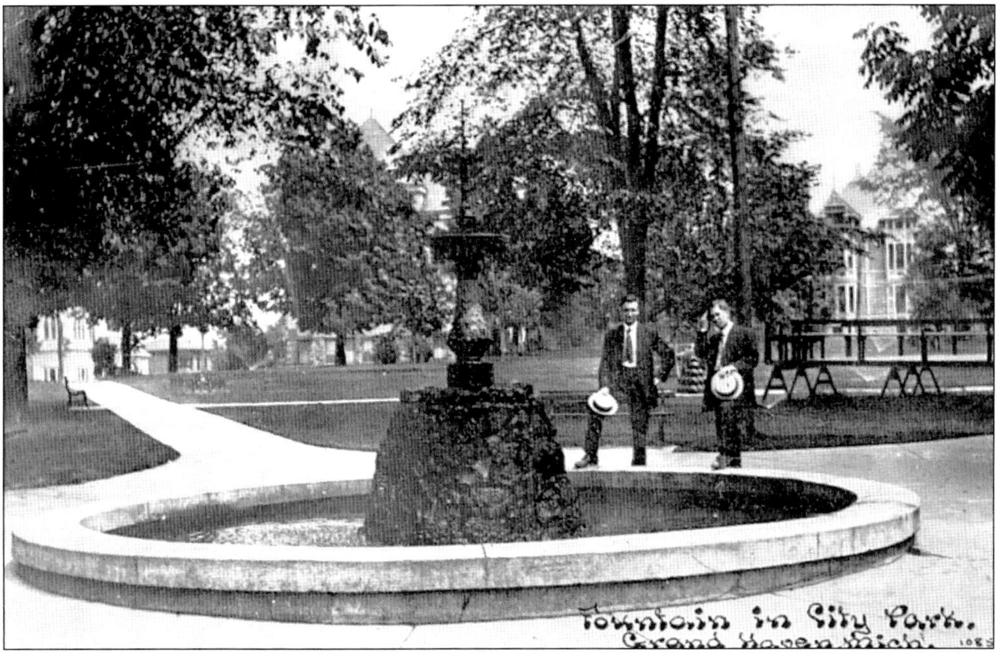

Formerly the site of the City Cemetery, Central Park was dedicated in 1901. Through the efforts of the City Park Board, the Grand Haven Women's Club, and the Garden Club, the park was sodded, shrubs planted, and walkways paved. The park's first fountain, shown in this 1918 card, was purchased by the city from Gerrit Bottje's Hardware Store for $42.40 in 1901. Just visible through the trees are buildings of Akeley School for Girls.

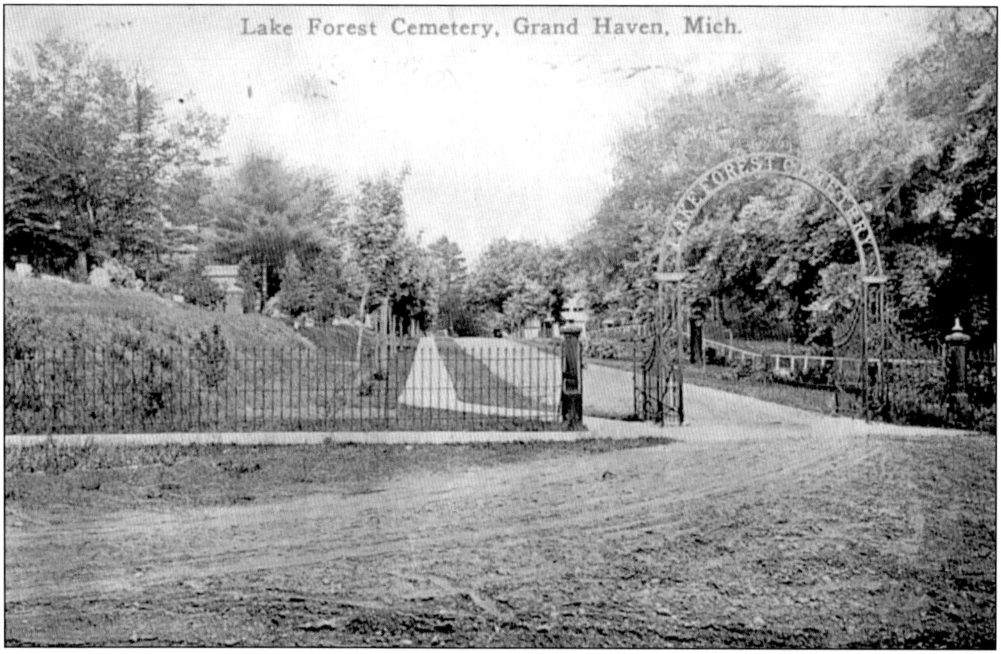

Grand Haven's cemetery was moved from Central Park to this site off Lake Avenue in the 1870s. The 1912 postcard shows the main entrance to the burial grounds, with the name Lake Forest Cemetery clearly outlined in the wrought iron arch at the gate. Lake Avenue was not yet paved.

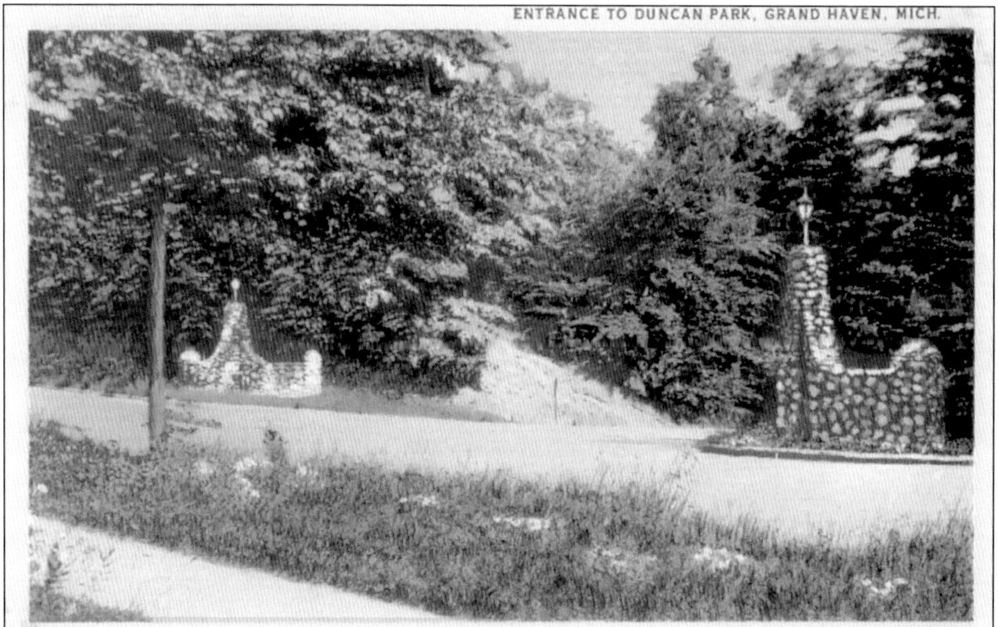

Duncan Memorial Park has been a 50-acre nature preserve since 1913, when widowed Martha Duncan presented it to the City of Grand Haven. The road continues through the Park to the Lake Avenue side, where it is gated to ensure tranquility. Shown in this undated card is the Park's entrance on Sheldon Road.

Nine

People and their Homes

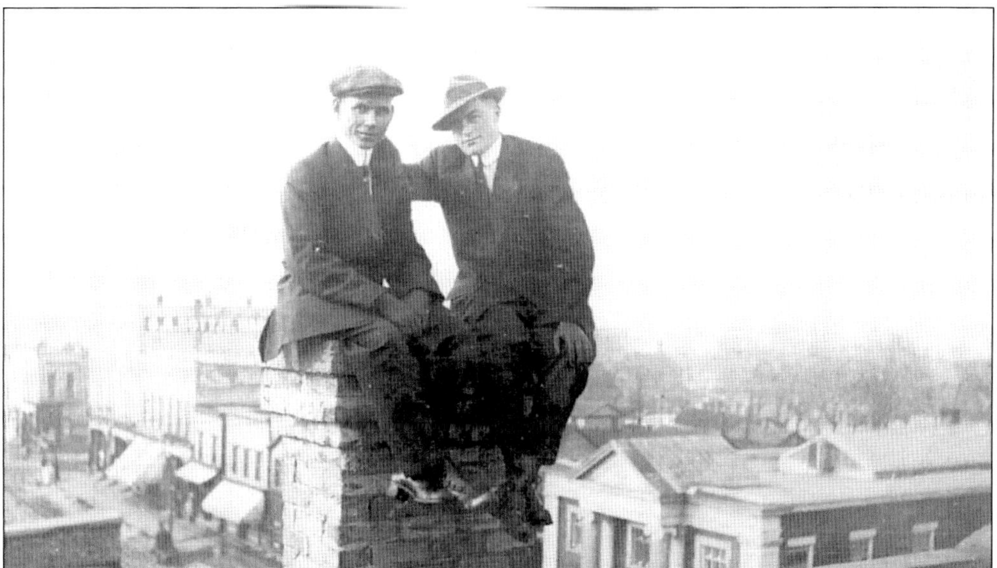

The two well-dressed men sitting on top of the chimney on the Oakes building are not identified, but they certainly had a panoramic view of rooftops! Behind them on the north side of Washington is the columned structure of Grand Haven State Bank, and farther down the 200 block are Justema's Shoe Store and Gerritt Bottje's Hardware Store. The card was not mailed.

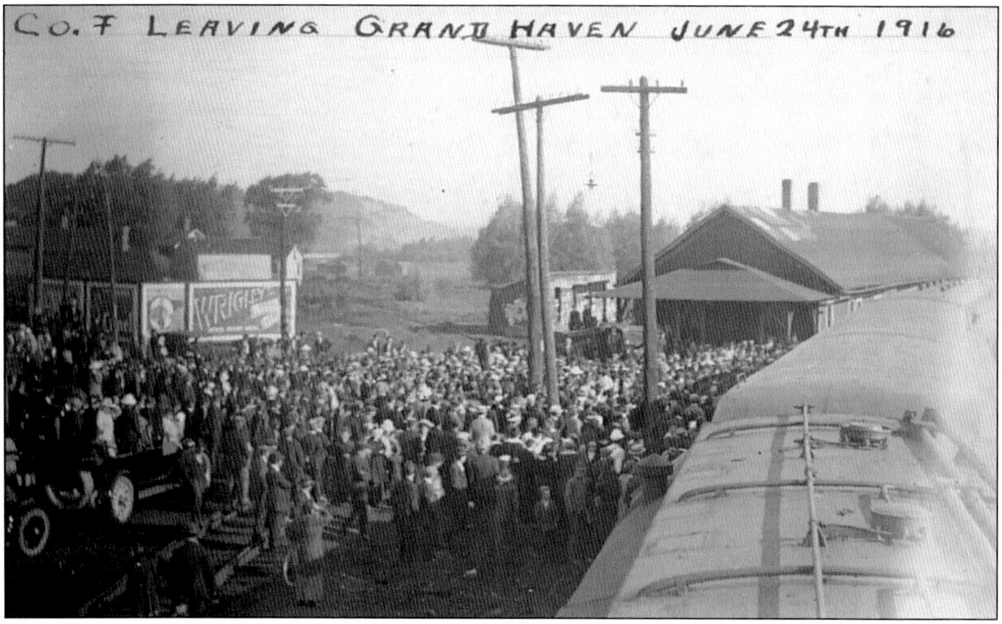

The large crowd pictured here jammed Jackson Street and the original Pere Marquette Railway Depot to say goodbye to Company F, on its way to Camp Grayling for training in preparation for the Mexican incursion. The date was June 24, 1916, two years before the local company was mobilized for action in France during World War I. One of the large billboard signs recommends Wrigley chewing gum "After Every Meal."

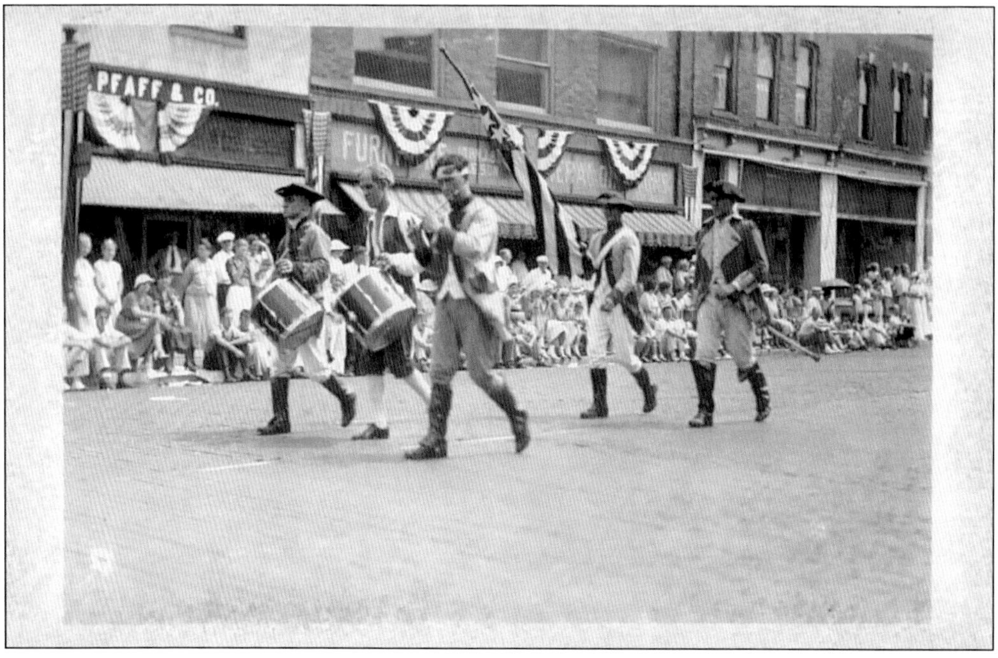

No parade would be complete without a drum and fife corps, and these six entrants in the 1934 Centennial parade were dressed in uniforms of the Revolutionary War to fill out the requirement. Pfaff's Hardware and Kiel's Furniture & Undertaking stores are in the background.

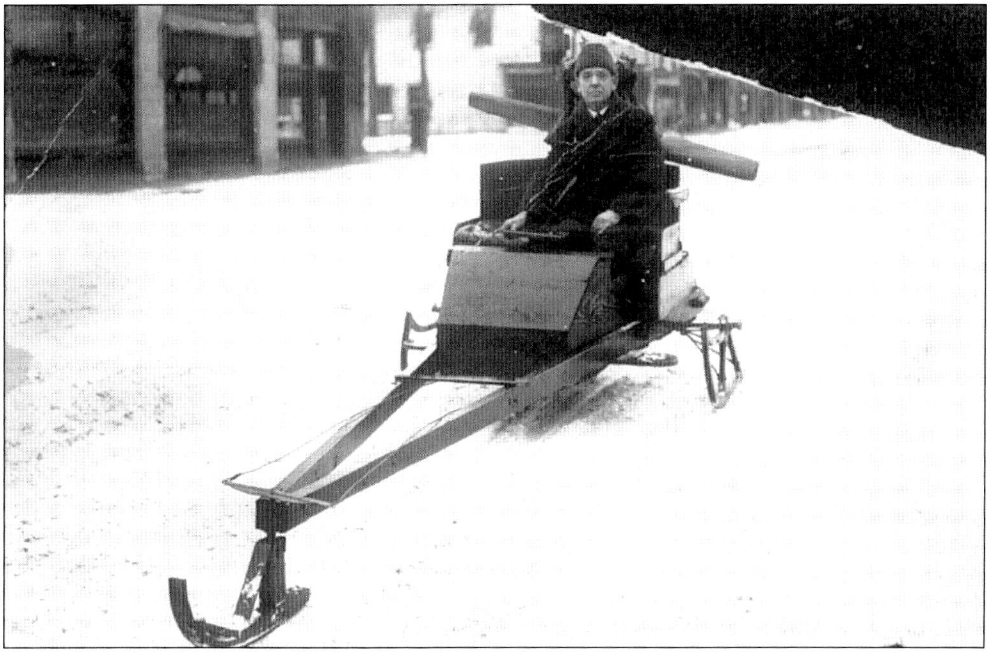

Grand Haven photographer Nathaniel E. Brown probably set up his own camera to pose for this wintertime shot. On the back he wrote, "These sleds propelled like an aeroplane could travel fast." The propeller can be seen behind him. The picture was taken near the corner of First and Washington Streets. The upper right corner of the card has broken off.

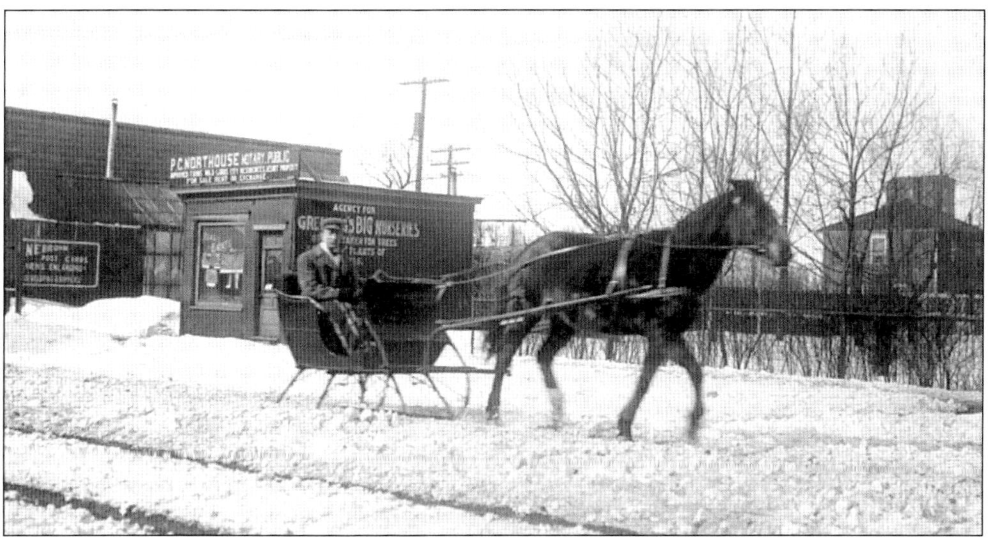

Ralph Ottenstraer rides his one-horse sleigh down Washington Avenue on this crisp winter day. Peter Northouse's real estate office is in the small building behind Ralph. Northouse was also a Notary Public. His sign advised the public that he offered "Improved Farms, Wild Lands, City Residences, Resort Property For Sale, Rent, or Exchange." Next to the real estate office is a sign advertising Nat Brown's photography business, and off to the right is the National Hotel on Harbor Drive. Not long after this picture was taken, Nat moved across the street to 22 Washington. The seven-story grain elevator can be seen behind the hotel at the corner of Columbus and Harbor.

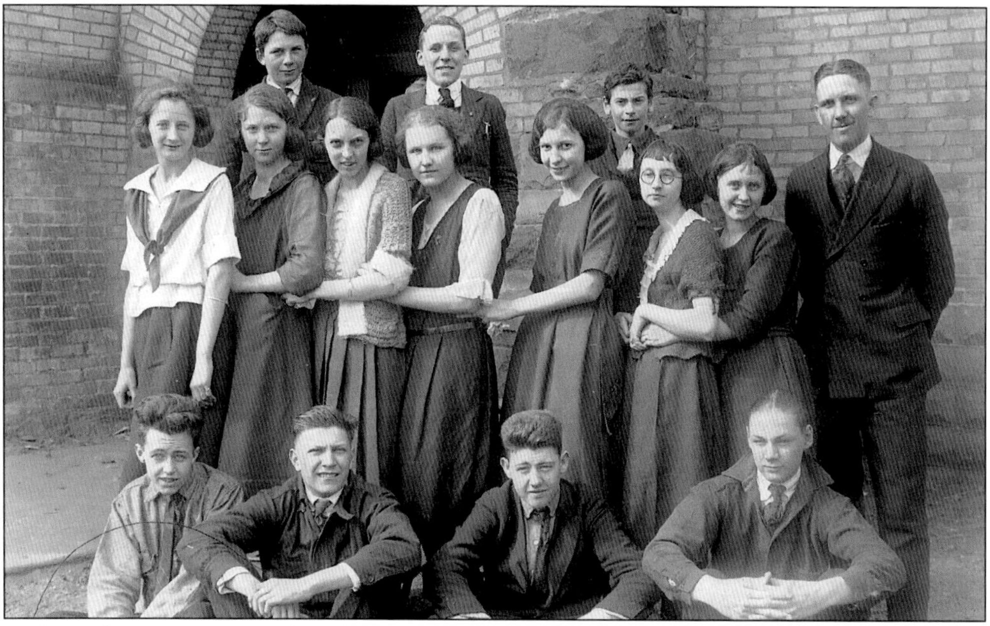

In the early years, Spring Lake schools educated students in grades kindergarten through twelve. In the 1920s grades nine to twelve were dropped and Spring Lake students traveled to Grand Haven for high school classes, until the village opened its own high school in 1963. This postcard shows the Spring Lake graduating class of 1922, perhaps one of the last before students were moved to Grand Haven, posing in front of their school on Exchange Street. From left to right and top to bottom, the students are Bartley Rider, Preston Bilz, James Rogers, Lillian Sankey, Dora Mergener, Dorothy Mulder, Marie Krueger, Kathryn Fox, Marjory Deremo, Ruth Hildebrant, Mr. Bos, Howard Spencer, August Tuey, Harold Katt, and Sidney Braak.

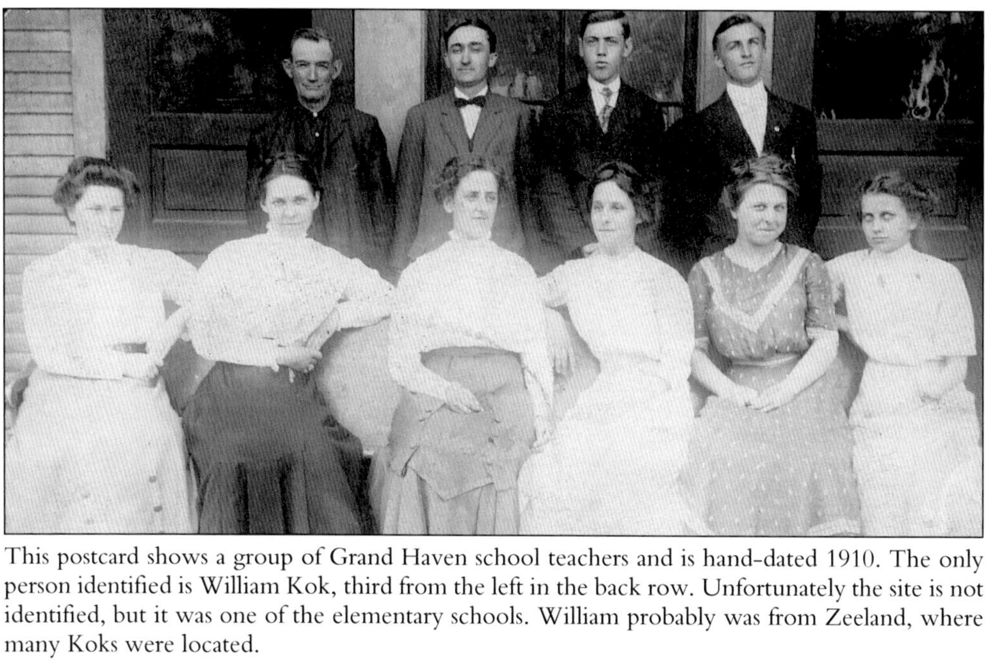

This postcard shows a group of Grand Haven school teachers and is hand-dated 1910. The only person identified is William Kok, third from the left in the back row. Unfortunately the site is not identified, but it was one of the elementary schools. William probably was from Zeeland, where many Koks were located.

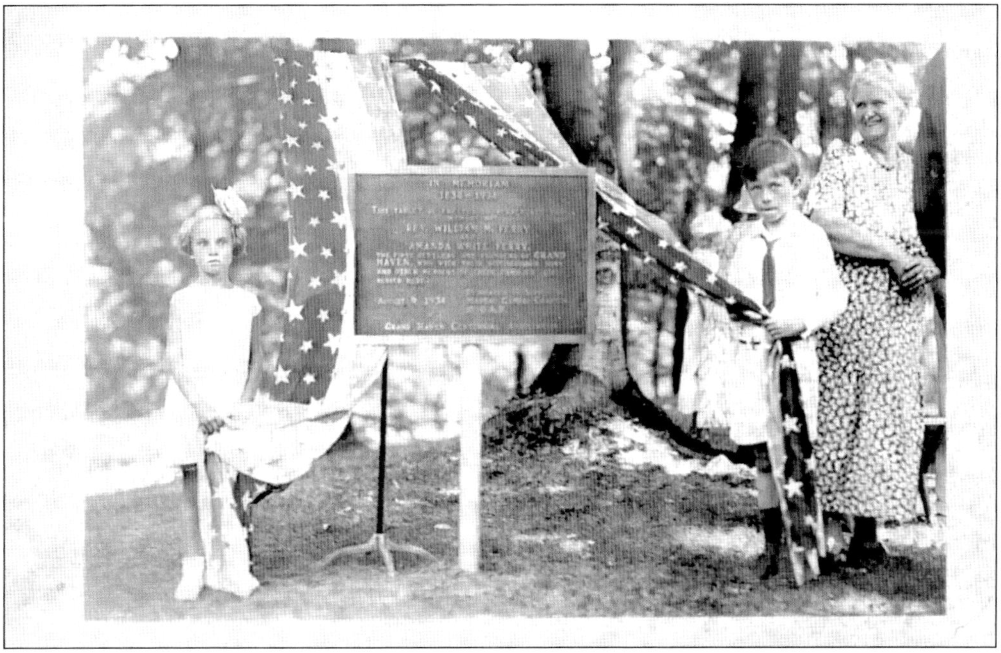

On August 9, 1934 in Lake Forest Cemetery, the Grand Haven Centennial Committee dedicated the plaque featured in this unmailed postcard to honor Rev. William Ferry and his wife as the founders of Grand Haven. Julian Hatton and Nancy Bowles had the privilege of holding the banners flanking the plaque.

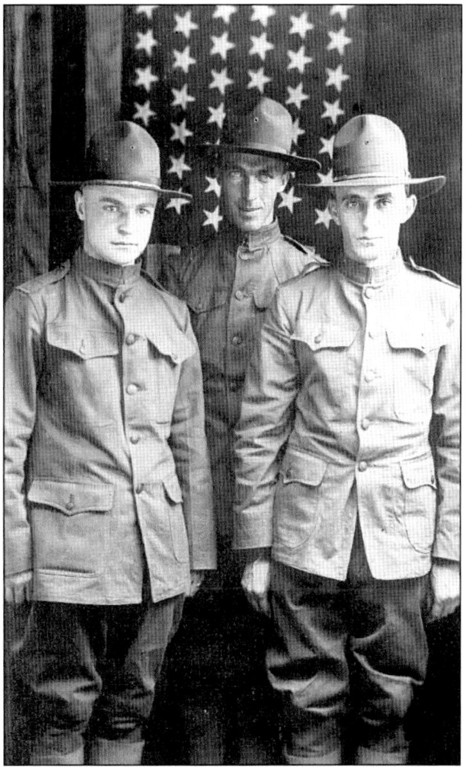

Young people from the Grand Haven area have responded patriotically to every armed conflict since the Civil War. These three Grand Haven residents were close to thirty years old when they donned Army uniforms and met their military obligation. Taking time to pose for this postcard portrait are Henry Verwoert, Henry Dykhouse, and David Nedervelt. The card was not mailed.

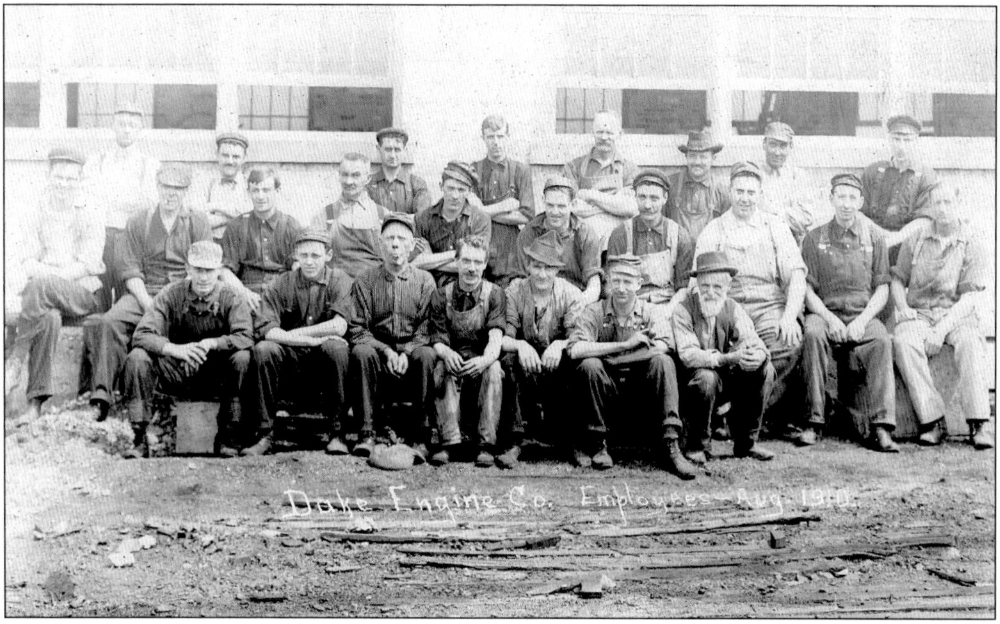

The caption on this unmailed postcard identifies the group of men as employees of the Dake Engine Company. Dake was founded in 1887 and is still in business, but in a different location. At the time of this photo, dated August of 1910, the company was located at the northwest corner of Monroe and Seventh Streets at the north end of Grand Haven. It is now on the south side of Robbins Road, west of U.S. 31. The men in the picture are not identified.

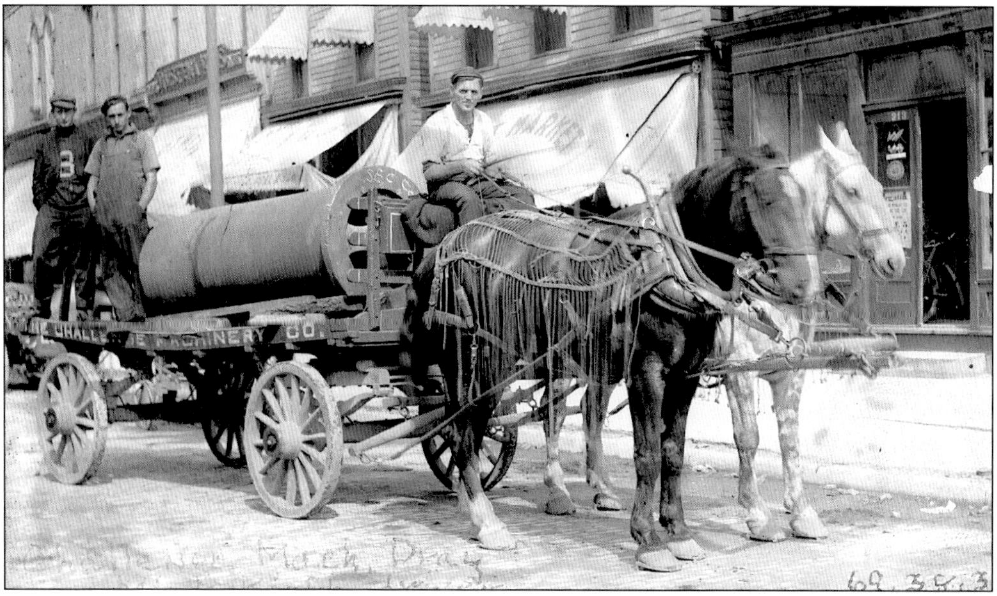

In this undated card, Mink Kieft is hauling a piece of equipment headed for Challenge Machinery. The photographer captured the scene in the 200 block of Washington Street. The store with the open door is Wilford Dake's bicycle shop. Next door is Ed Kinkema's meat market, and next to that was Lehman Brothers' City Barber Shop, today the Glo Barber Shop. Washington Street is still unpaved, indicating the picture predates 1910.

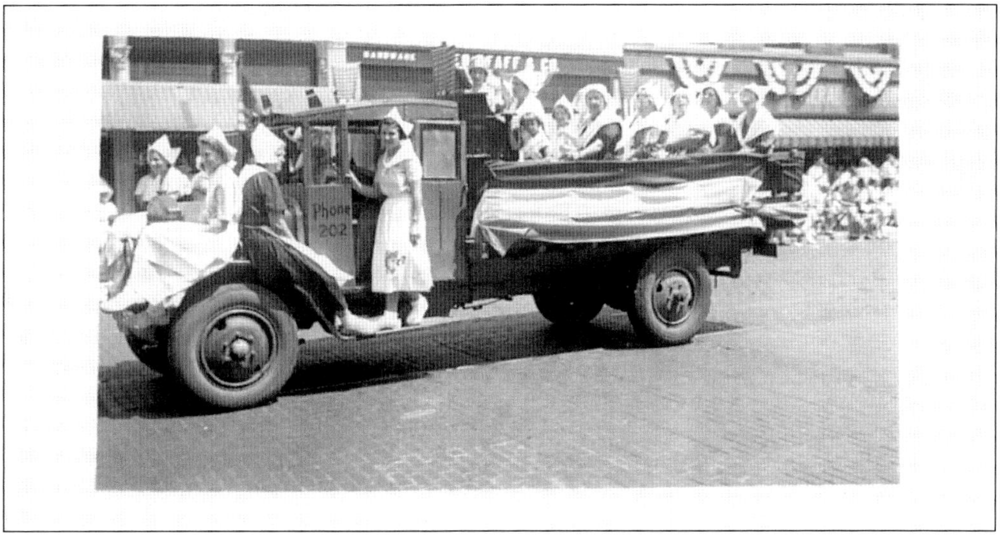

In August of 1934, Grand Haven celebrated 100 years as a community. It was a gala occasion and, of course, included a parade down Washington Street. One of the entries was the truck from Baker Lumber, pictured in this undated real photo card. Jennie Bolt is identified as the woman playing the organ in the truck's bed. The women behind her are singing psalms. Some of them are identified as "the Boon girls." Pfaff's Hardware at 117 Washington is in the background.

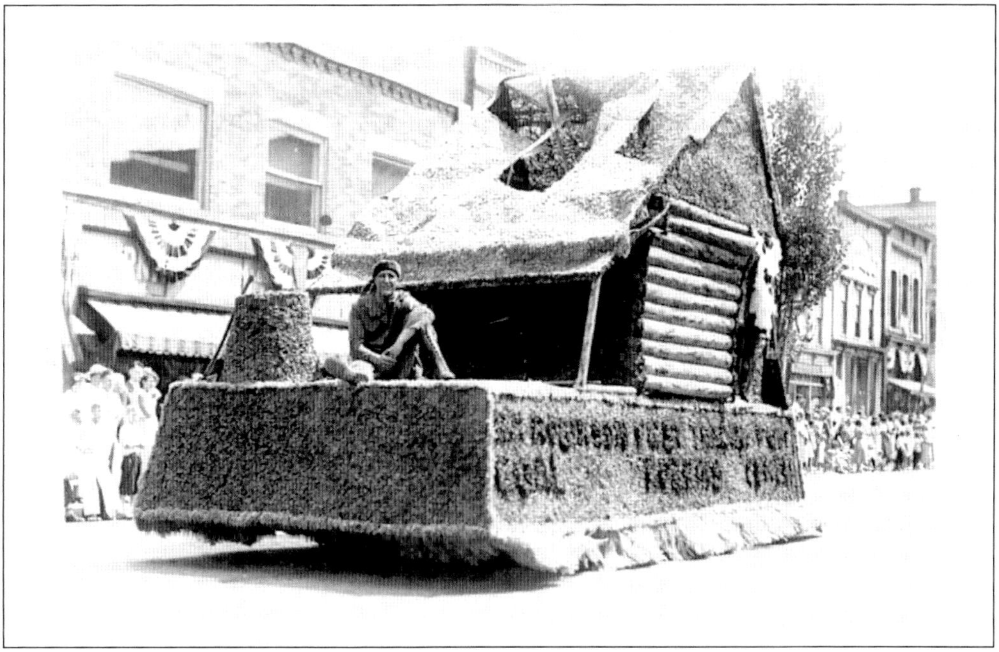

This float in the 1934 parade down Grand Haven's main street was a replica of Rix Robinson's fur trading post that he worked from in the early 1800s. It was the only structure in the area when the Ferry family arrived in 1834, and Robinson made the shelter available to the settlers that first winter. Larry Dornbos Sr. portrays Rix on the float. Kiel Furniture and Undertaking, located at 123–125 Washington, is in the background, and the building that now houses Hostetter's can be seen at the far right.

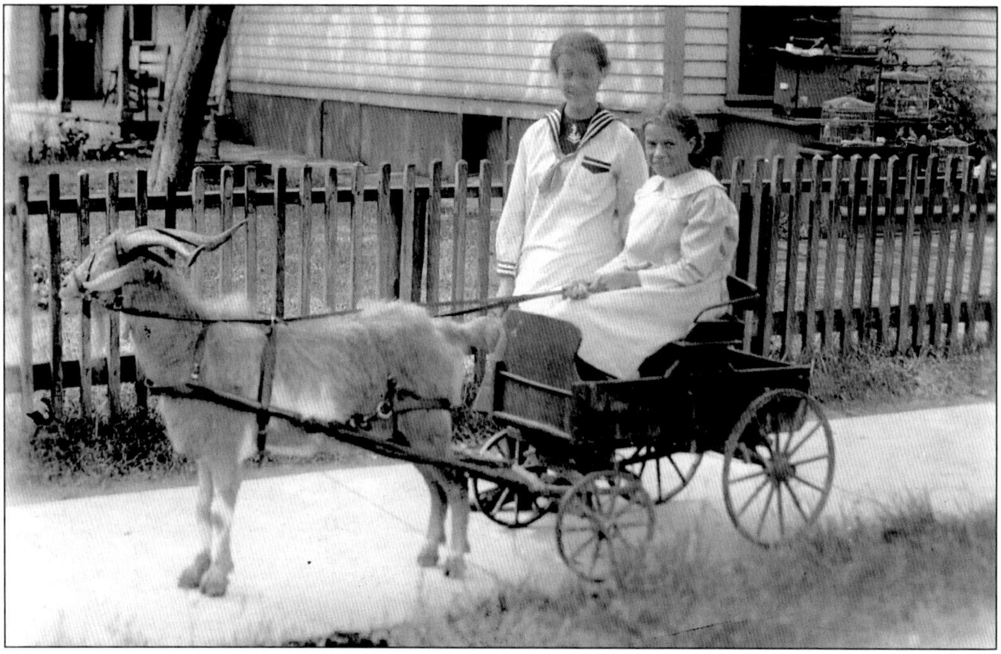

Jennie De Kiep and Henrietta Kiel must have been proud of their goat-drawn wagon as they went for an afternoon ride. Henrietta, the daughter of Lucy and Albert Kiel, resided at 315 Columbus. In the early 1900s Jennie lived with them. It's very likely they were cousins. There are at least six birdcages on the stoop of the house in the background.

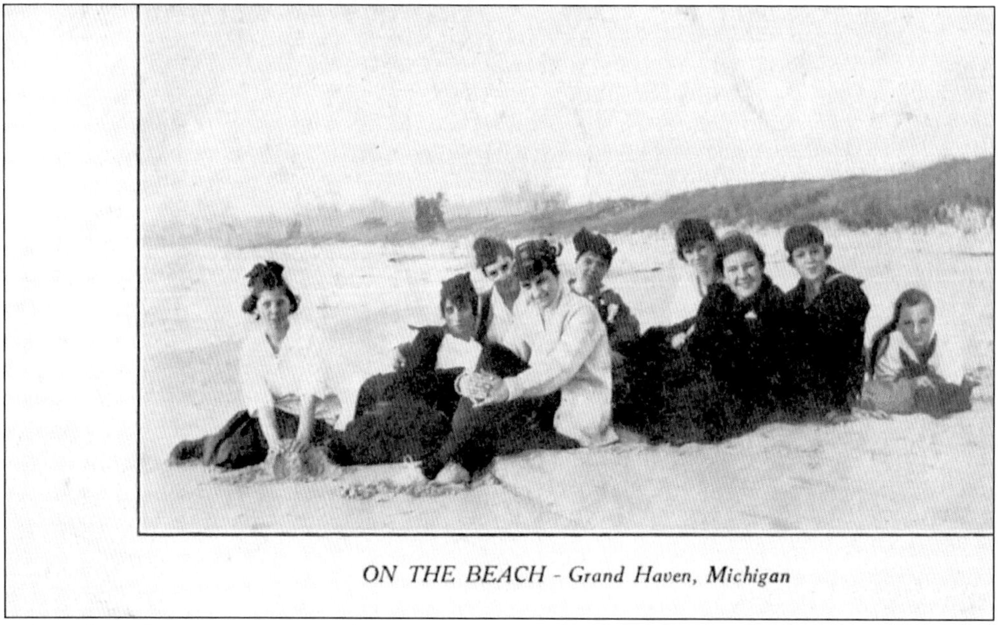

Where the girls are... chances are the boys aren't too far away. Neither the young women nor the exact location of this scene on the beach at Grand Haven are identified. However, the low foredunes give it the appearance of the Rosy Mound area. The card was not mailed and is not dated.

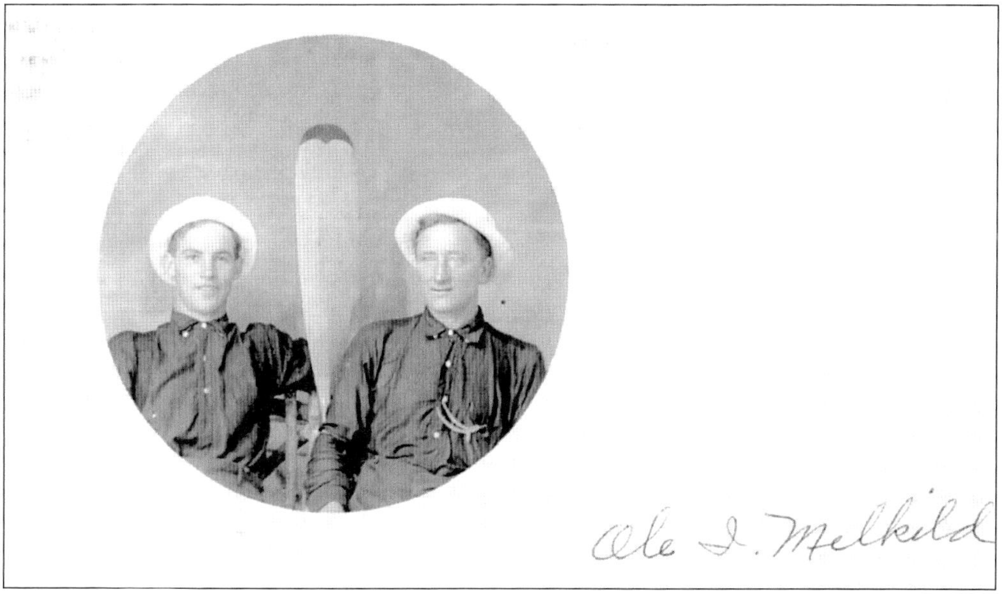

These two young men are dressed in the uniform of the United States Life Saving Service, with an oar between them to help identify their occupation. The man on the right is identified as Ole I. Melkild, Flora Thoma's brother-in-law. Flora and her husband, Jack, were residents of Grand Haven. Both were originally from Grand Rapids, also home to the Melkild family. The other man was William Fisher. Ole wrote the message, which is dated 1908.

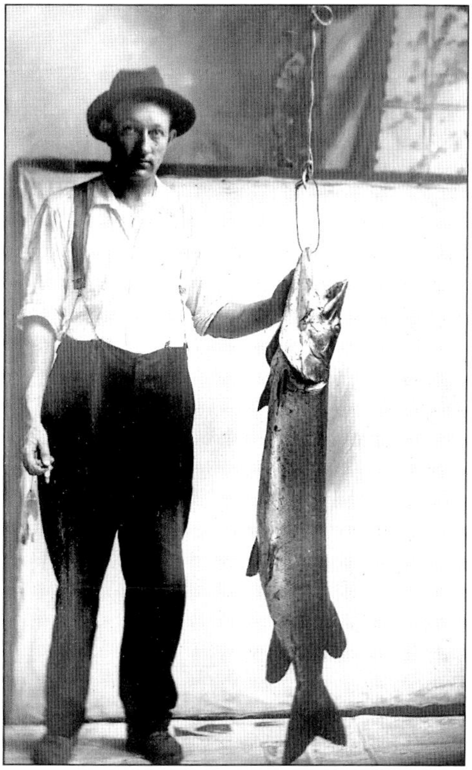

The man displaying his catch of the day is identified as Jerry Dykhuis of Grand Haven. The impressive muskellunge weighed in at 31 pounds. He landed the hefty critter with a cane pole, while fishing in the Sag off the Grand River.

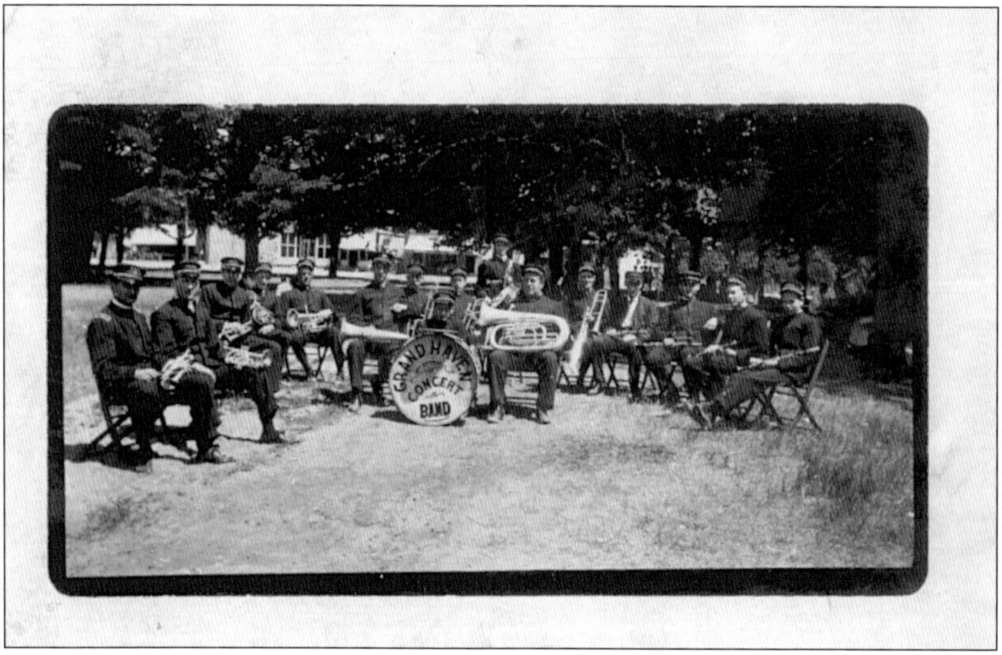

In the late 19th and early 20th century, brass bands provided summertime entertainment for young and old. The group in this postcard is identified on the drum as the Grand Haven Concert Band. It was formed in 1868 and played indoors as well as outdoors. The venue for this scene is not identified, but it does not appear to be Grand Haven.

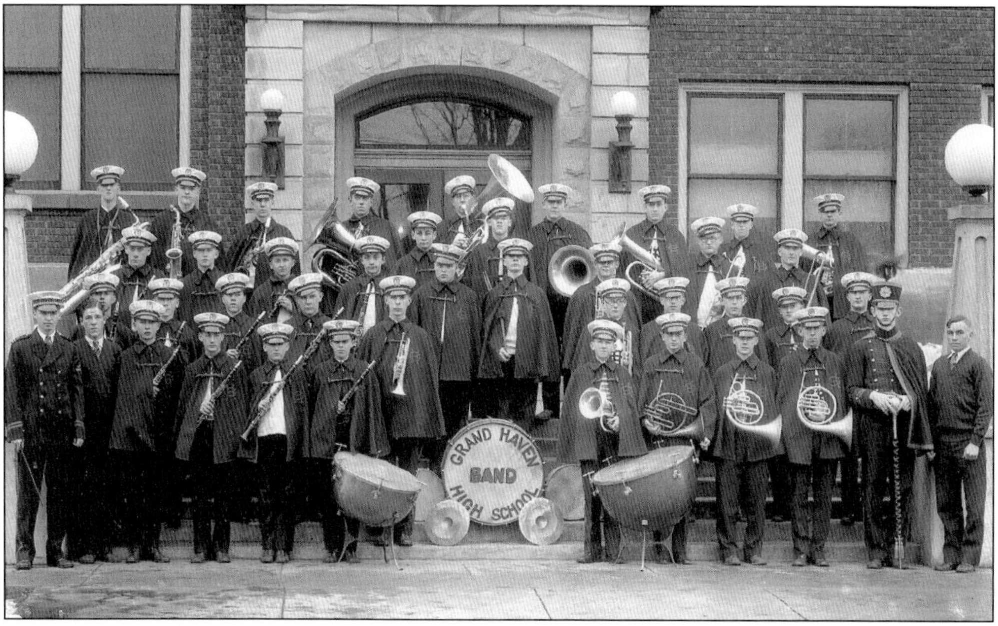

A band was formed not long after the new high school opened on Seventh Street in Grand Haven. This group gathered on the steps of the school in 1928 to pose for the camera. Marshall Richards, the band's director, is at the far left with baton in hand. This was the first year the 40 band members donned the blue and gold uniforms.

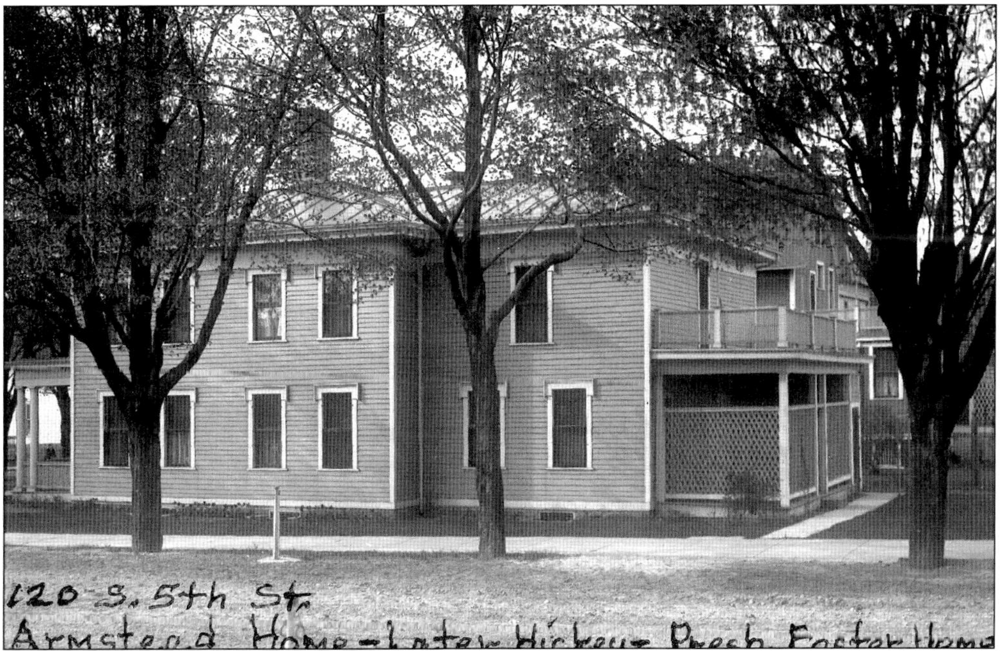

James and Myrtle Armstead built this lovely residence before 1900. Located at the corner of Fifth and Clinton Streets, the house was later purchased by the First Presbyterian Church, and in recent years was used as headquarters for Love INC. James Armstead was Secretary and Manager of Dake Engine Company.

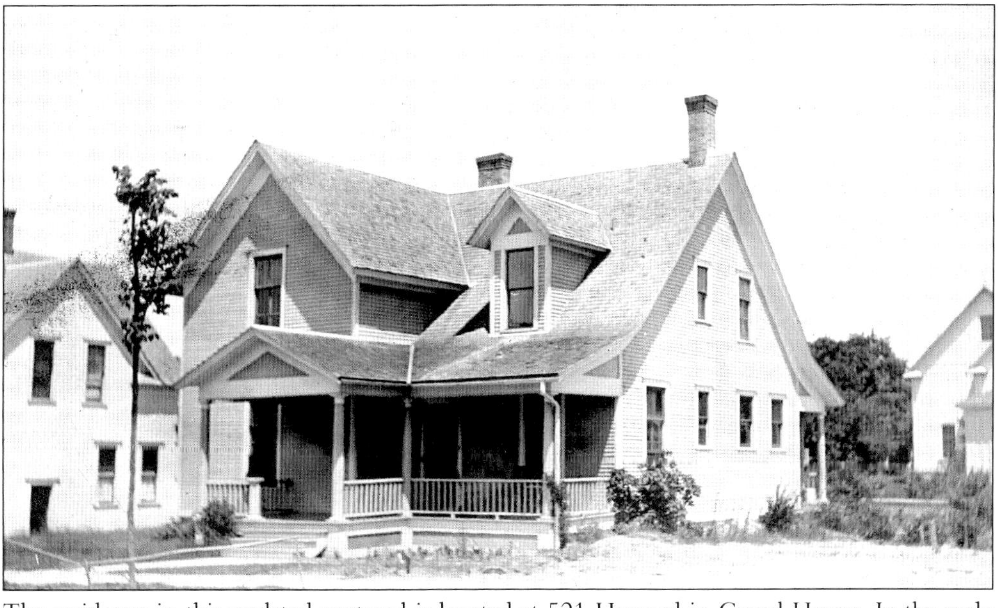

The residence in this undated postcard is located at 521 Howard in Grand Haven. In the early 1900s, Pennoyer Street was extended west to connect with Howard, but prior to that time this would have been the easternmost house on Howard. It remains a residence today. Pennoyer was originally platted to continue due west across Sheldon Road, rather than join Howard in the middle of the 500 block.

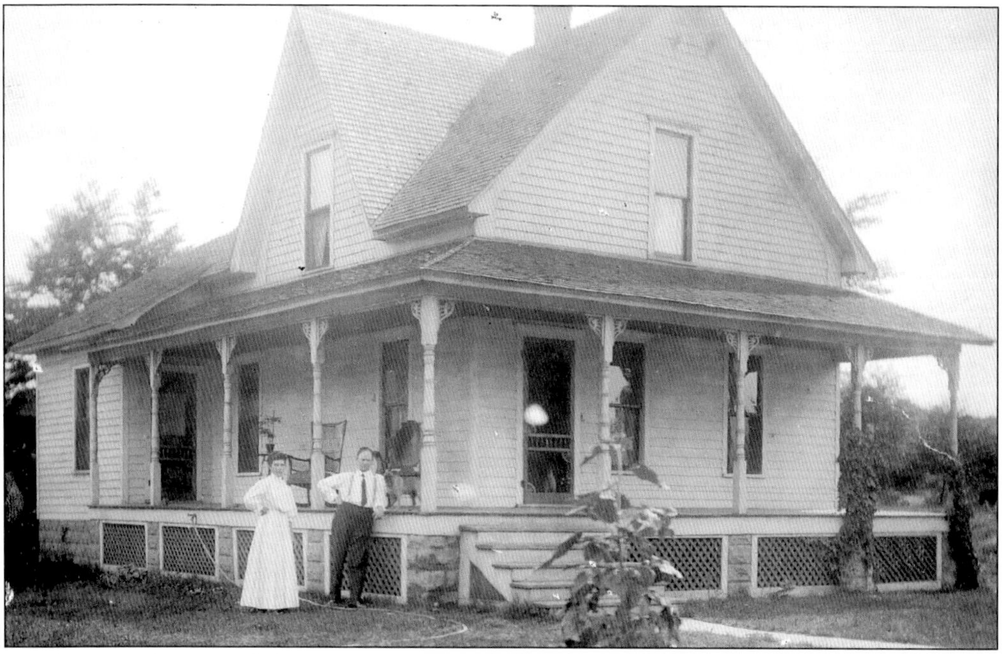

The house in this unmailed postcard is identified as the James and Amelia Vander Zalm residence at 108 Sherman in Grand Haven. The owners are posing in front of their home. James owned the Cheap Cash Department Store at 208 Washington.

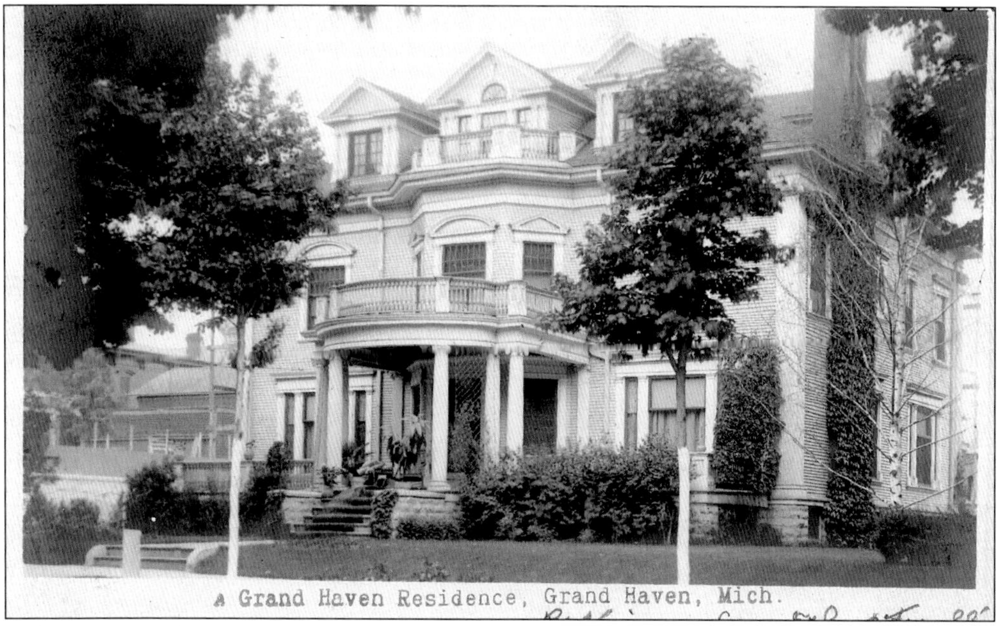

Titled "A Grand Haven Residence" on the card, this picture shows the spacious three-story home of Nat and Esther Robbins, constructed in 1898, just a few years after they were married. It cost $25,000 to build, an extravagant sum in those days. Among its many splendid features was a ballroom on the third floor. The house, located at the corner of Fifth and Franklin Streets, was recently restored to its original look. The card is undated.

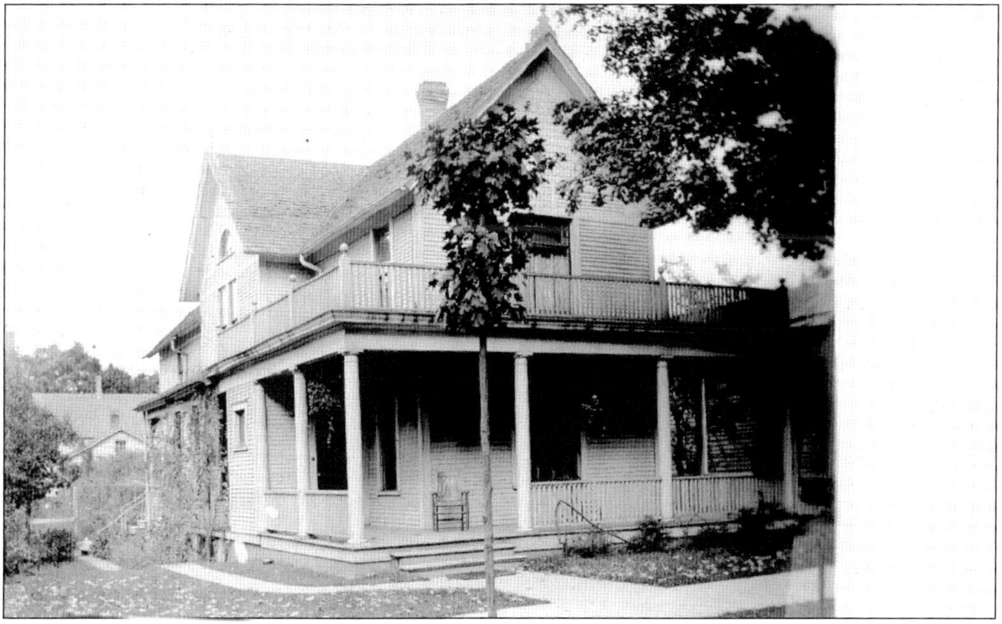

Captain Adrian O'Beck and his wife Johanna raised their family in this residence at 421 Clinton. O'Beck had his own commercial fishing business. His sons Adrian, Martin, and Ray O'Beck eventually took over the business, which continued until 1971. The older Adrian had been an early member of the United States Life Saving Service.

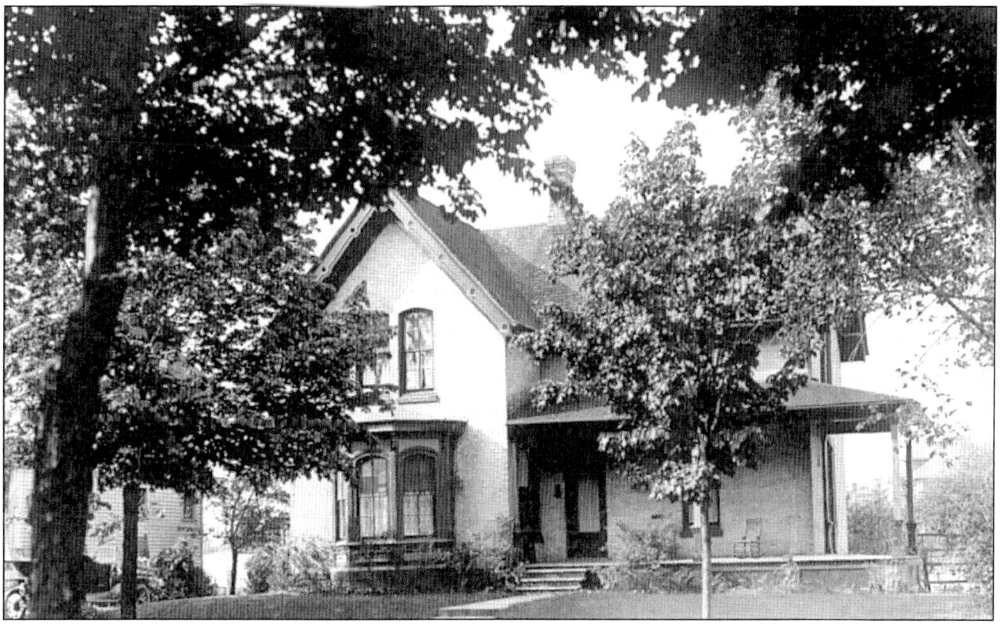

This brick home, the residence of John and May Angus, is located at 526 Lafayette Street in Grand Haven. The unmailed real photo postcard is hand dated October of 1920. An early Tin Lizzie sits in the driveway to the left.

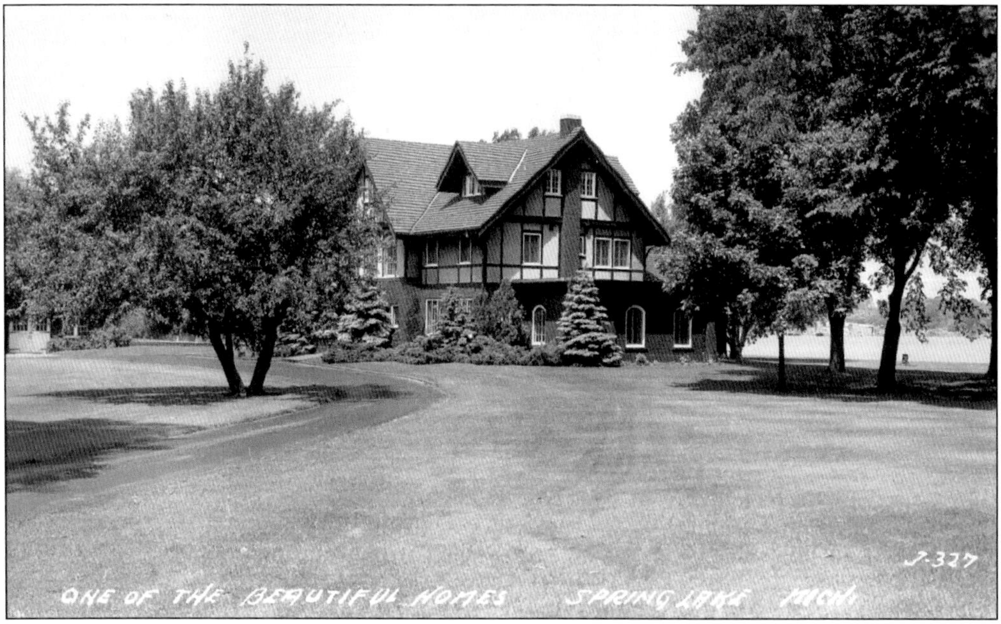

In the early 1920s, Nat and Esther Savidge Robbins constructed this fine home on the shores of Spring Lake for their son Hunter Savidge Robbins. The home was originally meant for occupancy during the summer months, when Hunter and his wife returned from their winter home in Pasadena, California. The current owners winterized it in 1977. The real photo card is postmarked 1946.

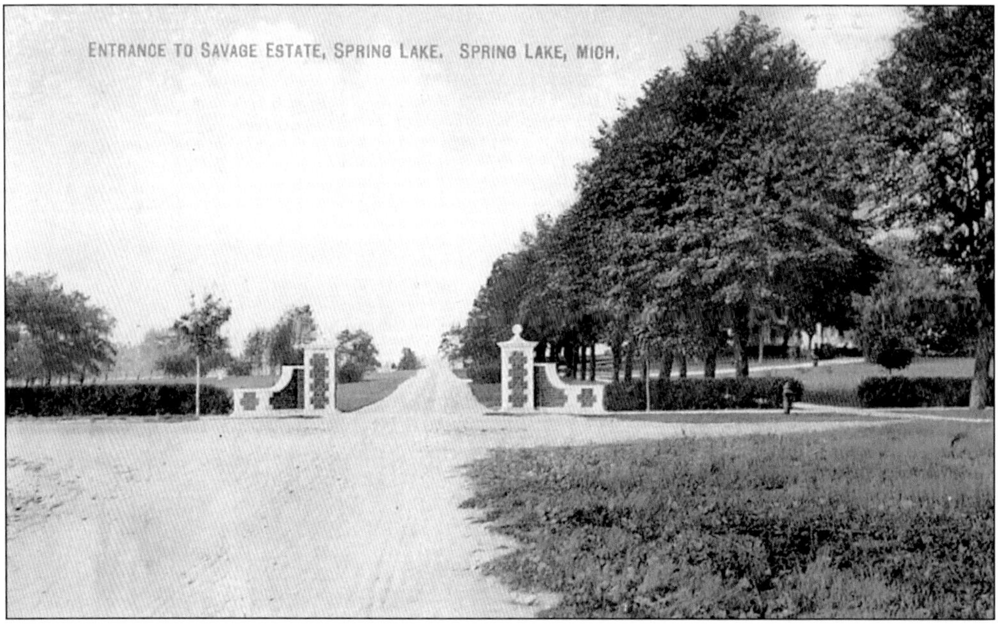

These two brick posts marked the entrance to the Savidge property in Spring Lake and location of the Hunter Robbins home. Hunter, the son of Nathaniel and Esther Savidge Robbins, was named for his grandfather, Hunter Savidge, a lumber baron and early settler in the village. The card is postmarked 1909.

Ten

As the Birds Saw Us

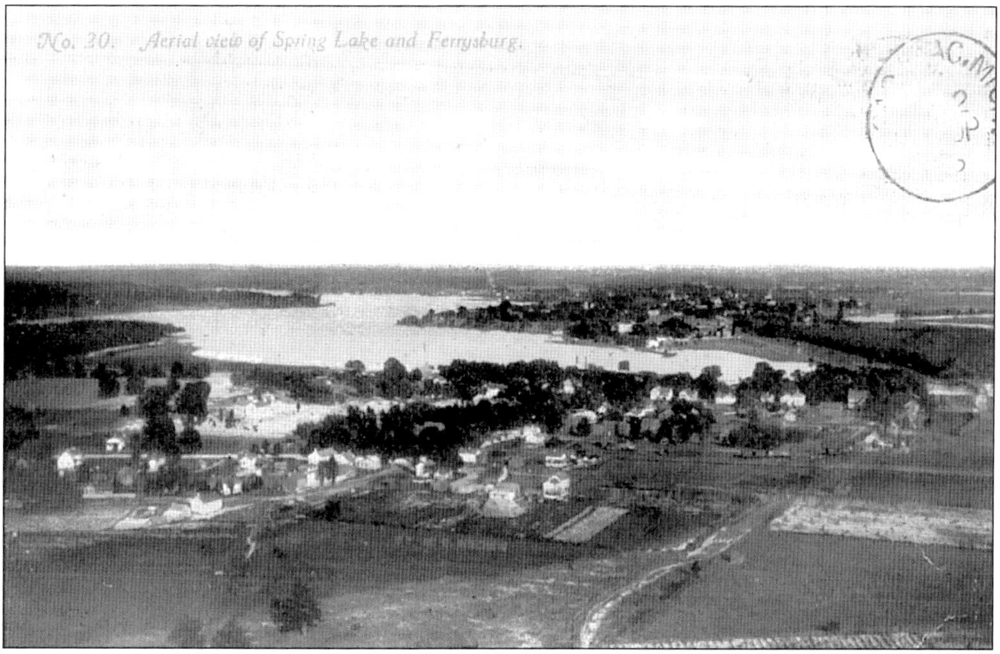

Mailed in 1912, this Nat Brown postcard shows an aerial view of Spring Lake, with Ferrysburg in the foreground and Spring Lake Village across the narrows. The tilled fields on the outskirts indicate that both communities remained primarily rural at the time of the photo. The chimneys and roof of Johnston Boiler barely peek above the tree tops.

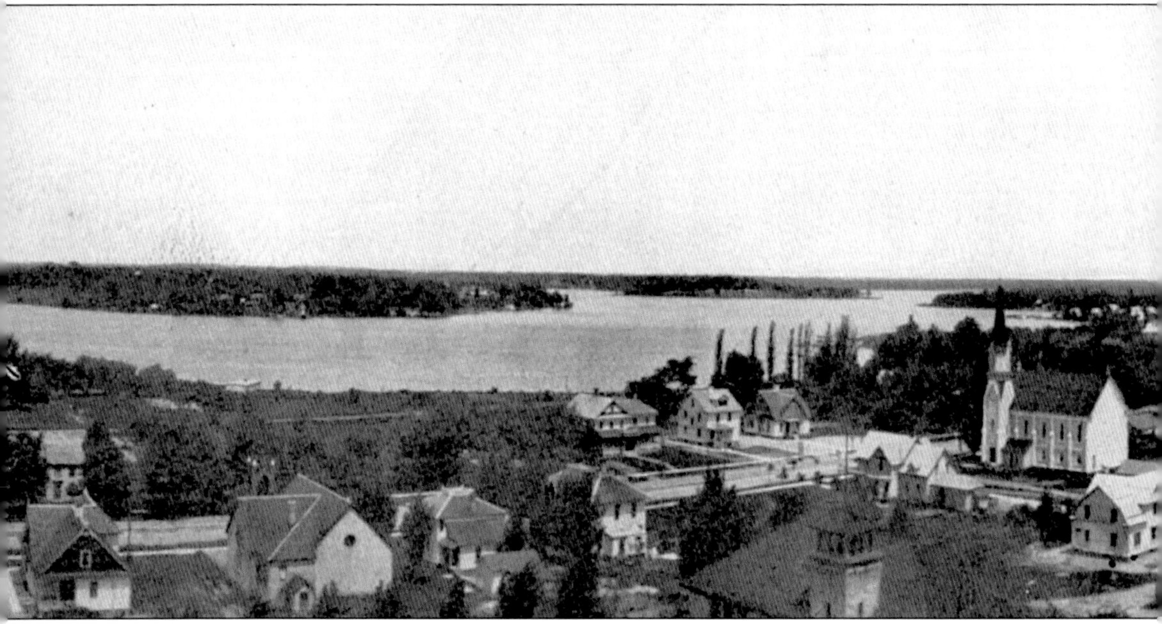

Nat Brown probably climbed a nearby water tower to take this panoramic, two-panel view of Spring Lake. Savidge Street runs close to the lake, and Exchange Street is little more than a path one block south of Savidge. The church near the center of the card is the First Presbyterian, at 212 East Savidge. The church farther to the right is the First Reformed, at 210 Summit. The

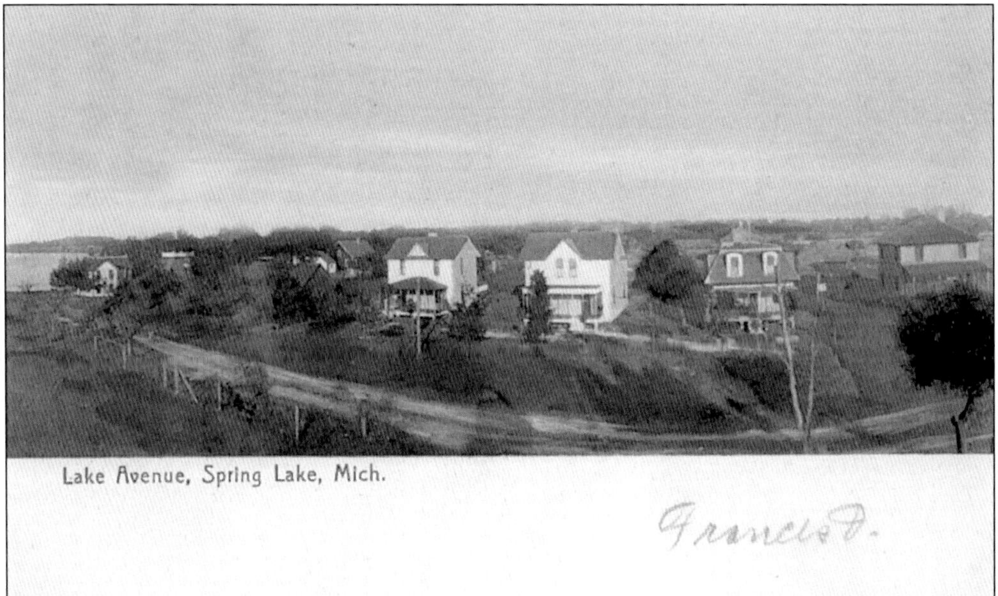

This is another one of Nat Brown's kite's eye views of Spring Lake, showing Lake Avenue between the railroad tracks and the lake. The card is a lithograph, printed in Germany for Felix Perl, who owned a pharmacy in the Village between 1905 and 1908. The postmark is faint, but it looks as if it is dated 1908.

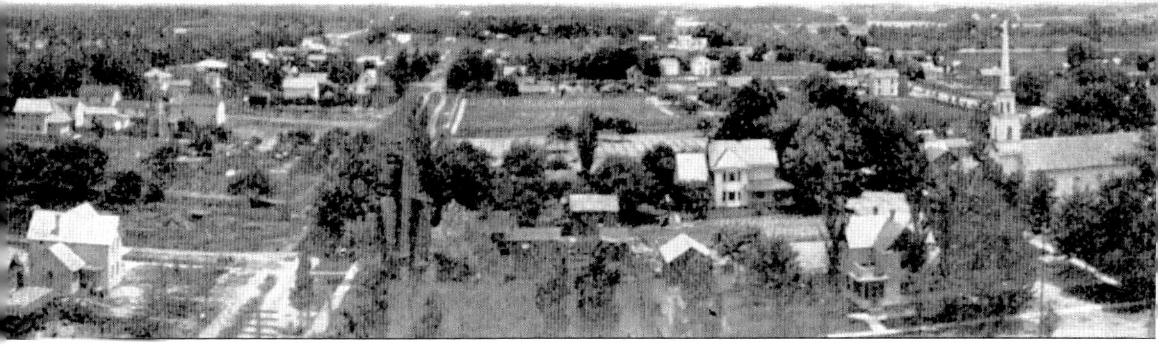

intersection of Buchanan and Savidge can be seen at the far left of the card. The roof and tower of the brick building in the foreground were part of the school built in the mid-1890s.

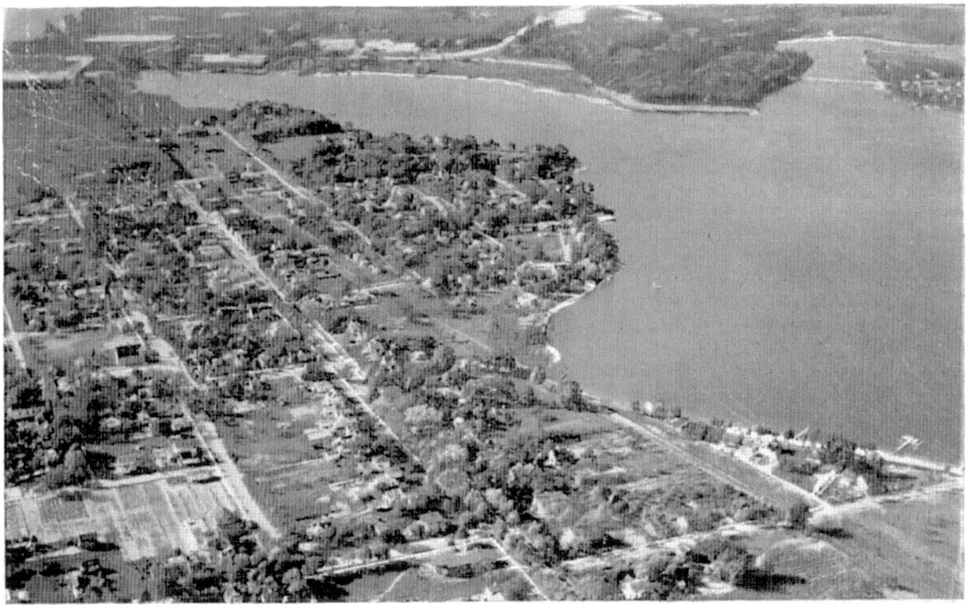

AERIAL VIEW OF SPRING LAKE, VILLAGE OF SPRING LAKE, FERRYSBURG AND MT. VERNON, MICH.

This view of the Spring Lake area, looking westward, was taken around the mid-1930s. Some tillable fields are evident in the lower left corner, but the Village had filled in considerably. The land between downtown Spring Lake and the bridge to Ferrysburg remained undeveloped. On the back of the card, Mount Vernon is identified as "Grand Haven's new summer community," and perhaps refers to the cluster of residences to the right of Smith's Bayou Bridge in the upper right corner.

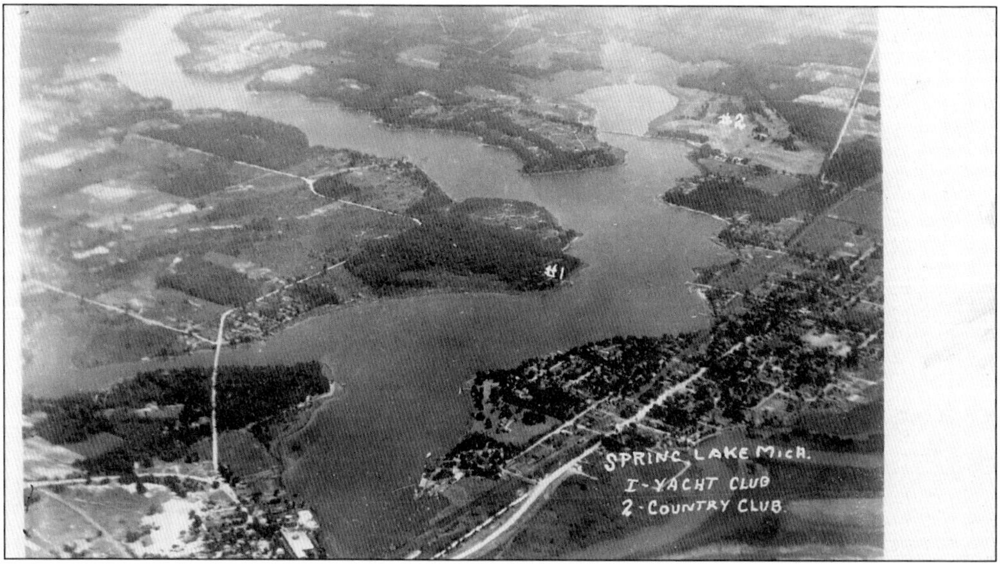

The plane was flying high when the picture on this undated postcard was taken. The camera is looking in a northeasterly direction and picks up the full length of Spring Lake and the bayous. Spring Lake Village and the City of Ferrysburg are in the foreground. The Yacht Club is marked in the center of the card, and the Country Club can be seen farther up and to the right. The bridge over Smith's Bayou is clearly visible at the left, but Bowen's Bridge over Petty's Bayou is more difficult to see.

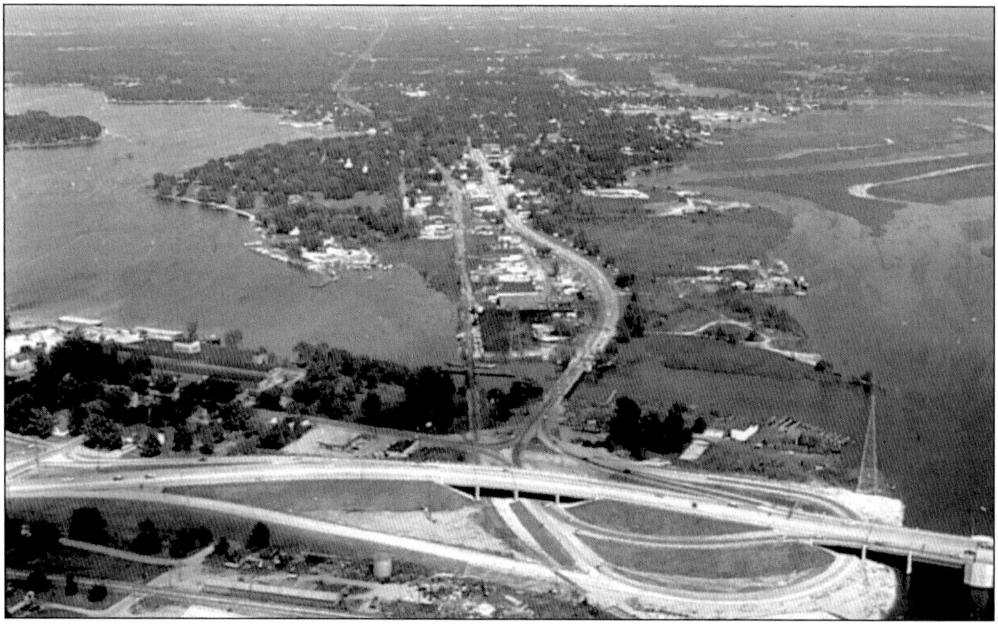

On July 9, 1959, the new U.S. 31 drawbridge began to carry vehicles over the Grand River, where the northbound vehicles could continue along the four-lane divided highway, or turn east to cross the fixed-span bridge to Spring Lake. Dan Barden's Marina, just to the right of the Spring Lake bridge, took the place of the State Police post, which moved to Grand Haven. The railroad tracks cut a clear path, running due east from Ferrysburg. The card is dated 1961.

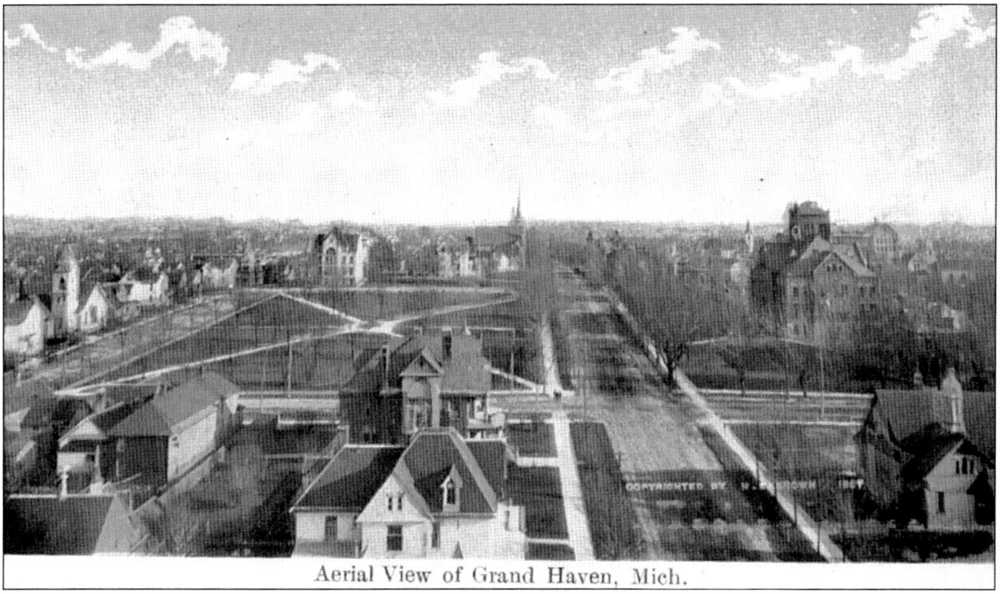

Another of Nat Brown's photographs taken from a kite, this view looks east over Central Park. W.C. Sheldon's home is in the foreground and William Loutit's mansion is just beyond it. To the right, across the street from those two houses, is the residence of Thomas and Ruth Parrish. Also in view are the 1894 Court House to the right and Akeley Hall just to left of center. The card has a 1907 copyright date.

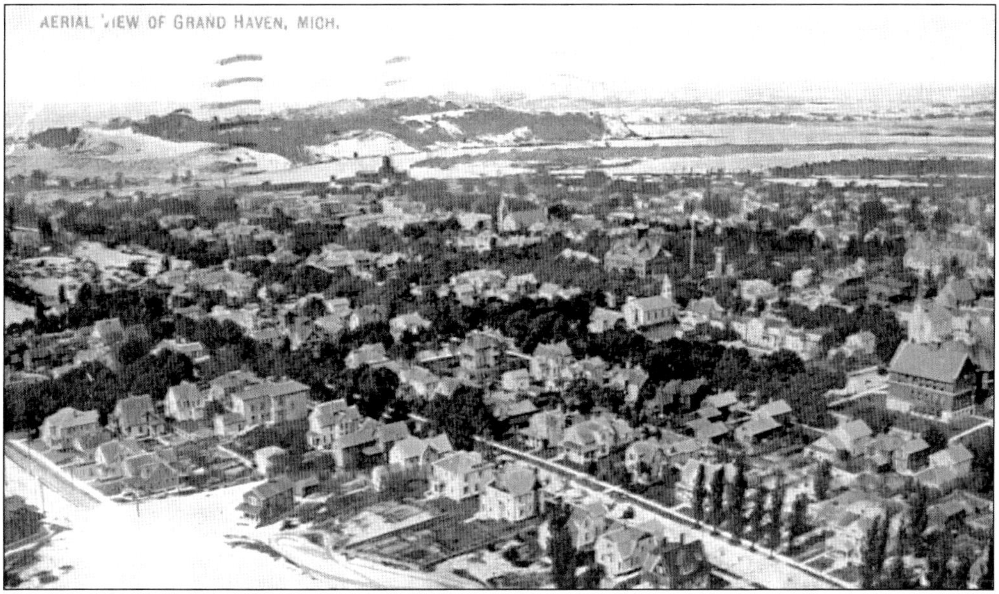

This aerial view of Nat Brown's survived several generations of postcard printings, but the original photograph evidently pre-dated 1907, the year the First Reformed Church, shown in this photograph, burned down. Pennoyer Street, in the lower left corner of the card, had not yet joined Howard Avenue. The Ferry home on Lafayette Street is clearly visible. Also easy to discern are Central School near the right edge, the Presbyterian Church and Court House near the center, and the grain elevator along the river bank.

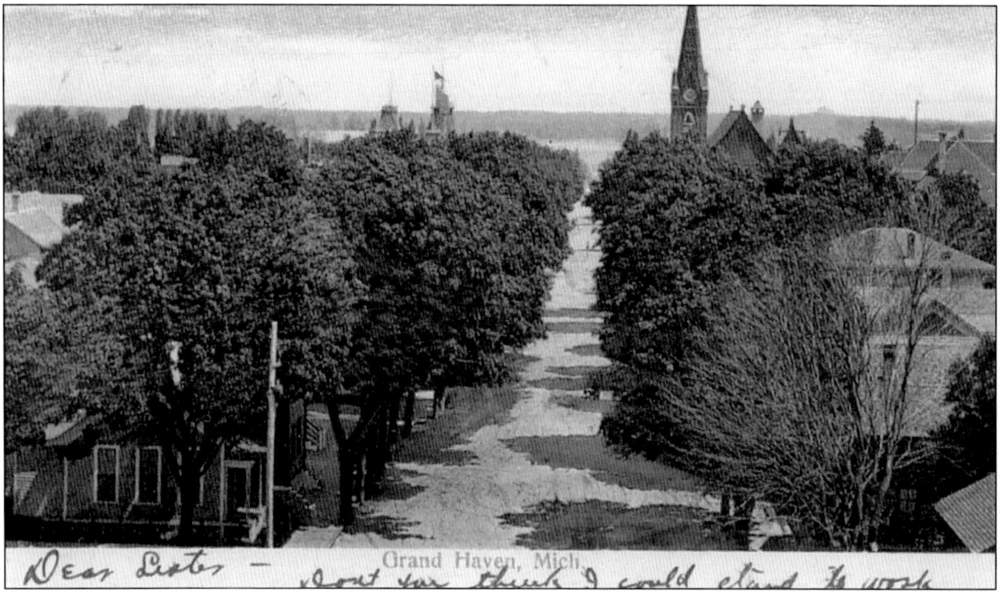

This early view looks north on Third Street from Clinton. The clock steeple of the First Reformed Church is visible to the right of center, and opposite it is the rooftop of the former Magnetic Mineral Springs Resort. At the time this photo was taken, the old spa was being used by Company F as a temporary armory while a new one was being constructed on Second Street. The Magnetic Mineral Springs building was torn down before 1905 to make room for the Federal Building/Post Office. The card is postmarked 1906.

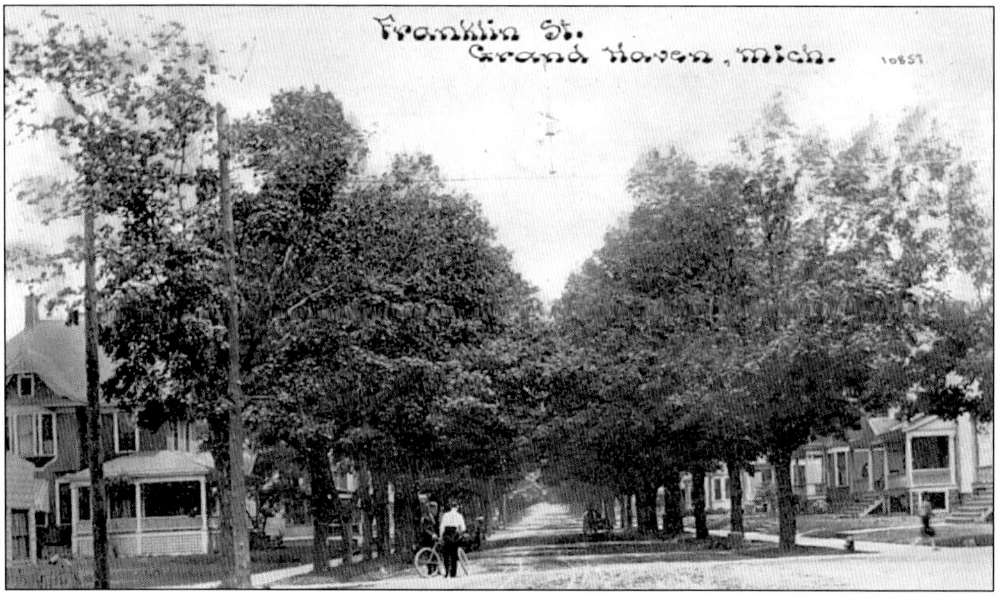

Dated 1910, this postcard shows a typical Grand Haven neighborhood, in this case Franklin Street. The maple trees have been in long enough to look fully mature, and they provided ample shade for the unpaved street. Sidewalks have been laid, but there is no curbing. A shallow ditch along side the street helped drain excess water. There is a fire hydrant on the corner to the right. One of the two gentlemen chatting in the street had been riding a bicycle.

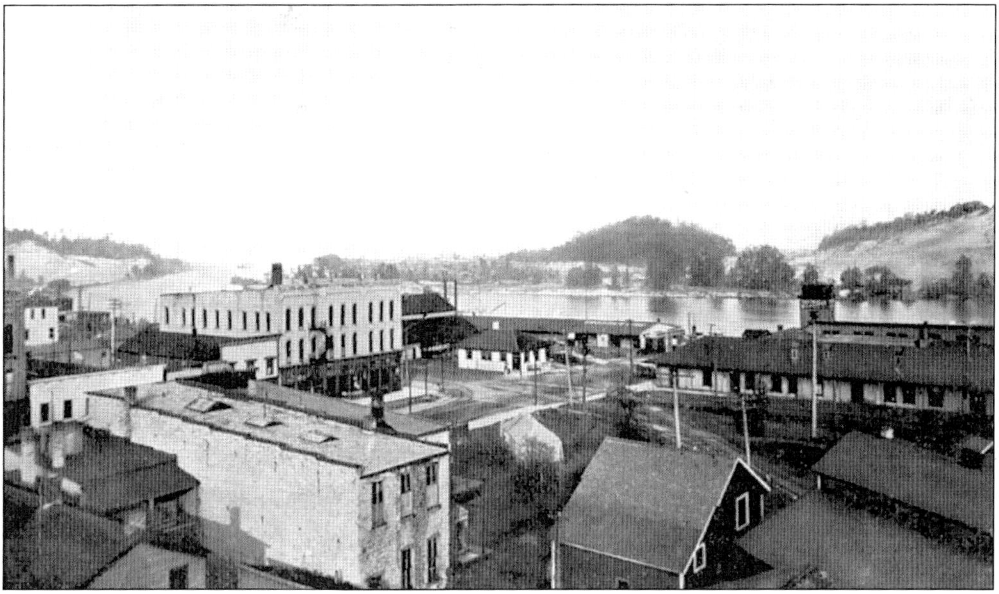

Looking over the rooftops toward Dewey Hill, this bird's-eye view catches a number of landmarks, including Nat Robbins Office at the southwest corner of Washington and Water Street (Harbor Drive). Behind it, lining the riverbank, is Nat's warehouse, with "Goodrich" woven into its roof. The long building on the right is the Grand Trunk Railway Station when it had an attached warehouse. The three-story building in the center is the Gildner Hotel, now known as Kirby's Grill. The picture may have been taken from the roof of the Story & Clark building, erected in 1905.

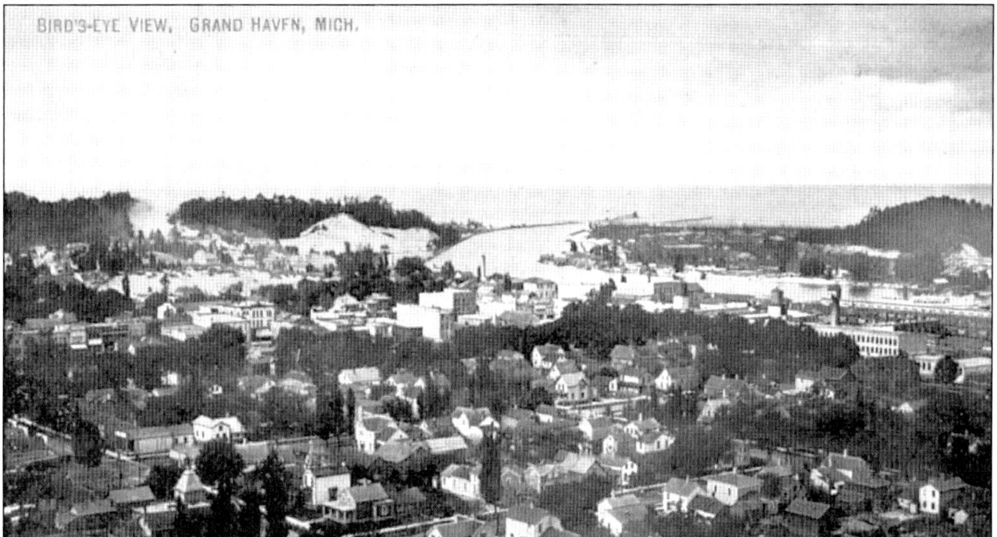

This view, looking southwest over Grand Haven, undoubtedly is another one of Nat Brown's kite shots, although his name does not appear on the unmailed card. It's fairly easy to pick out some of the large structures along Washington Street, such as the Akeley Building, the Grey Building, and the Gildner Hotel, as well as the first Story & Clark building on First Street. Concrete sidewalks were common, but the streets were not yet paved. The city had not yet expanded into the dunes to the west.

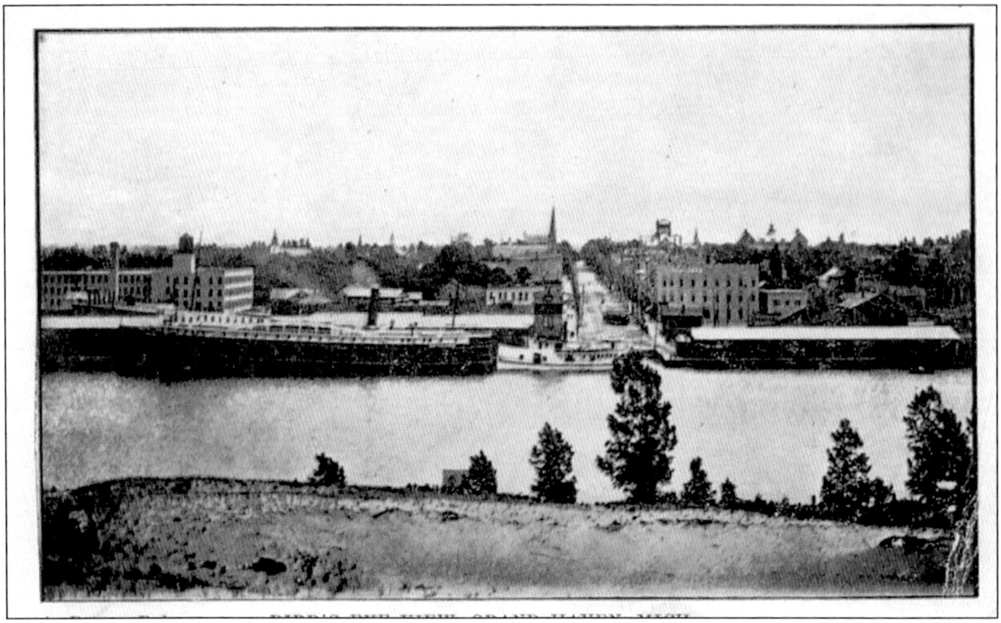

Dewey Hill provided photographers a wonderful vantage spot to view downtown Grand Haven. The white structure at the far left is the first building erected by the Story & Clark Piano Company in 1901. The company constructed the building between Columbus and Washington four years later, so this photo was taken between 1901 and 1905. Also visible is an Interurban coach, making the turn onto Washington. Punctuating the horizon are the steeple of the Congregational Church, the County Building, and Central School.

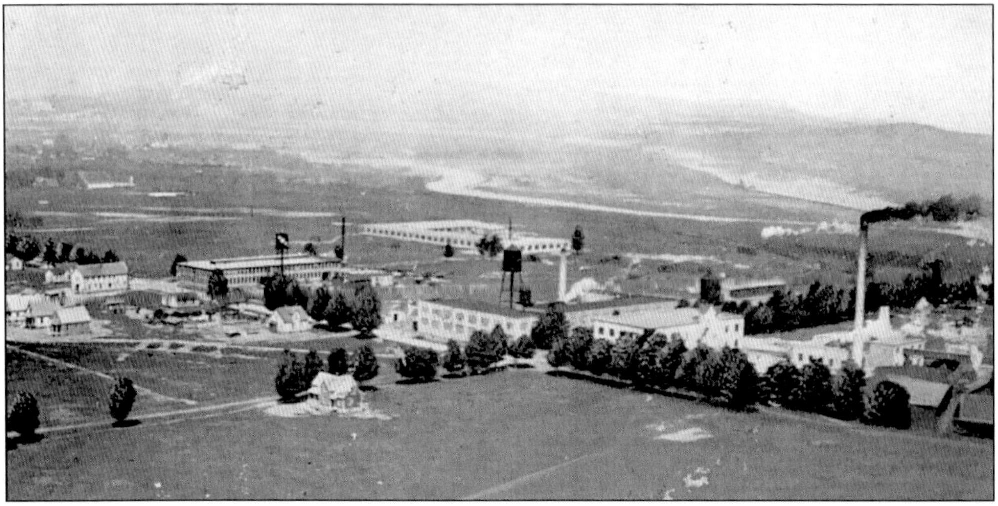

This is another of Nat Brown's "camera-on-a-kite" views. The intersection of Beechtree and Fulton is near the center of the card, with the grounds of Eagle Ottawa Leather Company on the right and Challenge Machinery Company to the left of it. The large building a bit farther to the west belonged to the William Heap Company, manufacturers of wooden plumbing ware. The two-story frame building across the street from Heap is the Ottawa Tavern, now known as Fricano's Pizza Tavern. The U-shaped building was the site of the Fountain Specialty Company, later known as Bastian Blessing. The card was not postmarked, but appears to date to about 1910.